THE BIBLE IS FOR YOU

THE BIBLE IS FOR YOU

A DEVOTIONAL JOURNEY THROUGH EVERY BOOK OF THE BIBLE

GENERAL EDITORS
RAECHEL MYERS & AMANDA BIBLE WILLIAMS
FOUNDERS OF SHE READS TRUTH

PUBLISHING®
BRENTWOOD, TENNESSEE

978-1-4336-8899-7

Published by B&H Publishing Group
Brentwood, Tennessee

Dewey Decimal Classification: 242.5
Subject Heading: DEVOTIONAL LITERATURE /BIBLE—READING / BIBLE—INSPIRATION

Cover design by B&H Publishing Group.
"The Garden of Eden" painting by Jan Brueghel the Elder/Bridgeman Images.
Author photos by Meshali Mitchell.

Authors are represented by Alive Literary Agency, www.aliveliterary.com.

1 2 3 4 5 6 7 • 28 27 26 25

To Etta and Hazel.
May the Word of Christ dwell in you richly.

TABLE OF CONTENTS

NEW TESTAMENT

A LETTER FROM THE EDITORS

The Bible is for you.

As two people who came to know Jesus when we were little kids and grew up to lead a worldwide community of Bible readers, you would think we've outgrown the need for this reminder. But the truth is, there are still days when we feel unqualified, uninspired, or simply unable to open our Bibles. The difference between now and when we founded She Reads Truth thirteen years ago is that we no longer have to rely on feelings, because now we have something better—we have proof.

Every day for thirteen years we've watched as women from all over the world have opened their Bibles and met God there. Whatever season of life they're in, whatever hard things are going on in the world, whatever they are celebrating or grieving or longing for—God's Word is for them, and it is constant and true. God has given us—all of us—the gift of Scripture so that we can know Him.

Reading the Bible might feel like a tall order. After all, it is the only book of its kind: sixty-six books but one story, ancient but also living, divinely inspired but also layered with historical context that can make it seem distant or even irrelevant. We created *The Bible Is for You* to show you how intimately, personally, and specifically the Bible is indeed for you. We say this with confidence now because reading it has shaped our hearts and our lives, not just once, but today and every day. Even as we curated the passages and essays you'll read in this devotional book, we found ourselves in awe yet again—high-fiving over connections in Scripture we'd never seen before, or tears streaming, staggered and hopeful at God's unshakable promises. The Word of God is an endless well of truth, and we are determined to keep lowering our buckets.

Wherever you are in your journey with the Bible, we hope this devotional book will serve as a warm welcome into the pages of Scripture. From Genesis to Revelation, you'll get a glimpse into each book of the Bible and how it fits into the whole. One book at a time, you'll read key sections from that book along with curated passages from other parts of Scripture, to help you connect the dots and see how it all tells one story: the story of a holy God and His merciful pursuit of the people He created and loves.

We pray these sixty-six devotions will give you a bigger window into the beauty, goodness, and truth of the Bible. It is a story that is as vast as it is personal, as powerful as it is precious. It is a gift, and it is for you.

Read on,

Raechel & Amanda

DESIGN ON PURPOSE

At She Reads Truth, we believe design says and does so much in a book before a single word is read, so we always seek to design with purpose. This is our chance to tell you, our reader, why the book you're holding looks and feels like it does and, if we did our jobs right, how your experience will be shaped because of the purpose in our design. Mind if we show you around?

To start, the cover art is a seventeenth-century work titled "The Garden of Eden" by Belgian painter Jan Brueghel. Just like the story of humanity is bookended by gardens—with Eden in Genesis and the new heavens and new earth in Revelation—we used a canvas-like cover paper to wrap the garden painting from front to back. This reminds us that, despite (and because of) everything that happens in the middle of the story, we begin and end with the presence of God in a garden. This centuries-old painting is overlaid with the book's title in a modern type and bright color to juxtapose the old and new, much like the ancient words of Scripture that still have power to transform our lives today.

You have probably noticed that this book doesn't have a typical covered spine or binding. We left the bound pages of the book exposed on the spine as a visual reminder that the Bible is both one book and a collection of sixty-six books written and assembled over time to complete God's special revelation of Scripture.

Moving inside to the sixty-six devotionals, you will see things are set up a little differently than a typical devotional book. Each book of the Bible begins with a key verse and a curated Scripture reading that will give you a good idea of what is happening in that particular book, followed by related passages from other parts of the Bible. And we don't simply list the references—we've put the actual words of the text right there on the page. Reading Scripture is our main thing at She Reads Truth, and it's important to us that we invite you to read the words God Himself inspired before offering words of our own.

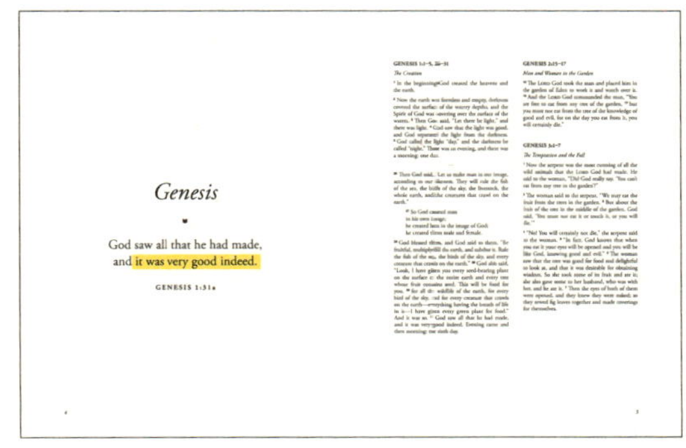

Genesis

God saw all that he had made,
and it was very good indeed.

GENESIS 1:31a

After you've read the Scripture, we invite you to read the devotional that follows. These essays are meant to be a response to God's Word, arrows pointing back to Scripture. They're even presented in a different typeface to make it extra clear which words are ours and which are His. The yellow highlighter is there not just to draw attention to key words or phrases, but to encourage you to engage fully with what you're reading.

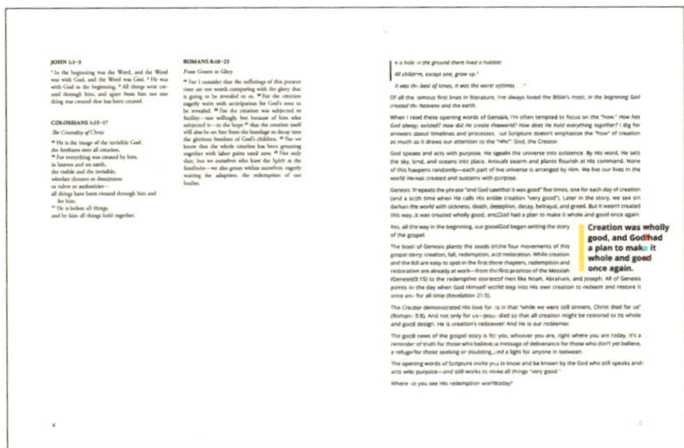

Creation was wholly good, and God had a plan to make it whole and good once again.

We hope each of these individual design choices combine to help you draw connections as you read and discover that yes, *The Bible Is for You.*

Genesis

God saw all that he had made,
and it was very good indeed.

GENESIS 1:31a

GENESIS 1:1–5, 26–31

The Creation

1 In the beginning God created the heavens and
the earth.

2 Now the earth was formless and empty, darkness
covered the surface of the watery depths, and the
Spirit of God was hovering over the surface of the
waters. 3 Then God said, "Let there be light," and
there was light. 4 God saw that the light was good,
and God separated the light from the darkness.
5 God called the light "day," and the darkness he
called "night." There was an evening, and there was
a morning: one day.

. . .

26 Then God said, "Let us make man in our image,
according to our likeness. They will rule the fish
of the sea, the birds of the sky, the livestock, the
whole earth, and the creatures that crawl on the
earth."

> 27 So God created man
> in his own image;
> he created him in the image of God;
> he created them male and female.

28 God blessed them, and God said to them, "Be
fruitful, multiply, fill the earth, and subdue it. Rule
the fish of the sea, the birds of the sky, and every
creature that crawls on the earth." 29 God also said,
"Look, I have given you every seed-bearing plant
on the surface of the entire earth and every tree
whose fruit contains seed. This will be food for
you, 30 for all the wildlife of the earth, for every
bird of the sky, and for every creature that crawls
on the earth—everything having the breath of life
in it—I have given every green plant for food."
And it was so. 31 God saw all that he had made,
and it was very good indeed. Evening came and
then morning: the sixth day.

GENESIS 2:15–17

Man and Woman in the Garden

15 The LORD God took the man and placed him in
the garden of Eden to work it and watch over it.
16 And the LORD God commanded the man, "You
are free to eat from any tree of the garden, 17 but
you must not eat from the tree of the knowledge of
good and evil, for on the day you eat from it, you
will certainly die."

GENESIS 3:1–7

The Temptation and the Fall

1 Now the serpent was the most cunning of all the
wild animals that the LORD God had made. He
said to the woman, "Did God really say, 'You can't
eat from any tree in the garden'?"

2 The woman said to the serpent, "We may eat the
fruit from the trees in the garden. 3 But about the
fruit of the tree in the middle of the garden, God
said, 'You must not eat it or touch it, or you will
die.'"

4 "No! You will certainly not die," the serpent said
to the woman. 5 "In fact, God knows that when
you eat it your eyes will be opened and you will be
like God, knowing good and evil." 6 The woman
saw that the tree was good for food and delightful
to look at, and that it was desirable for obtaining
wisdom. So she took some of its fruit and ate it;
she also gave some to her husband, who was with
her, and he ate it. 7 Then the eyes of both of them
were opened, and they knew they were naked; so
they sewed fig leaves together and made coverings
for themselves.

JOHN 1:1–3

1 In the beginning was the Word, and the Word
was with God, and the Word was God. 2 He was
with God in the beginning. 3 All things were created through him, and apart from him not one
thing was created that has been created.

COLOSSIANS 1:15–17

The Centrality of Christ

15 He is the image of the invisible God,
the firstborn over all creation.
16 For everything was created by him,
in heaven and on earth,
the visible and the invisible,
whether thrones or dominions
or rulers or authorities—
all things have been created through him and
for him.
17 He is before all things,
and by him all things hold together.

ROMANS 8:18–23

From Groans to Glory

18 For I consider that the sufferings of this present
time are not worth comparing with the glory that
is going to be revealed to us. 19 For the creation
eagerly waits with anticipation for God's sons to
be revealed. 20 For the creation was subjected to
futility—not willingly, but because of him who
subjected it—in the hope 21 that the creation itself
will also be set free from the bondage to decay into
the glorious freedom of God's children. 22 For we
know that the whole creation has been groaning
together with labor pains until now. 23 Not only
that, but we ourselves who have the Spirit as the
firstfruits—we also groan within ourselves, eagerly
waiting for adoption, the redemption of our
bodies.

In a hole in the ground there lived a hobbit.[1]

All children, except one, grow up.[2]

It was the best of times, it was the worst of times . . .[3]

Of all the famous first lines in literature, I've always loved the Bible's most: *In the beginning God created the heavens and the earth.*

When I read these opening words of Genesis, I'm often tempted to focus on the "how." *How has God always existed? How did He create the world? How does He hold everything together?* I dig for answers about timelines and processes. But Scripture doesn't emphasize the "how" of creation as much as it draws our attention to the "who": God, the Creator.

God speaks and acts with purpose. He speaks the universe into existence. By His word, He sets the sky, land, and oceans into place. Animals swarm and plants flourish at His command. None of this happens randomly—each part of the universe is arranged by Him. We live our lives in the world He has created and sustains with purpose.

Genesis 1 repeats the phrase "and God saw that it was good" five times, one for each day of creation (and a sixth time when He calls His entire creation "very good"). Later in the story, we see sin darken the world with sickness, death, deception, decay, betrayal, and greed. But it wasn't created this way. It was created wholly good, and God had a plan to make it whole and good once again.

Yes, all the way in the beginning, our good God began writing the story of the gospel.

Creation was wholly good, and God had a plan to make it whole and good once again.

The book of Genesis plants the seeds of the four movements of this gospel story: creation, fall, redemption, and restoration. While creation and the fall are easy to spot in the first three chapters, redemption and restoration are already at work—from the first promise of the Messiah (Genesis 3:15) to the redemptive stories of men like Noah, Abraham, and Joseph. All of Genesis points to the day when God Himself would step into His own creation to redeem and restore it once and for all time (Revelation 21:5).

The Creator demonstrated His love for us in that "while we were still sinners, Christ died for us" (Romans 5:8). And not only for us—Jesus died so that all creation might be restored to its whole and good design. He is creation's redeemer! And He is our redeemer.

The good news of the gospel story is for you, whoever you are, right where you are today. It's a reminder of truth for those who believe, a message of deliverance for those who don't yet believe, a refuge for those seeking or doubting, and a light for anyone in between.

The opening words of Scripture invite you to know and be known by the God who still speaks and acts with purpose—and still works to make all things "very good."

Where do you see His redemption work today?

Exodus

"I am the Lord your God, who brought you out of the land of Egypt, out of the place of slavery."

EXODUS 20:2

EXODUS 6:2–8

God Promises Freedom

2 Then God spoke to Moses, telling him, "I am the Lord. 3 I appeared to Abraham, Isaac, and Jacob as God Almighty, but I was not known to them by my name 'the Lord.' 4 I also established my covenant with them to give them the land of Canaan, the land they lived in as aliens. 5 Furthermore, I have heard the groaning of the Israelites, whom the Egyptians are forcing to work as slaves, and I have remembered my covenant.

6 "Therefore tell the Israelites: I am the Lord, and I will bring you out from the forced labor of the Egyptians and rescue you from slavery to them. I will redeem you with an outstretched arm and great acts of judgment. 7 I will take you as my people, and I will be your God. You will know that I am the Lord your God, who brought you out from the forced labor of the Egyptians. 8 I will bring you to the land that I swore to give to Abraham, Isaac, and Jacob, and I will give it to you as a possession. I am the Lord."

EXODUS 15:1–3

Israel's Song

1 Then Moses and the Israelites sang this song to the Lord. They said:

> I will sing to the Lord,
> for he is highly exalted;
> he has thrown the horse
> and its rider into the sea.
> 2 The Lord is my strength and my song;
> he has become my salvation.
> This is my God, and I will praise him,
> my father's God, and I will exalt him.
> 3 The Lord is a warrior;
> the Lord is his name.

EXODUS 19:1–6

Israel at Sinai

1 In the third month from the very day the Israelites left the land of Egypt, they came to the Sinai Wilderness. 2 They traveled from Rephidim, came to the Sinai Wilderness, and camped in the wilderness. Israel camped there in front of the mountain.

3 Moses went up the mountain to God, and the Lord called to him from the mountain: "This is what you must say to the house of Jacob and explain to the Israelites: 4 'You have seen what I did to the Egyptians and how I carried you on eagles' wings and brought you to myself. 5 Now if you will carefully listen to me and keep my covenant, you will be my own possession out of all the peoples, although the whole earth is mine, 6 and you will be my kingdom of priests and my holy nation.' These are the words that you are to say to the Israelites."

EXODUS 20:1–6

The Ten Commandments

1 Then God spoke all these words:

> 2 I am the Lord your God, who brought you out of the land of Egypt, out of the place of slavery.
>
> 3 Do not have other gods besides me.
>
> 4 Do not make an idol for yourself, whether in the shape of anything in the heavens above or on the earth below or in the waters under the earth. 5 Do not bow in worship to them, and do not serve them; for I, the Lord your God, am a jealous God, bringing the consequences of the fathers' iniquity on the children to the third and fourth generations of those who hate me, 6 but showing faithful love to a thousand generations of those who love me and keep my commands.

HOSEA 13:4

"I have been the Lord your God
ever since the land of Egypt;
you know no God but me,
and no Savior exists besides me."

MATTHEW 5:17–18

Christ Fulfills the Law

17 "Don't think that I came to abolish the Law or
the Prophets. I did not come to abolish but to fulfill. 18 For truly I tell you, until heaven and earth
pass away, not the smallest letter or one stroke of
a letter will pass away from the law until all things
are accomplished."

HEBREWS 2:14–15

Jesus and Humanity

14 Now since the children have flesh and blood
in common, Jesus also shared in these, so that
through his death he might destroy the one holding the power of death—that is, the devil— 15 and
free those who were held in slavery all their lives by
the fear of death.

One Saturday when my kids were little, I listened to the book of Exodus all the way through. I'd never read the book in one sitting before, and I wanted to get a sense of Exodus as a piece of literature, rather than a series of chapters and verses. By the end I was moved to tears.

There were plenty of interruptions, so it took the entire day, but there was a sweetness in our home as the story of God's salvation filled the air from breakfast to dinner. For a while, my young daughter lay at my feet and fiddled with toys, listening to the story while it played. As the Israelites crossed the Red Sea and Miriam sang her song, my girl sang a version she'd learned in school: "Sing to the LORD, for he is highly exalted; he has thrown the horse and its rider into the sea" (Exodus 15:21).

In the afternoon, I listened as God gave instructions to build the tabernacle. I noticed my husband find a place on the nearby sofa to listen as God appointed and equipped Bezalel to be the chief designer and executor of the process. I could tell by my husband's interest that these chapters hold a special place in his design-loving heart.

I wanted to get a sense of Exodus as a piece of literature, rather than a series of chapters and verses.

As evening set in, I moved to our back porch to listen to the final chapters. God sweetly gathered my family to listen with me as "the glory of the LORD filled the tabernacle" (Exodus 40:35). I replayed the last few paragraphs several times, in awe of the nearness of God to His people then and His nearness to us still. God seemed more holy and magnificent than ever before. But in reality, He's the same—yesterday, today, forever (Hebrews 13:8).

Exodus is a story of salvation. And it's our heritage—*our* story of salvation. It starts with God delivering the Israelites from slavery in Egypt, Pharaoh and his army in hot pursuit, and Moses saying to God's people, "Don't be afraid. Stand firm and see the LORD's salvation that he will accomplish for you today" (Exodus 14:13). But it doesn't end there. The story unfolds in our lives, too. God saved His people that day through Moses, and He saves us even now, through the completed work of Jesus Christ.

As believers, we have been set free—this time not from Egypt, but from sin and death. Like Israel did, we encounter God's presence—this time not because we built a tabernacle for Him to dwell in, but because He came to "tabernacle" among us and in us, through the work of His Son and by the power of His Spirit (1 Corinthians 3:16; Ephesians 2:22).

Yes, the Exodus story is our story, and it is a story worth sharing. Let it ring out in your home! Let the truth of God's salvation move you to tears of praise. The Lord, He is God. And you—you are free.

Leviticus

"You are to be holy
to me because I,
the LORD, am holy,
and I have set you
apart from the nations
to be mine."

LEVITICUS 20:26

LEVITICUS 20:22–26

Holiness in the Land

22 “You are to keep all my statutes and all my ordinances, and do them, so that
the land where I am bringing you to live will not vomit you out. 23 You must not
follow the statutes of the nations I am driving out before you, for they did all
these things, and I abhorred them. 24 And I promised you: You will inherit their
land, since I will give it to you to possess, a land flowing with milk and honey.
I am the LORD your God who set you apart from the peoples. 25 Therefore you
are to distinguish the clean animal from the unclean one, and the unclean bird
from the clean one. Do not become contaminated by any land animal, bird, or
whatever crawls on the ground; I have set these apart as unclean for you. 25 You
are to be holy to me because I, the LORD, am holy, and I have set you apart from
the nations to be mine.”

HEBREWS 7:26–28

A Superior Priesthood

26 For this is the kind of high priest we need: holy, innocent, undefiled, separated from sinners, and exalted above the heavens. 27 He doesn't need to offer sacrifices every day, as high priests do—first for their own sins, then for those of the people. He did this once for all time when he offered himself. 28 For the law appoints as high priests men who are weak, but the promise of the oath, which came after the law, appoints a Son, who has been perfected forever.

HEBREWS 10:1–18

The Perfect Sacrifice

1 Since the law has only a shadow of the good things to come, and not the reality itself of those things, it can never perfect the worshipers by the same sacrifices they continually offer year after year. 2 Otherwise, wouldn't they have stopped being offered, since the worshipers, purified once and for all, would no longer have any consciousness of sins? 3 But in the sacrifices there is a reminder of sins year after year. 4 For it is impossible for the blood of bulls and goats to take away sins.

5 Therefore, as he was coming into the world, he said:

> "You did not desire sacrifice and offering,
> but you prepared a body for me.
> 6 You did not delight
> in whole burnt offerings and sin offerings.
> 7 Then I said, 'See—
> it is written about me
> in the scroll—
> I have come to do your will, God.'"

8 After he says above, "You did not desire or delight in sacrifices and offerings, whole burnt offerings and sin offerings" (which are offered according to the law), 9 he then says, "See, I have come to do your will." He takes away the first to establish the second. 10 By this will, we have been sanctified through the offering of the body of Jesus Christ once for all time.

11 Every priest stands day after day ministering and offering the same sacrifices time after time, which can never take away sins. 12 But this man, after offering one sacrifice for sins forever, sat down at the right hand of God. 13 He is now waiting until his enemies are made his footstool. 14 For by one offering he has perfected forever those who are sanctified. 15 The Holy Spirit also testifies to us about this. For after he says:

> 16 "This is the covenant I will make with them
> after those days,"

the Lord says,

> "I will put my laws on their hearts
> and write them on their minds,"

17 and "I will never again remember

> their sins" and their lawless acts.

18 Now where there is forgiveness of these, there is no longer an offering for sin.

1 PETER 1:13–21

A Call to Holy Living

13 Therefore, with your minds ready for action, be sober-minded and set your hope completely on the grace to be brought to you at the revelation of Jesus Christ. 14 As obedient children, do not be conformed to the desires of your former ignorance. 15 But as the one who called you is holy, you also are to be holy in all your conduct; 16 for it is written, "Be holy, because I am holy." 17 If you appeal to the Father who judges impartially according to each one's work, you are to conduct yourselves in reverence during your time living as strangers. 18 For you know that you were redeemed from your empty way of life inherited from your ancestors, not with perishable things like silver or gold, 19 but with the precious blood of Christ, like that of an unblemished and spotless lamb. 20 He was foreknown before the foundation of the world but was revealed in these last times for you. 21 Through him you believe in God, who raised him from the dead and gave him glory, so that your faith and hope are in God.

Tuesdays were the designated cleaning day at our small church growing up. Every week, a group of members would arrive at the familiar brick building, greeting each other with "Praise the Lord!" and "How's your week going?" The sound of gospel music filled every room as we cleaned and bopped our heads to the beat. Aged, wooden pews were polished and dining room floors were mopped, the scents of lemon and pine permeating the church.

I didn't understand it as a kid, but as an adult I now realize the significance of what we were doing. There was something almost holy, priestly even, about our routine of care for that space. Even though we knew the church is a people more than a building, it was still appropriate and meaningful to prepare a place for our close-knit congregation to gather and worship God—to ready ourselves for His presence.

The book of Leviticus is about God preparing His people for His presence. It shows us how God readies the people of Israel, making it possible for them to come near Him without compromising His holiness and without excusing their sin. The instructions, systems, and processes God established in order to remove their sins are key for understanding how God still frees people from sin today.

There was something almost priestly about our routine.

On behalf of the people, the high priest offered a sacrifice to God to pay for their sins and restore them to God. A priest was a mediator; after being purified, he stood between Israel and God, offering a sacrifice on their behalf. The sacrifice was an unblemished animal, often a lamb (Exodus 29:38–42). Atonement, or payment, for sin was complete when the blood of this lamb or other animal was sprinkled in the place of atonement, also called the mercy seat, where God dwelled. This had to be done day after day, year after year, to cover the continual sins of God's people.

It's this context—this language of *sacrifice, priesthood, atonement,* and *mercy seat*—that the New Testament writers use to describe who Jesus is and what He has done for us. He is the "*Lamb* of God, who takes away the sin of the world" (John 1:29). He is our Great *High Priest* (Hebrews 4:15–16). He is our *atoning sacrifice* (1 John 2:2). He's the atonement place itself—the *mercy seat* (Romans 3:25). And His sacrifice lasts!

Old Testament believers needed animal sacrifices year after year, but for New Testament believers, "we have been sanctified through the offering of the body of Jesus Christ once for all time" (Hebrews 10:1–3, 10). In other words, animal sacrifices are now obsolete, not because God abolished the concept of an atoning sacrifice, but because it has been fulfilled in Christ—and that fulfillment endures forever.

Leviticus is a can't-miss book because it introduces us to this imagery, helping us see its truest fulfillment in Jesus. Without Leviticus, the full significance of these metaphors and analogies is lost to us, but with it, we can appreciate all God has done to ready us for His presence in our lives.

Today, remember there's no need to clean yourself up before approaching God. In Christ, you are already prepared.

Numbers

The LORD is slow to anger and
abounding in faithful love,
forgiving iniquity and rebellion.
But he will not leave the guilty
unpunished, bringing the
consequences of the fathers'
iniquity on the children to the
third and fourth generation.

NUMBERS 14:18

NUMBERS 13:1–2, 26–28, 32

Scouting Out Canaan

1 The Lord spoke to Moses: 2 "Send men to scout out the land of Canaan I am giving to the Israelites. Send one man who is a leader among them from each of their ancestral tribes."

. . .

26 The men went back to Moses, Aaron, and the entire Israelite community in the Wilderness of Paran at Kadesh. They brought back a report for them and the whole community, and they showed them the fruit of the land. 27 They reported to Moses, "We went into the land where you sent us. Indeed it is flowing with milk and honey, and here is some of its fruit. 28 However, the people living in the land are strong, and the cities are large and fortified. We also saw the descendants of Anak there.

. . .

32 So they gave a negative report to the Israelites about the land they had scouted: "The land we passed through to explore is one that devours its inhabitants, and all the people we saw in it are men of great size."

NUMBERS 14:1–4, 11–24

Israel's Refusal to Enter Canaan

1 Then the whole community broke into loud cries, and the people wept that night. 2 All the Israelites complained about Moses and Aaron, and the whole community told them, "If only we had died in the land of Egypt, or if only we had died in this wilderness! 3 Why is the Lord bringing us into this land to die by the sword? Our wives and children will become plunder. Wouldn't it be better for us to go back to Egypt?" 4 So they said to one another, "Let's appoint a leader and go back to Egypt."

. . .

God's Judgment of Israel's Rebellion

11 The Lord said to Moses, "How long will these people despise me? How long will they not trust in me despite all the signs I have performed among them? 12 I will strike them with a plague and destroy them. Then I will make you into a greater and mightier nation than they are."

13 But Moses replied to the Lord, "The Egyptians will hear about it, for by your strength you brought up this people from them. 14 They will tell it to the inhabitants of this land. They have heard that you, Lord, are among these people, how you, Lord, are seen face to face, how your cloud stands over them, and how you go before them in a pillar of cloud by day and in a pillar of fire by night. 15 If you kill this people with a single blow, the nations that have heard of your fame will declare, 16 'Since the Lord wasn't able to bring this people into the land he swore to give them, he has slaughtered them in the wilderness.'

17 "So now, may my Lord's power be magnified just as you have spoken: 18 The Lord is slow to anger and abounding in faithful love, forgiving iniquity and rebellion. But he will not leave the guilty unpunished, bringing the consequences of the fathers' iniquity on the children to the third and fourth generation. 19 Please pardon the iniquity of this people, in keeping with the greatness of your faithful love, just as you have forgiven them from Egypt until now."

20 The Lord responded, "I have pardoned them as you requested. 21 Yet as I live and as the whole earth is filled with the Lord's glory, 22 none of the men who have seen my glory and the signs I performed in Egypt and in the wilderness, and have tested me these ten times and did not obey me, 23 will ever see the land I swore to give their ancestors. None of those who have despised me will see it. 24 But since my servant Caleb has a different spirit and has remained loyal to me, I will bring him into the land where he has gone, and his descendants will inherit it."

PSALM 105:7–11

God's Faithfulness to His People

7 He is the LORD our God;
his judgments govern the whole earth.
8 He remembers his covenant forever,
the promise he ordained
for a thousand generations—
9 the covenant he made with Abraham,
swore to Isaac,
10 and confirmed to Jacob as a decree
and to Israel as a permanent covenant:
11 "I will give the land of Canaan to you
as your inherited portion."

HEBREWS 3:7–14

Warning Against Unbelief

7 Therefore, as the Holy Spirit says:

> "Today, if you hear his voice,
> 8 do not harden your hearts as in the rebellion,
> on the day of testing in the wilderness,
> 9 where your ancestors tested me, tried me,
> and saw my works 10 for forty years.
> Therefore I was provoked to anger with that generation
> and said, 'They always go astray in their hearts,
> and they have not known my ways.'
> 11 So I swore in my anger,
> 'They will not enter my rest.'"

12 Watch out, brothers and sisters, so that there
won't be in any of you an evil, unbelieving heart
that turns away from the living God. 13 But
encourage each other daily, while it is still called
"today," so that none of you is hardened by sin's
deception. 14 For we have become participants in
Christ if we hold firmly until the end the reality
that we had at the start.

My friend Sissy is a family counselor with more than thirty years of experience. Recently she told me about an exercise where she asks kids to make a map of their life so far, drawing mountains and valleys to represent the happy and hard things they've walked through. It's sobering to realize that even young children deal with the aches and uncertainties of being human, often in seasons they can look back on and name.

When I consider what a map of my life might look like, there are detours and dark places, unexpected joys and mountaintop moments. There's also an invisible thread running through it all—one I trust my own children will discover in their stories: God's character is constant, and His presence pursues me.

The book of Numbers is like my friend Sissy's map. It records Israel's indirect journey from Mount Sinai to the Jordan River, the time between their rescue from Egypt and their arrival at the promised land. Their wilderness wandering—a consequence of their disobedience to enter the land the way God instructed—testifies to God's holiness. As Numbers 14:18 reveals, God is not one to let wrongdoing go without consequences. Instead, He warns us that the aftermath of sin never stays contained or private; it always spills onto our loved ones, both in our generation and some that follow.

God's character is constant.

But God's grace and faithfulness are also on full display during Israel's wandering. It's the setting in which God demonstrates His unwavering commitment to His people by pursuing them with His presence. They endure a season of wilderness, but on the other side of it, God will fulfill His promise to plant them in a forever home. He may extend discipline for sin for a few generations, but He extends grace for a *thousand* generations (Exodus 20:5–6).

Numbers is a redemption story, but not just for the generation of Israelites who ate manna and drank water from the rock. It is a redemption story for all nations and generations. Through the person and work of Jesus, we are all invited into the presence of the God whose holiness and compassion are unparalleled. Jesus Christ is the Bread of Life (John 6:35), the reviving Rock we drink from (1 Corinthians 10:4), and the one whose perfect obedience redeems our wandering souls (Romans 5:19).

We are all like Israel as we wander through this fallen world, awaiting the inheritance promised to us. Only this time, it's not simply a stretch of land we're promised. It's the new heavens and the new earth—the whole world (Revelation 21:1–7).

Wherever you stand in the map of your life— even if it's a wilderness season— you can celebrate the God who gives daily bread, treats sin justly, blesses obedience lavishly, and pursues you with His presence.

How do you sense Him pursuing you today?

Deuteronomy

Know that the LORD your God is God, the faithful God who keeps his gracious covenant loyalty for a thousand generations with those who love him and keep his commands.

DEUTERONOMY 7:9

DEUTERONOMY 4:1–9

Call to Obedience

1 "Now, Israel, listen to the statutes and ordinances I am teaching you to follow,
so that you may live, enter, and take possession of the land the LORD, the God of
your ancestors, is giving you. 2 You must not add anything to what I command
you or take anything away from it, so that you may keep the commands of the
LORD your God I am giving you. 3 Your eyes have seen what the LORD did at
Baal-peor, for the LORD your God destroyed every one of you who followed Baal
of Peor. 4 But you who have remained faithful to the LORD your God are all alive
today. 5 Look, I have taught you statutes and ordinances as the LORD my God has
commanded me, so that you may follow them in the land you are entering to possess. 6 Carefully follow them, for this will show your wisdom and understanding
in the eyes of the peoples. When they hear about all these statutes, they will say,
'This great nation is indeed a wise and understanding people.' 7 For what great
nation is there that has a god near to it as the LORD our God is to us whenever we
call to him? 8 And what great nation has righteous statutes and ordinances like this
entire law I set before you today?

9 "Only be on your guard and diligently watch yourselves, so that you don't forget
the things your eyes have seen and so that they don't slip from your mind as long
as you live. Teach them to your children and your grandchildren."

DEUTERONOMY 7:7–11

7 "The LORD had his heart set on you and chose you, not because you were more
numerous than all peoples, for you were the fewest of all peoples. 8 But because
the LORD loved you and kept the oath he swore to your ancestors, he brought
you out with a strong hand and redeemed you from the place of slavery, from the
power of Pharaoh king of Egypt. 9 Know that the LORD your God is God, the
faithful God who keeps his gracious covenant loyalty for a thousand generations
with those who love him and keep his commands. 10 But he directly pays back
and destroys those who hate him. He will not hesitate to pay back directly the one
who hates him. 11 So keep the command—the statutes and ordinances—that I am
giving you to follow today."

ROMANS 8:1–6

The Life-Giving Spirit

1 Therefore, there is now no condemnation for
those in Christ Jesus, 2 because the law of the Spirit
of life in Christ Jesus has set you free from the law
of sin and death. 3 For what the law could not do
since it was weakened by the flesh, God did. He
condemned sin in the flesh by sending his own
Son in the likeness of sinful flesh as a sin offering,
4 in order that the law's requirement would be fulfilled in us who do not walk according to the flesh
but according to the Spirit. 5 For those who live
according to the flesh have their minds set on the
things of the flesh, but those who live according to
the Spirit have their minds set on the things of the
Spirit. 6 Now the mindset of the flesh is death, but
the mindset of the Spirit is life and peace.

2 TIMOTHY 1:9–10

Not Ashamed of the Gospel

9 He has saved us and called us with a holy calling,
not according to our works, but according to his
own purpose and grace, which was given to us in
Christ Jesus before time began. 10 This has now
been made evident through the appearing of our
Savior Christ Jesus, who has abolished death and
has brought life and immortality to light through
the gospel.

HEBREWS 8:1–6

A Heavenly Priesthood

1 Now the main point of what is being said is this:
We have this kind of high priest, who sat down at
the right hand of the throne of the Majesty in the
heavens, 2 a minister of the sanctuary and the true
tabernacle that was set up by the Lord and not man.
3 For every high priest is appointed to offer gifts
and sacrifices; therefore, it was necessary for this
priest also to have something to offer. 4 Now if he
were on earth, he wouldn't be a priest, since there
are those offering the gifts prescribed by the law.
5 These serve as a copy and shadow of the heavenly
things, as Moses was warned when he was about to
complete the tabernacle. For God said, "Be careful
that you make everything according to the pattern
that was shown to you on the mountain." 6 But
Jesus has now obtained a superior ministry, and to
that degree he is the mediator of a better covenant,
which has been established on better promises.

Early in our marriage, my husband and I became overnight parents to three little girls by way of foster care. We were brand new to parenting, so we paid very careful attention to all of the agency requirements, including the suggestion to write and post a list of simple household rules. On the day the girls arrived, we began our season together by giving a tour of our home and reading over those rules.

These girls had just been uprooted from their family and home. Ours was a brand-new place with brand-new people and expectations, where everything from the food we served to the smell of the shampoo was unfamiliar. Describing with clarity what life would be like in this new environment wasn't a replacement for building a relationship—it was an essential part of establishing structure in a season of overwhelming transition.

In many ways, the book of Deuteronomy is the Lord's way of establishing a similar structure with His people. The law given by Moses in these pages are the conditions of a covenant, or agreement, between Israel and God. It most closely follows the pattern of Ancient Near Eastern marriage and adoption covenants, where two previously unconnected groups established themselves as a new family.

Before he explains the laws and structure that would frame their new society, Moses begins by reminding Israel of their history with God. God brought the Israelites out of Egyptian slavery to the edge of the promised land, but they rebelled, refusing to enter it. Their fear and discouragement took precedence over trusting the Lord. Yet, God remained faithful to the exodus generation and their children as they wandered in the desert for forty years.

Now at the doorstep of the promised land with all that wandering behind them, this new generation is finally ready to enter a brand-new environment. It's a season of overwhelming transition, a second chance to live as an obedient people in response to a good God.

Deuteronomy contains many laws and specific instructions to the people of Israel. It can be tempting to read these rules from a modern-day perspective, raising an eyebrow at what seem like confusing or confining commands. But to nomads without a criminal justice system or legal code, these instructions were necessary and steadying. After all, the gods of surrounding regions were considered fickle, sometimes cruel, and constantly changing their minds on what pleased them. In giving His Law to Israel, the one true God offers His people clarity and stability—no games, no walking on eggshells, no guessing what pleases Him.

No games, no walking on eggshells.

God had always been faithful to Israel—from Egypt to the exodus and through the wilderness. And now, as they finally enter into this promised land under covenant with God, He formally promises to continue being the "faithful God who keeps his gracious covenant loyalty for a thousand generations with those who love him and keep his commands" (Deuteronomy 7:9).

By entering into the promised land under the conditions of this covenant, Israel was entering into a new kind of life—one that demonstrated God's goodness and love to the entire world, bearing witness to the only One who makes a family out of wanderers.

Joshua

"Haven't I commanded you:
be strong and courageous?
Do not be afraid or discouraged,
for the LORD your God is
with you wherever you go."

JOSHUA 1:9

JOSHUA 1:1–11

Encouragement of Joshua

1 After the death of Moses the LORD's servant, the LORD spoke to Joshua son of
Nun, Moses's assistant: 2 "Moses my servant is dead. Now you and all the people
prepare to cross over the Jordan to the land I am giving the Israelites. 3 I have given
you every place where the sole of your foot treads, just as I promised Moses. 4 Your
territory will be from the wilderness and Lebanon to the great river, the Euphrates
River—all the land of the Hittites—and west to the Mediterranean Sea. 5 No one
will be able to stand against you as long as you live. I will be with you, just as I was
with Moses. I will not leave you or abandon you.

6 "Be strong and courageous, for you will distribute the land I swore to their ancestors to give them as an inheritance. 7 Above all, be strong and very courageous to
observe carefully the whole instruction my servant Moses commanded you. Do
not turn from it to the right or the left, so that you will have success wherever
you go. 8 This book of instruction must not depart from your mouth; you are
to meditate on it day and night so that you may carefully observe everything
written in it. For then you will prosper and succeed in whatever you do. 9 Haven't
I commanded you: be strong and courageous? Do not be afraid or discouraged,
for the LORD your God is with you wherever you go."

Joshua Prepares the People

10 Then Joshua commanded the officers of the people, 11 "Go through the camp
and tell the people, 'Get provisions ready for yourselves, for within three days you
will be crossing the Jordan to go in and take possession of the land the LORD your
God is giving you to inherit.'"

PSALM 73:23–26

God's Ways Vindicated

[23] Yet I am always with you;
you hold my right hand.
[24] You guide me with your counsel,
and afterward you will take me up in glory.
[25] Who do I have in heaven but you?
And I desire nothing on earth but you.
[26] My flesh and my heart may fail,
but God is the strength of my heart,
my portion forever.

MATTHEW 28:16–20

The Great Commission

[16] The eleven disciples traveled to Galilee, to
the mountain where Jesus had directed them.
[17] When they saw him, they worshiped, but some
doubted. [18] Jesus came near and said to them, "All
authority has been given to me in heaven and on
earth. [19] Go, therefore, and make disciples of all
nations, baptizing them in the name of the Father
and of the Son and of the Holy Spirit, [20] teaching
them to observe everything I have commanded
you. And remember, I am with you always, to the
end of the age."

HEBREWS 13:5–6

Final Exhortations

[5] Keep your life free from the love of money. Be
satisfied with what you have, for he himself has
said, "I will never leave you or abandon you."
[6] Therefore, we may boldly say,

> "The Lord is my helper;
> I will not be afraid.
> What can man do to me?"

Imagine a terrible road trip on the way to a tropical resort.

After enduring three bouts of standstill traffic, a flat tire, and a broken transmission, you finally arrive at paradise—only to face worse. Due to regional flooding, a 2-mile-wide moat surrounds the resort. What's more, the local guide who was supposed to help you never shows up. And to top it off, you call the resort and hear, "Sorry! I see your guaranteed reservation here, but other people have taken your room, activities, and dinner reservations." You're stranded, seeing paradise before you, but with no way through the water, no guide, and strangers occupying your room.

Israel faced something similar, but far worse.

God had delivered Israel to the promised land and also, in His Law, given them the ground rules for navigating life within it. All that was left to do? Enter. Except for three problems: the Jordan River blocked their entrance, Israel's leader (Moses) had died, and there were already occupants in the land. Their destination was within eyeshot, but with no bridge to reach it, no leader to guide them, and no ability to conquer it.

Good thing God specializes in appointing leaders, parting waters, and winning battles.

In the book of Joshua, God overcomes each obstacle. First, He gives the people a new leader: Joshua. With Joshua installed, God instructs him directly: "Now you and all the people prepare to cross over the Jordan to the land I am giving the Israelites" (Joshua 1:2).

What must it have been like to receive instructions straight from the mouth of the Lord? We can't know for sure, but we can infer from what God said next that Joshua was apprehensive about the enormous task ahead of him: "I will be with you, just as I was with Moses. I will not leave you or abandon you" (Joshua 1:5).

God specializes in appointing leaders, parting waters, and winning battles.

Put yourself in Joshua's place, the weight of a nation's survival on your shoulders and impossible battles before you. Let God's promise sink in.

God was indeed with Joshua as he faced Israel's remaining obstacles. God stopped the flow of the river, and Joshua successfully led the Israelites across it, accompanied by the tangible presence of God in the ark of the covenant. God also fought for Israel as they took possession of the promised land under Joshua's command. Everyone who followed Joshua benefited from God's presence with him.

Joshua's life and mission point to someone greater: Jesus Christ. As God's work through Joshua was for the benefit of all those who followed and obeyed Joshua, God's work through Christ is extended today to all those who follow and obey Jesus. As Joshua led Israel through the Jordan, Jesus leads us through the waters of death and into resurrection life. As Joshua ushered Israel into a new land, Jesus will one day usher us into a renewed world. As Joshua defeated Israel's enemies, Jesus defeats our true enemies: the world, the flesh, and the devil.

Knowing this we can rejoice, free from fear. "The Lord is my helper; I will not be afraid. What can man do to me?" (Hebrews 13:6).

Judges

In those days there was no king in Israel; everyone did whatever seemed right to him.

JUDGES 21:25

JUDGES 2:1–23

Pattern of Sin and Judgment

1 The angel of the LORD went up from Gilgal to Bochim and said, "I brought you out of Egypt and led you into the land I had promised to your ancestors. I also said: I will never break my covenant with you. 2 You are not to make a covenant with the inhabitants of this land. You are to tear down their altars. But you have not obeyed me. What have you done? 3 Therefore, I now say: I will not drive out these people before you. They will be thorns in your sides, and their gods will be a trap for you." 4 When the angel of the LORD had spoken these words to all the Israelites, the people wept loudly. 5 So they named that place Bochim and offered sacrifices there to the LORD.

Joshua's Death

6 Previously, when Joshua had sent the people away, the Israelites had gone to take possession of the land, each to his own inheritance. 7 The people worshiped the LORD throughout Joshua's lifetime and during the lifetimes of the elders who outlived Joshua. They had seen all the LORD's great works he had done for Israel.

8 Joshua son of Nun, the servant of the LORD, died at the age of 110. 9 They buried him in the territory of his inheritance, in Timnath-heres, in the hill country of Ephraim, north of Mount Gaash. 10 That whole generation was also gathered to their ancestors. After them another generation rose up who did not know the LORD or the works he had done for Israel.

11 The Israelites did what was evil in the LORD's sight. They worshiped the Baals 12 and abandoned the LORD, the God of their ancestors, who had brought them out of Egypt. They followed other gods from the surrounding peoples and bowed down to them. They angered the LORD, 13 for they abandoned him and worshiped Baal and the Ashtoreths.

14 The LORD's anger burned against Israel, and he handed them over to marauders who raided them. He sold them to the enemies around them, and they could no longer resist their enemies. 15 Whenever the Israelites went out, the LORD was against them and brought disaster on them, just as he had promised and sworn to them. So they suffered greatly.

16 The LORD raised up judges, who saved them from the power of their marauders, 17 but they did not listen to their judges. Instead, they prostituted themselves with other gods, bowing down to them. They quickly turned from the way of their ancestors, who had walked in obedience to the LORD's commands. They did not do as their ancestors did. 18 Whenever the LORD raised up a judge for the Israelites, the LORD was with him and saved the people from the power of their enemies while the judge was still alive. The LORD was moved to pity whenever they groaned because of those who were oppressing and afflicting them. 19 Whenever the judge died, the Israelites would act even more corruptly than their ancestors, following other gods to serve them and bow in worship to them. They did not turn from their evil practices or their obstinate ways.

20 The LORD's anger burned against Israel, and he declared, "Because this nation has violated my covenant that I made with their ancestors and disobeyed me, 21 I will no longer drive out before them any of the nations Joshua left when he died. 22 I did this to test Israel and to see whether or not they would keep the LORD's way by walking in it, as their ancestors had." 23 The LORD left these nations and did not drive them out immediately. He did not hand them over to Joshua.

JUDGES 21:25

In those days there was no king in Israel; everyone did whatever seemed right to him.

PROVERBS 21:2–3

2 All a person's ways seem right to him,
but the LORD weighs hearts.

3 Doing what is righteous and just
is more acceptable to the LORD than sacrifice.

MARK 12:28–31

The Primary Commands

28 One of the scribes approached. When he heard
them debating and saw that Jesus answered them
well, he asked him, "Which command is the most
important of all?"

29 Jesus answered, "The most important is 'Listen,
Israel! The Lord our God, the Lord is one. 30 Love
the Lord your God with all your heart, with all
your soul, with all your mind, and with all your
strength.' 31 The second is, 'Love your neighbor as
yourself.' There is no other command greater than
these."

Have you ever grown complacent in a relationship that means the world to you? Unfortunately, it's an easy thing to do. Even in relationships with a long history of hard work to get to a healthy place, we can get comfortable and start to just, well, coast. And the thing about coasting is, it rarely ends well.

I'm guilty of this in big and small ways, whether it's slipping into a season of living parallel lives with my husband rather than intentionally connecting with him, or letting a treasured friendship fade away because I'm consumed with the urgencies of everyday life. We get comfortable, we forget what's most important to us, and we might even look elsewhere for something shiny and new.

This is what happens to Israel's relationship with God in the book of Judges, only in a much more severe way.

Joshua had faithfully led God's people into the promised land, and at first, the Israelites remembered God's steadfast love. "They had seen all the LORD's great works he had done for Israel" (Judges 2:7). But soon they grew complacent and, enticed by the false gods of their new neighbors, they forgot God—the one who had just proven His deity by delivering them through the waters of the Jordan. After wandering for decades in the desert, they now wandered with their hearts.

And they didn't do this just once. Over and over, Israel forgot God, and over and over, the Lord sent a leader, called a judge, to call them back to Himself and to right living. No matter how many times they returned, though, it was only a matter of time before Israel went right back to doing "whatever seemed right to him" (Judges 21:25), worshiping the pagan gods of their neighbors. This choice to follow false gods was no neutral matter—it always resulted in Israel becoming increasingly compromised and cruel, instead of the holy and honorable people God called them to be.

> **We get comfortable, we forget what's most important, and we might even look elsewhere for something shiny and new.**

What amazes me about this book is that despite Israel's failures, God remained faithful. He continued to send judge after judge, knowing His people would still turn away. It's a dark era in Israel's story, but it reveals the goodness and mercy of a God who will continue to pursue His people, calling them back to their true God and their true identity.

The cycle of the judges seemed unending, and cycles of sin and repentance will continue in our human hearts until we are at home with Christ. Sometimes I draw close to God's heart and enjoy His steadfast love, and other times, like Israel, I chase after false gods and lesser loves. But there is hope! In a show of ultimate mercy and pursuit, God sent Jesus, the faithful and final Judge. Jesus is able to justify us not because of our faithfulness, but because of His. He alone reconciles us to God, no matter how many times we forget Him.

What kind of season are you in? Do you find yourself drifting? Are you pursuing what is "right in your own eyes"? Stop the cycle and run to Christ.

Ruth

The women said to Naomi, "Blessed be the LORD, who has not left you without a family redeemer today. May his name become well known in Israel."

RUTH 4:14

RUTH 1:1–5

Naomi's Family in Moab

1 During the time of the judges, there was a famine in the land. A man left Bethlehem in Judah with his wife and two sons to stay in the territory of Moab for a while. 2 The man's name was Elimelech, and his wife's name was Naomi. The names of his two sons were Mahlon and Chilion. They were Ephrathites from Bethlehem in Judah. They entered the fields of Moab and settled there. 3 Naomi's husband, Elimelech, died, and she was left with her two sons. 4 Her sons took Moabite women as their wives: one was named Orpah and the second was named Ruth. After they lived in Moab about ten years, 5 both Mahlon and Chilion also died, and the woman was left without her two children and without her husband.

RUTH 2:1–3, 8–12

Ruth and Boaz Meet

1 Now Naomi had a relative on her husband's side. He was a prominent man of noble character from Elimelech's family. His name was Boaz.

2 Ruth the Moabitess asked Naomi, "Will you let me go into the fields and gather fallen grain behind someone with whom I find favor?"

Naomi answered her, "Go ahead, my daughter." 3 So Ruth left and entered the field to gather grain behind the harvesters. She happened to be in the portion of the field belonging to Boaz, who was from Elimelech's family.

. . .

8 Then Boaz said to Ruth, "Listen, my daughter. Don't go and gather grain in another field, and don't leave this one, but stay here close to my female servants. 9 See which field they are harvesting, and follow them. Haven't I ordered the young men not to touch you? When you are thirsty, go and drink from the jars the young men have filled."

10 She fell facedown, bowed to the ground, and said to him, "Why have I found favor with you, so that you notice me, although I am a foreigner?"

11 Boaz answered her, "Everything you have done for your mother-in-law since your husband's death has been fully reported to me: how you left your father and mother and your native land, and how you came to a people you didn't previously know. 12 May the Lord reward you for what you have done, and may you receive a full reward from the Lord God of Israel, under whose wings you have come for refuge."

RUTH 4:1–6

Ruth and Boaz Marry

1 Boaz went to the gate of the town and sat down there. Soon the family redeemer Boaz had spoken about came by. Boaz said, "Come over here and sit down." So he went over and sat down. 2 Then Boaz took ten men of the town's elders and said, "Sit here." And they sat down. 3 He said to the redeemer, "Naomi, who has returned from the territory of Moab, is selling the portion of the field that belonged to our brother Elimelech. 4 I thought I should inform you: Buy it back in the presence of those seated here and in the presence of the elders of my people. If you want to redeem it, do it. But if you do not want to redeem it, tell me so that I will know, because there isn't anyone other than you to redeem it, and I am next after you."

"I want to redeem it," he answered.

5 Then Boaz said, "On the day you buy the field from Naomi, you will acquire Ruth the Moabitess, the wife of the deceased man, to perpetuate the man's name on his property."

6 The redeemer replied, "I can't redeem it myself, or I will ruin my own inheritance. Take my right of redemption, because I can't redeem it."

RUTH 4:13–17

Ruth and Boaz Marry

13 Boaz took Ruth and she became his wife. He
slept with her, and the LORD granted conception
to her, and she gave birth to a son. 14 The women
said to Naomi, "Blessed be the LORD, who has not
left you without a family redeemer today. May
his name become well known in Israel. 15 He will
renew your life and sustain you in your old age.
Indeed, your daughter-in-law, who loves you and
is better to you than seven sons, has given birth to
him." 16 Naomi took the child, placed him on her
lap, and became a mother to him. 17 The neighbor
women said, "A son has been born to Naomi," and
they named him Obed. He was the father of Jesse,
the father of David.

ISAIAH 54:4–5

Future Glory for Israel

4 "Do not be afraid, for you will not be put
to shame;
don't be humiliated, for you will not be disgraced.
For you will forget the shame of your youth,
and you will no longer remember
the disgrace of your widowhood.
5 Indeed, your husband is your Maker—
his name is the LORD of Armies—
and the Holy One of Israel is your Redeemer;
he is called the God of the whole earth."

TITUS 2:11–14

Sound Teaching and Christian Living

11 For the grace of God has appeared, bringing
salvation for all people, 12 instructing us to deny
godlessness and worldly lusts and to live in a sensible, righteous, and godly way in the present age,
13 while we wait for the blessed hope, the appearing of the glory of our great God and Savior, Jesus
Christ. 14 He gave himself for us to redeem us from
all lawlessness and to cleanse for himself a people
for his own possession, eager to do good works.

I sometimes feel caught off guard by the harsh reality of living under a curse. A broken world in need of redemption means I shouldn't be surprised when I or the people I love suffer loss, injury, and danger. I know these hardships are happening in every corner of the globe, but when I receive a text that a dear friend is having a miscarriage, or sit with a loved one whose anxiety I'm powerless to ease, or read reports of devastating tragedy happening in my own town—it feels personal. And yes, still somehow surprising.

Ruth lived in a broken world too. In fact, she lived during the darkest days of Israel's history—the time of the Judges. And it wasn't just her nation in turmoil—it was her personal life too. Her Israelite-born husband had died, and she lived now as a widow in a land far from Israel. Along with her mother-in-law, Naomi, Ruth was completely isolated and desolate.

In those days, if a man died, it was customary and honorable in Israel for his nearest brother, or kinsman, to take responsibility for the man's widow—to ensure her wellbeing, marry her, and continue his brother's bloodline through their marriage. This person was called a "kinsman redeemer." But Ruth's brother-in-law and father-in-law were both dead. And Ruth wasn't even in Israel—she was a foreigner in Moab. Where would she begin?

Ruth and Naomi did eventually arrive in Israel, and they arrived hungry. Ruth gathered grain for the two of them on the outskirts of a field that belonged to a man named Boaz, who just so happened to be a relative of her late husband. By God's sovereignty, Ruth found herself in the backyard of her family's kinsman redeemer.

Boaz was honorable—he found many ways to care for Ruth, not the least of which was a proposal of marriage. Boaz married Ruth, and they had a son named Obed, who would be the father of Jesse, who would be the father of King David, Israel's great and mighty king. Ruth, the Moabite widow, became part of the very lineage of Christ!

Boaz isn't the hero of this story.

As much as I love his heroic love, Boaz isn't the hero of this story. Jesus is our true and better kinsman redeemer who takes those who are far from God, "foreigners to the covenants of promise" (Ephesians 2:12), and brings us in and gives us new life in Him. While Boaz was the kinsman redeemer for Ruth, making her part of a family again, Jesus is the Kinsman Redeemer who makes us His family, giving true, abundant, and eternal life to everyone who puts their trust in Him.

What are the hardest parts of your story? What areas of life feel too far gone for anything good to happen? Where do you find yourself isolated or hungry for help? Remember Ruth and take heart. God's sovereignty rules the day. Trust Him to work in seen and unseen ways, and rest in the joy of Jesus Christ, your eternal hope and your redeemer.

1 Samuel

But the Lord told him, "Listen to the people and everything they say to you. They have not rejected you; they have rejected me as their king."

1 SAMUEL 8:7

1 SAMUEL 8:1–22

Israel's Demand for a King

1 When Samuel grew old, he appointed his sons as judges over Israel. 2 His
firstborn son's name was Joel and his second was Abijah. They were judges in
Beer-sheba. 3 However, his sons did not walk in his ways—they turned toward
dishonest profit, took bribes, and perverted justice.

4 So all the elders of Israel gathered together and went to Samuel at Ramah.
5 They said to him, "Look, you are old, and your sons do not walk in your ways.
Therefore, appoint a king to judge us the same as all the other nations have."

6 When they said, "Give us a king to judge us," Samuel considered their demand
wrong, so he prayed to the LORD. 7 But the LORD told him, "Listen to the people
and everything they say to you. They have not rejected you; they have rejected
me as their king. 8 They are doing the same thing to you that they have done to
me, since the day I brought them out of Egypt until this day, abandoning me and
worshiping other gods. 9 Listen to them, but solemnly warn them and tell them
about the customary rights of the king who will reign over them."

10 Samuel told all the LORD's words to the people who were asking him for a king.
11 He said, "These are the rights of the king who will reign over you: He will take
your sons and put them to his use in his chariots, on his horses, or running in front
of his chariots. 12 He can appoint them for his use as commanders of thousands
or commanders of fifties, to plow his ground and reap his harvest, or to make his
weapons of war and the equipment for his chariots. 13 He can take your daughters
to become perfumers, cooks, and bakers. 14 He can take your best fields, vineyards,
and olive orchards and give them to his servants. 15 He can take a tenth of your
grain and your vineyards and give them to his officials and servants. 16 He can take
your male servants, your female servants, your best cattle, and your donkeys and
use them for his work. 17 He can take a tenth of your flocks, and you yourselves
can become his servants. 18 When that day comes, you will cry out because of the
king you've chosen for yourselves, but the LORD won't answer you on that day."

19 The people refused to listen to Samuel. "No!" they said. "We must have a king
over us. 20 Then we'll be like all the other nations: our king will judge us, go out
before us, and fight our battles."

21 Samuel listened to all the people's words and then repeated them to the LORD.
22 "Listen to them," the LORD told Samuel. "Appoint a king for them."

Then Samuel told the men of Israel, "Each of you, go back to your city."

PROVERBS 1:29–33

Wisdom's Plea

29 Because they hated knowledge,
didn't choose to fear the LORD,
30 were not interested in my counsel,
and rejected all my correction,
31 they will eat the fruit of their way
and be glutted with their own schemes.
32 For the apostasy of the inexperienced will
kill them,
and the complacency of fools will destroy them.
33 But whoever listens to me will live securely
and be undisturbed by the dread of danger.

PROVERBS 14:12

There is a way that seems right to a person,
but its end is the way to death.

1 TIMOTHY 1:15–17

Paul's Testimony

15 This saying is trustworthy and deserving of full
acceptance: "Christ Jesus came into the world to
save sinners"—and I am the worst of them. 16 But
I received mercy for this reason, so that in me, the
worst of them, Christ Jesus might demonstrate his
extraordinary patience as an example to those who
would believe in him for eternal life. 17 Now to the
King eternal, immortal, invisible, the only God, be
honor and glory forever and ever. Amen.

"Mom. We look like tourists!"

As typical human teenagers, one of my kids' deepest desires is to blend in. So when I walked the streets of Paris with them last spring, holding up my phone to follow the maps app, or stopping a stranger to ask her to take our photo in front of the Eiffel Tower, they were understandably mortified. They're sweet and they'll indulge me, but I know my kids, and it goes against their human instincts to draw attention to anything about themselves that is different.

Israel was in a similar position. They'd come all this way and they were set apart from the nations, but what they really wanted was to blend in.

They may not have looked like much, but Israel was head and shoulders above all other nations. They were God's chosen people—led by Him, protected by Him, and ruled by Him. Yet, they desired something less, hoping it might be something more. Tired of rotating leaders who only held the status of judge, Israel wanted a king, and they wanted one now. What kind of king? "The same as all the other nations have" (1 Samuel 8:5). *Moms of teens, does this sound familiar?*

With a warning against their choice, God gave Israel her first king. King Saul was, "an impressive young man. There was no one more impressive among the Israelites than he. He stood a head taller than anyone else" (1 Samuel 9:2). Israel liked the idea of Saul fighting their battles. They wanted someone they could see—someone who looked like them, and someone that made them look like everyone else. Israel trusted Saul to be kind and fair. But no one is good like God.

I think of another time a crowd demanded a similar trade. Offering the Son of God Himself, the people of Israel followed Him all the way to the cross, shouting, "We have no king but Caesar!" (John 19:15). Even with God incarnate in their midst, they wanted the same kind of king as their neighbors.

Why are we so afraid to look like tourists?

It's a habit we have as God's people. We want to blend in and rule our lives like the people around us, and it never stops getting us in trouble. We have a privileged position as God's chosen people, led by Him, protected by Him, and ruled by Him. So why are we afraid to look like tourists? Afraid to look different or like we don't belong?

The truth? The earth is the Lord's and everything in it (Psalm 24:1). As coheirs with Christ, this is our turf. Our ultimate home is with God in a renewed world, but we are appointed to live in the fallen version of it right now—in allegiance to our King.

Who or what are we trusting to rule our lives and fight our battles? Are we crying out for man to be our defense, or are we believing—and living like—our God is King?

Believe today that He will fight your battles. Pray even now that He will go before you. Know that He alone is your sure defense (Psalm 94:22).

2 Samuel

"The LORD declares to you:
The LORD himself will
make a house for you."

2 SAMUEL 7:11b

2 SAMUEL 7:1–17

The LORD's Covenant with David

1 When the king had settled into his palace and the LORD had given him rest on
every side from all his enemies, 2 the king said to the prophet Nathan, "Look I am
living in a cedar house while the ark of God sits inside tent curtains."

3 So Nathan told the king, "Go and do all that is on your mind, for the LORD is
with you."

4 But that night the word of the LORD came to Nathan: 5 "Go to my servant David
and say, 'This is what the LORD says: Are you to build me a house to dwell in?
6 From the time I brought the Israelites out of Egypt until today I have not dwelt
in a house; instead, I have been moving around with a tent as my dwelling. 7 In all
my journeys with all the Israelites, have I ever spoken a word to one of the tribal
leaders of Israel, whom I commanded to shepherd my people Israel, asking: Why
haven't you built me a house of cedar?'

8 "So now this is what you are to say to my servant David: 'This is what the LORD
of Armies says: I took you from the pasture, from tending the flock, to be ruler
over my people Israel. 9 I have been with you wherever you have gone, and I have
destroyed all your enemies before you. I will make a great name for you like that of
the greatest on the earth. 10 I will designate a place for my people Israel and plant
them, so that they may live there and not be disturbed again. Evildoers will not
continue to oppress them as they have done 11 ever since the day I ordered judges
to be over my people Israel. I will give you rest from all your enemies.

"'The LORD declares to you: The LORD himself will make a house for you. 12 When
your time comes and you rest with your ancestors, I will raise up after you your
descendant, who will come from your body, and I will establish his kingdom.
13 He is the one who will build a house for my name, and I will establish the
throne of his kingdom forever. 14 I will be his father, and he will be my son. When
he does wrong, I will discipline him with a rod of men and blows from mortals.
15 But my faithful love will never leave him as it did when I removed it from Saul,
whom I removed from before you. 16 Your house and kingdom will endure before
me forever, and your throne will be established forever.'"

17 Nathan reported all these words and this entire vision to David.

PSALM 84:10

Longing for God's House

Better a day in your courts
than a thousand anywhere else.
I would rather stand at the threshold of the
  house of my God
than live in the tents of wicked people.

REVELATION 22:16

The Time Is Near

"I, Jesus, have sent my angel to attest these things to you for the churches. I am the Root and descendant of David, the bright morning star."

Author and theologian C. S. Lewis called it "the scent of a flower we have not found, the echo of a tune we have not heard, news from a country we have never yet visited."[5] It's that deep longing in us that tells us that this world as we experience it can't be all there is. There must be something more. Something better. Something right. You feel it, don't you?

This feeling is God-given and true. It's one the Israelites experienced, and one we do, too. Each of us longs for a perfect world—a world which could not exist without a perfect King.

In most every case in history, the pursuit of a better kingdom has involved finding and crowning a new and better leader. Sometimes this happens through a peaceful transition of power, other times it comes by way of a coup, but throughout world history, people have been restless to find a better world.

There must be something more. Something better.

Here's how God's kingdom is different: The goal is not to keep looking for kings who are better than the ones we have now—always searching, always coming up short. In God's kingdom, the true and perfect King has existed since before the dawn of time. His eternal rule has never been in doubt, and neither have His qualifications.

In the book of 1 Samuel, Israel asked God for someone to rule over them. And of course, God's plan was even better. He intended to give them not just one king, but a kingly line that would last forever. After King Saul took the throne and failed, the Lord used the ministry of the prophet Samuel to anoint David as Israel's new king. And God told King David that one would come from his line who would rule for all eternity as a perfect and just King.

Israel longed for this king. But the one God had in mind wouldn't be just another man. The King who was coming to them would be God Himself (Isaiah 9:6). He would be the Savior born in Bethlehem to the wonder of the shepherds and the exaltation of the angelic host. He would be the King the wise men sought so they could worship at His feet, and the threat to Herod's iron fist of control. He would be Isaiah's Suffering Servant crucified for the iniquities of the people, atoning for their sins through His blood.

Every move Jesus made was to establish the kingdom over which He would reign forever. That's what our hearts are longing for—an eternally secure and established kingdom, ruled by a perfect, eternal King.

Are you aching today for a place you've never been? Have courage! Christ, your King, is already on His throne, and His kingdom is already underway. One day He will establish it fully and forevermore.

Your longing is not in vain. Your King reigns, and His kingdom is at hand.

1 Kings

When all the people saw
it, they fell facedown and
said, "The LORD, he is God!
The LORD, he is God!"

1 KINGS 18:39

1 KINGS 18:20–21, 30–39

Elijah at Mount Carmel

20 So Ahab summoned all the Israelites and gathered the prophets at Mount
Carmel. 21 Then Elijah approached all the people and said, "How long will you
waver between two opinions? If the LORD is God, follow him. But if Baal, follow
him." But the people didn't answer him a word.

. . .

30 Then Elijah said to all the people, "Come near me." So all the people approached
him. Then he repaired the LORD's altar that had been torn down: 31 Elijah took
twelve stones—according to the number of the tribes of the sons of Jacob, to
whom the word of the LORD had come, saying, "Israel will be your name"—
32 and he built an altar with the stones in the name of the LORD. Then he made
a trench around the altar large enough to hold about four gallons. 33 Next, he
arranged the wood, cut up the bull, and placed it on the wood. He said, "Fill four
water pots with water and pour it on the offering to be burned and on the wood."
34 Then he said, "A second time!" and they did it a second time. And then he said,
"A third time!" and they did it a third time. 35 So the water ran all around the altar;
he even filled the trench with water.

36 At the time for offering the evening sacrifice, the prophet Elijah approached
the altar and said, "LORD, the God of Abraham, Isaac, and Israel, today let it be
known that you are God in Israel and I am your servant, and that at your word I
have done all these things. 37 Answer me, LORD! Answer me so that this people will
know that you, the LORD, are God and that you have turned their hearts back."

38 Then the LORD's fire fell and consumed the burnt offering, the wood, the stones,
and the dust, and it licked up the water that was in the trench. 39 When all the
people saw it, they fell facedown and said, "The LORD, he is God! The LORD, he
is God!"

REVELATION 19:11–16

The Rider on a White Horse

11 Then I saw heaven opened, and there was a white horse. Its rider is called
Faithful and True, and with justice he judges and makes war. 12 His eyes were like
a fiery flame, and many crowns were on his head. He had a name written that no
one knows except himself. 13 He wore a robe dipped in blood, and his name is
called the Word of God. 14 The armies that were in heaven followed him on white
horses, wearing pure white linen. 15 A sharp sword came from his mouth, so that
he might strike the nations with it. He will rule them with an iron rod. He will
also trample the winepress of the fierce anger of God, the Almighty. 16 And he has
a name written on his robe and on his thigh: KING OF KINGS AND LORD OF LORDS.

I took a sabbatical-style break from work a couple of summers ago. I desperately needed the downshift in pace, and I was looking forward to more time in my garden and kitchen, being a more available mama to my teenagers, and connecting with my friends. What surprised me was the restlessness I began to feel with this new slower pace. I was accustomed to having every minute of my days spoken for, with high-capacity work, important meetings, and big-impact decisions. But during this break, I had days when my family was buzzing in and out around me, and I was much less busy, struggling to find a sense of purpose.

Elijah was a man with a clear purpose. If he'd had a mission statement, it would have been something like: *Promote loyalty to God in a pagan culture.* Elijah also knew Israel had a purpose: *Worship God alone, and make God known to the world.*

Part of Israel's call to loyalty included the responsibility to preserve their one true faith. Preserving that faith meant opposing the infiltration of idolatry or the blending of their worship with pagan practices and traditions, especially in the stories of 1 Kings.

Having a call like Elijah's meant living a life of opposition—all the time. Apart from the protection of God, he would have been doomed. But as we see in his confrontation with the prophets of Baal, God displayed His power through Elijah's ministry in ways that not only prevailed over the false prophets, but caused people to think twice before opposing Elijah or his God.

I've heard it said that if the gospel you're preaching can't resonate around the globe and across time, you aren't preaching a true gospel. The gospel of covenant loyalty and divine purpose we see in Elijah's story is one that preached a thousand years before Christ and continues to preach today, both on Mount Carmel in Israel and in my home in Nashville. Whether you're a high-capacity CEO or dropping off a cooler full of bottled waters at a lacrosse game, the truth is, every believer has a purpose. Always. And our purpose isn't far off from Elijah's. It may look different (no calling down fire on a drenched altar for me in Nashville), but the spirit is the same.

As followers of Jesus Christ, you and I may face seasons of restlessness—but it should never be because we don't know our ultimate aim in life. No matter where we find ourselves, we are called to promote loyalty to God in a pagan culture. And we are absolutely called to worship God alone, and to make God known to the world. While that's going to look different for me than it does for you, and it's going to look different for all of us than it did for Elijah, we're invited into a high calling that can give us purpose and vision every day of our lives.

Every believer has a purpose. Always.

What holy work has God placed before you today?

"Lord, You have made us for Yourself,
and our heart is restless until it finds its rest in You."[4]

–The Confessions of St. Augustine

2 Kings

For the sake of his servant David, the LORD was unwilling to destroy Judah, since he had promised to give a lamp to David and his sons forever.

2 KINGS 8:19

2 KINGS 8:16–19

Judah's King Jehoram

16 In the fifth year of Israel's King Joram son of Ahab, Jehoram son of Jehoshaphat became king of Judah, replacing his father. 17 He was thirty-two years old when he became king, and he reigned eight years in Jerusalem. 18 He walked in the ways of the kings of Israel, as the house of Ahab had done, for Ahab's daughter was his wife. He did what was evil in the LORD's sight. 19 For the sake of his servant David, the LORD was unwilling to destroy Judah, since he had promised to give a lamp to David and his sons forever.

2 KINGS 22:1–11

Judah's King Josiah

1 Josiah was eight years old when he became king, and he reigned thirty-one years in Jerusalem. His mother's name was Jedidah the daughter of Adaiah; she was from Bozkath. 2 He did what was right in the LORD's sight and walked in all the ways of his ancestor David; he did not turn to the right or the left.

Josiah Repairs the Temple

3 In the eighteenth year of King Josiah, the king sent the court secretary Shaphan son of Azaliah, son of Meshullam, to the LORD's temple, saying, 4 "Go up to the high priest Hilkiah so that he may total up the silver brought into the LORD's temple—the silver the doorkeepers have collected from the people. 5 It is to be given to those doing the work—those who oversee the LORD's temple. They in turn are to give it to the workmen in the LORD's temple to repair the damage. 6 They are to give it to the carpenters, builders, and masons to buy timber and quarried stone to repair the temple. 7 But no accounting is to be required from them for the silver given to them since they work with integrity."

The Book of the Law Found

8 The high priest Hilkiah told the court secretary Shaphan, "I have found the book of the law in the LORD's temple," and he gave the book to Shaphan, who read it.

9 Then the court secretary Shaphan went to the king and reported, "Your servants have emptied out the silver that was found in the temple and have given it to those doing the work—those who oversee the LORD's temple." 10 Then the court secretary Shaphan told the king, "The priest Hilkiah has given me a book," and Shaphan read it in the presence of the king.

11 When the king heard the words of the book of the law, he tore his clothes.

2 KINGS 23:1–3

Covenant Renewal

1 So the king sent messengers, and they gathered all the elders of Judah and Jerusalem to him. 2 Then the king went to the LORD's temple with all the men of Judah and all the inhabitants of Jerusalem, as well as the priests and the prophets—all the people from the youngest to the oldest. He read in their hearing all the words of the book of the covenant that had been found in the LORD's temple. 3 Next, the king stood by the pillar, and made a covenant in the LORD's presence to follow the LORD and to keep his commands, his decrees, and his statutes with all his heart and with all his soul in order to carry out the words of this covenant that were written in this book; all the people agreed to the covenant.

PSALM 119:55

Delight in God's Word

LORD, I remember your name in the night,
and I obey your instruction.

MATTHEW 2:1–6

Wise Men Visit the King

1 After Jesus was born in Bethlehem of Judea in the days of King Herod, wise men from the east arrived in Jerusalem,
2 saying, "Where is he who has been born king of the Jews? For we saw his star at its rising and have come to worship him."

3 When King Herod heard this, he was deeply disturbed, and all Jerusalem with him.
4 So he assembled all the chief priests and scribes of the people and asked them where the Messiah would be born.

5 "In Bethlehem of Judea," they told him, "because this is what was written by the prophet:

> 6 'And you, Bethlehem,' in the land of Judah,
> are by no means 'least among the rulers
> of Judah:
> Because out of you will come a ruler
> who will shepherd my people Israel.'"

JOHN 14:23–24

23 Jesus answered, "If anyone loves me, he will keep my word. My Father will love him, and we will come to him and make our home with him.
24 The one who doesn't love me will not keep my words. The word that you hear is not mine but is from the Father who sent me."

In a former season of life, I worked for a real estate developer. In addition to keeping my boss relatively organized and sane, my job was to keep our buyers happy and, more importantly, keep their contracts intact.

This was easier said than done for a myriad of reasons, the primary one being time. Condo developments are often sold before they are built, and it is not uncommon for a buyer—a person who has contractually agreed to purchase one of the condo units—to wait upwards of a year or even two for their home to be ready. Two years is a long time to wait for something you've already partially paid for, and it's ample time to overthink every detail. You can imagine the number of emails a buyer might send to the developer's assistant (hi, that's me) about anything from finish selections and timeline updates, to contract addendums and pricing adjustments. Yep, two years' worth.

(Did I mention the emails continued after the condos were finished and the contracts closed? Construction punch lists and buyer warranties are not for the faint of heart, my friend.)

Truth be told, I loved that job. I like to hear people out, listen to their concerns, and help them reach a solution. I enjoyed the challenge of turning a frustrated buyer into a happy one. But I also learned that contracts exist for a reason. If the world ran on handshakes and feelings, it would be one rough ride.

The covenant God made with Israel through King David was like a contract—each party made a promise to the other. Israel promised to worship God alone, obeying His commands and living as His people. God promised to be their God and make them His people, establishing for them a kingdom that would reign forever (2 Samuel 7:16). The problem that we see over and over again in the Old Testament is that God's people did not uphold their part of the agreement. Based on Israel's actions, the contract should have been null and void.

But God.

"For the sake of his servant David, the Lord was unwilling to destroy Judah, since he had promised to give a lamp to David and his sons forever" (2 Kings 8:19). God kept His covenant with His people, even when they didn't do the same.

The contract should have been null and void.

The book of 2 Kings continues the roll call of rulers who failed to lead Israel in the ways of the one true God, landing them in a long and painful season of exile. But discouraging as it is to read, we can see God's gracious and merciful character displayed throughout Israel's unfaithful history. Even King Josiah, who "did what was right in the Lord's sight and walked in all the ways of his ancestor David" (2 Kings 22:2) realized after unearthing the book of the Law that his own obedience fell woefully short of God's holiness. Even good kings need God's mercy.

Does your faithfulness ever wane? Turn your eyes to the great Covenant Keeper. His love and mercy never fail. His promises are ironclad. We can trust Him to hold us as we hold on to Him.

1 Chronicles

Yours, Lord, is the greatness and the power and the glory and the splendor and the majesty, for everything in the heavens and on earth belongs to you. Yours, Lord, is the kingdom, and you are exalted as head over all.

1 CHRONICLES 29:11

1 CHRONICLES 29:10–22

David's Prayer

10 Then David blessed the LORD in the sight of all the assembly. David said,

May you be blessed, LORD God of our father Israel, from eternity to eternity. 11 Yours, LORD, is the greatness and the power and the glory and the splendor and the majesty, for everything in the heavens and on earth belongs to you. Yours, LORD, is the kingdom, and you are exalted as head over all. 12 Riches and honor come from you, and you are the ruler of everything. Power and might are in your hand, and it is in your hand to make great and to give strength to all. 13 Now therefore, our God, we give you thanks and praise your glorious name.

14 But who am I, and who are my people, that we should be able to give as generously as this? For everything comes from you, and we have given you only what comes from your own hand. 15 For we are aliens and temporary residents in your presence as were all our ancestors. Our days on earth are like a shadow, without hope. 16 LORD our God, all this wealth that we've provided for building you a house for your holy name comes from your hand; everything belongs to you. 17 I know, my God, that you test the heart and that you are pleased with what is right. I have willingly given all these things with an upright heart, and now I have seen your people who are present here giving joyfully and willingly to you. 18 LORD God of Abraham, Isaac, and Israel, our ancestors, keep this desire forever in the thoughts of the hearts of your people, and confirm their hearts toward you. 19 Give my son Solomon an undivided heart to keep and to carry out all your commands, your decrees, and your statutes, and to build the building for which I have made provision.

20 Then David said to the whole assembly, "Blessed be the LORD your God." So the whole assembly praised the LORD God of their ancestors. They knelt low and paid homage to the LORD and the king.

21 The following day they offered sacrifices to the LORD and burnt offerings to the LORD: a thousand bulls, a thousand rams, and a thousand lambs, along with their drink offerings, and sacrifices in abundance for all Israel. 22 They ate and drank with great joy in the LORD's presence that day.

The Enthronement of Solomon

Then, for a second time, they made David's son Solomon king; they anointed him as the LORD's ruler, and Zadok as the priest.

PSALM 132:11–12

David and Zion Chosen

11 The LORD swore an oath to David,
a promise he will not abandon:
"I will set one of your offspring
on your throne.
12 If your sons keep my covenant
and my decrees that I will teach them,
their sons will also sit on your throne forever."

REVELATION 5:13

I heard every creature in heaven, on earth, under the earth, on the sea, and everything in them say,

> Blessing and honor and glory and power
> be to the one seated on the throne,
> and to the Lamb, forever and ever!

I go to a church where forty percent of the congregation is made up of children ages ten and under. This means that on any given Sunday there are nearly as many kids in attendance as there are adults. It also means that the perimeter of the sanctuary doubles as a running track before and after the service, the bowl of mints in the lobby is regularly emptied by tiny hands, and church picnics are never, ever boring.

My favorite part of our child-filled church service is always the last sixty seconds: the Doxology. If your church's doxology isn't punctuated by tiny voices yell-singing "praise Father, Son, and Holy Ghost . . . AHHH-MENNNN"—well. You're missing out on something special.

Amen is a versatile word. It's a word of agreement *(Amen. So be it.)*, a word of surety *(Amen. It is true.)*, and even a word of hope *(Amen. May it be so.)*. It can be a word of prayer, of praise, of worship, or—as with our rather raucous weekly doxology—it can be all of the above.

The book of 1 Chronicles reads like a long and loud "amen."

The book of 1 Chronicles reads like a long and loud "amen." Written as the Israelites returned home after seventy years in captivity in Babylon, it was a testimony to them of God's faithfulness, His covenant promises, and their identity as His people. The exile was a national, personal, and religious crisis for the Israelites, after all, and their return was fraught with questions we all resonate with:

> *How do I trust God after my life has gone so much differently than I expected?*
>
> *How do we live rightly as the people of God here and now?*
>
> *How do we trust that the Messiah will come, thousands of years after we first were promised He would?*

The author of Chronicles answers these questions with a breathtaking view of God's work to restore His people over lifetimes of rebellion. From Adam to Enoch, Abraham to David and beyond, the Chronicler lays out the record of the God who holds all "the greatness and the power and the glory and the splendor and the majesty" and still cares intimately for His people (1 Chronicles 29:11). These are true stories of the God whose faithfulness precedes us and will long outlast us, stories that turn our hearts back to Him and prompt our praise.

God's restoration after rebellion is our story too. We know what it's like to be disoriented by our disobedience, to suffer the consequences of our choices and the choices of others, and to forget our identity as beloved children of God. Chronicles teaches us to look back on God's faithfulness when we don't know how to move forward. It shows us how to turn and return to Him as we wait in anticipation for Christ to come back. It reminds us that we are children of the always-loving, always-working, always-present God who is above all and over all.

To this we say, "Amen. So be it."

2 Chronicles

“If I shut the sky so there is no rain, or if I command the grasshopper to consume the land, or if I send pestilence on my people, and my people, who bear my name, humble themselves, pray and seek my face, and turn from their evil ways, then I will hear from heaven, forgive their sin, and heal their land.”

2 CHRONICLES 7:13–14

2 CHRONICLES 6:12–17

Solomon's Prayer

[12] Then Solomon stood before the altar of the LORD in front of the entire congregation of Israel and spread out his hands. [13] For Solomon had made a bronze platform 7½ feet long, 7½ feet wide, and 4½ feet high and put it in the court. He stood on it, knelt down in front of the entire congregation of Israel, and spread out his hands toward heaven. [14] He said:

> LORD God of Israel,
> there is no God like you
> in heaven or on earth,
> who keeps his gracious covenant
> with your servants who walk before you
> with all their heart.
> [15] You have kept what you promised
> to your servant, my father David.
> You spoke directly to him,
> and you fulfilled your promise by your power,
> as it is today.
> [16] Therefore, LORD God of Israel,
> keep what you promised
> to your servant, my father David:
> "You will never fail to have a man
> to sit before me on the throne of Israel,
> if only your sons take care to walk in my Law
> as you have walked before me."
> [17] Now, LORD God of Israel, please confirm
> what you promised to your servant David.

2 CHRONICLES 7:1–5, 12–18

The Dedication Ceremonies

[1] When Solomon finished praying, fire descended from heaven and consumed the burnt offering and the sacrifices, and the glory of the LORD filled the temple. [2] The priests were not able to enter the LORD's temple because the glory of the LORD filled the temple of the LORD. [3] All the Israelites were watching when the fire descended and the glory of the LORD came on the temple. They bowed down on the pavement with their faces to the ground. They worshiped and praised the LORD:

> For he is good,
> for his faithful love endures forever.

[4] The king and all the people were offering sacrifices in the LORD's presence. [5] King Solomon offered a sacrifice of twenty-two thousand cattle and one hundred twenty thousand sheep and goats. In this manner the king and all the people dedicated God's temple.

. . .

The LORD's Response

[12] Then the LORD appeared to Solomon at night and said to him:

I have heard your prayer and have chosen this place for myself as a temple of sacrifice. [13] If I shut the sky so there is no rain, or if I command the grasshopper to consume the land, or if I send pestilence on my people, [14] and my people, who bear my name, humble themselves, pray and seek my face, and turn from their evil ways, then I will hear from heaven, forgive their sin, and heal their land. [15] My eyes will now be open and my ears attentive to prayer from this place. [16] And I have now chosen and consecrated this temple so that my name may be there forever; my eyes and my heart will be there at all times.

[17] As for you, if you walk before me as your father David walked, doing everything I have commanded you, and if you keep my statutes and ordinances, [18] I will establish your royal throne, as I promised your father David: You will never fail to have a man ruling in Israel.

JOHN 1:14

The Word became flesh and dwelt among us. We observed his glory, the glory as the one and only Son from the Father, full of grace and truth.

1 JOHN 1:8–9

Fellowship with God

8 If we say, "We have no sin," we are deceiving
ourselves, and the truth is not in us. 9 If we confess
our sins, he is faithful and righteous to forgive us
our sins and to cleanse us from all unrighteousness.

Sometimes my children ask me questions when my brain is in some other hemisphere—like deadlines, laundry piles, and remembering to order school lunches. "Can we go to the park later?" "Can we eat ice cream for dinner?" "Can we fly to the moon?" Okay, maybe not that last one. But it doesn't matter what they ask me; when I reply with a half-listening "Yes," they expect whatever I promised. Only, I often completely forget.

But God never forgets His promises (2 Chronicles 6:10, 15–16). The writer of Chronicles reminded the returning-from-exile Judeans that even though they didn't hold up their end of the covenant relationship with God, the Holy One of Israel never skipped town.

This particular passage is recounting the details of God's continuation of the Davidic covenant by David's son Solomon, who built the temple of the Lord. I imagine the people listening to this story could almost smell the countless thousands of cattle, sheep, and goats being offered to God (2 Chronicles 7:5). They could almost hear the blowing trumpets and envision the glory of the Lord consuming the sacrifices with fire from heaven, and His glory filling the temple (2 Chronicles 7:1).

I appreciate the details of this record of Israel's history because they needed to remember their origin story as they started a new chapter back in the land. Just as they did the first time they entered this land of promise, these returning, humbled people needed to recount who God was and who they were so they could move forward as God's people.

The Holy One of Israel never skipped town.

Sometimes we need to re-enter the story of God too. We easily forget who we once were, how God rescued us, and who the story of our lives should be centered around now. We may not like to admit it, but we all tend to forget the gospel of Jesus Christ at times and start hoping we can find the good news we're longing for in other things. We try to work toward our own self-made good news by hustling for the promotion, curating a perfect home, or making our name great in some sphere in which we desperately want to be respected. Over time, we forget whose story we are living in, and we are lured away from the one, big, eternal story of God—and of our Savior, who is full of grace and truth (John 1:14).

Maybe this is one of the reasons the writer of Chronicles thought it necessary to include God's promise to Solomon after the dedication of the temple: If Israel turns from God again (which they will), but then turns back to God, He would hear their prayer, forgive their sin, and bless the land (2 Chronicles 7:14).

This is the story I need to return to over and over again, especially when I mess up. This is the gospel of grace, right here in the pages of Chronicles. Is there something in your life distancing you from God? Do you feel like you're in a season of exile? If we turn from our sin, seek His face, and ask for forgiveness, we once again find our home in God's story (1 John 1:9)—because God keeps His promises.

Ezra

They sang with praise and thanksgiving to the LORD: "For he is good; his faithful love to Israel endures forever." Then all the people gave a great shout of praise to the LORD because the foundation of the LORD's house had been laid.

EZRA 3:11

EZRA 1:1–5

The Decree of Cyrus

1 In the first year of King Cyrus of Persia, in order
to fulfill the word of the LORD spoken through
Jeremiah, the LORD roused the spirit of King Cyrus
to issue a proclamation throughout his entire kingdom and to put it in writing:

> 2 This is what King Cyrus of Persia says:
> "The LORD, the God of the heavens, has
> given me all the kingdoms of the earth and
> has appointed me to build him a house
> at Jerusalem in Judah. 3 Any of his people
> among you, may his God be with him, and
> may he go to Jerusalem in Judah and build
> the house of the LORD, the God of Israel, the
> God who is in Jerusalem. 4 Let every survivor,
> wherever he resides, be assisted by the men
> of that region with silver, gold, goods, and
> livestock, along with a freewill offering for
> the house of God in Jerusalem."

Return from Exile

5 So the family heads of Judah and Benjamin,
along with the priests and Levites—everyone
whose spirit God had roused—prepared to go up
and rebuild the LORD's house in Jerusalem.

EZRA 3:8–13

Rebuilding the Temple

8 In the second month of the second year after they
arrived at God's house in Jerusalem, Zerubbabel
son of Shealtiel, Jeshua son of Jozadak, and the
rest of their brothers, including the priests, the
Levites, and all who had returned to Jerusalem
from the captivity, began to build. They appointed
the Levites who were twenty years old or more to
supervise the work on the LORD's house. 9 Jeshua
with his sons and brothers, Kadmiel with his sons,
and the sons of Judah and of Henadad, with their
sons and brothers, the Levites, joined together to
supervise those working on the house of God.

Temple Foundation Completed

10 When the builders had laid the foundation of the
LORD's temple, the priests, dressed in their robes
and holding trumpets, and the Levites descended
from Asaph, holding cymbals, took their positions
to praise the LORD, as King David of Israel had
instructed. 11 They sang with praise and thanksgiving to the LORD: "For he is good; his faithful
love to Israel endures forever." Then all the people
gave a great shout of praise to the LORD because
the foundation of the LORD's house had been laid.

12 But many of the older priests, Levites, and family
heads, who had seen the first temple, wept loudly
when they saw the foundation of this temple, but
many others shouted joyfully. 13 The people could
not distinguish the sound of the joyful shouting
from that of the weeping, because the people were
shouting so loudly. And the sound was heard far
away.

JEREMIAH 29:10–14

Jeremiah's Letter to the Exiles

10 For this is what the Lord says: "When seventy
years for Babylon are complete, I will attend to
you and will confirm my promise concerning
you to restore you to this place. 11 For I know the
plans I have for you"—this is the Lord's declaration—"plans for your well-being, not for disaster,
to give you a future and a hope. 12 You will call to
me and come and pray to me, and I will listen to
you. 13 You will seek me and find me when you
search for me with all your heart. 14 I will be found
by you"—this is the Lord's declaration—"and I
will restore your fortunes and gather you from all
the nations and places where I banished you"—
this is the Lord's declaration. "I will restore you to
the place from which I deported you."

1 CORINTHIANS 3:9–11

The Role of God's Servants

9 For we are God's coworkers. You are God's field,
God's building.

10 According to God's grace that was given to me,
I have laid a foundation as a skilled master builder,
and another builds on it. But each one is to be
careful how he builds on it. 11 For no one can lay
any foundation other than what has been laid
down. That foundation is Jesus Christ.

Is there a season in your life that you look back on and think, *Those were the good old days?*

I remember the summer I was seventeen—old enough to have a driver's license and a job; young enough to have no serious expenses or responsibilities. My friends and I spent those months before senior year on the lakes (Michigan has more than 11,000 of them!), creating scavenger hunts around town, swimming in the downtown fountain, and buying half-price Chinese food at closing time. They were glory days for sure.

We love how things were. Sometimes we even love how things are. And, boy, does time have a way of softening our memories. When things are good, we want them to stay that way forever. And when things are bad, we long for the good old days.

But here's the thing: If I had stayed seventeen forever, I would have missed out on having a seventeen-year-old of my own—a child I now indeed have. He's tall enough to give me big bear hugs, he drives his sister to school, and he meets his friends for a burrito almost every day before lacrosse practice because his metabolism demands five square meals a day. These may be his glory days, but they somehow feel like mine all over again, too.

If we insist now that these are the best days of our life, we end up doubting that God has new, good things for us still ahead. We end up forgetting that with God, our good old days are always ahead of us.

In the book of Ezra, the returning exiles recalled the glory days of Jerusalem, some with firsthand memories. God's presence was with them in the temple, the city was protected, and the favor of the Lord was on them and against their enemies. As they returned to the city, they found themselves caught in the tension of looking backwards to what used to be—even relearning the law they had forgotten—while believing God would carry them into a new future. There's a wonderful moment when they reestablish Passover and confess their sin. But that would also mean continuing to trust God with their future as they walked forward in obedience.

With God, our good old days are always ahead of us.

Not unlike the Israelites in Ezra, you and I have the opportunity to look back to relearn and remember what God has done. It is always wise and faith-building to "remember the LORD's works" (Psalm 77:11). But after that, don't keep gazing into the past. Turn around, believing God's presence and provision will follow you into the future. Keep your eyes up—at the yet-unfulfilled promises God has made in His Word. For God's people in Ezra, that meant looking forward toward Christ. For we who are in Christ, this means we look forward to His work in the Church throughout the globe, and His promise that He is making all things new.

God has "good old days" and new things ahead for us. Onward and upward!

Nehemiah

So I said to them, "You see the trouble we are in. Jerusalem lies in ruins and its gates have been burned. Come, let's rebuild Jerusalem's wall, so that we will no longer be a disgrace."

NEHEMIAH 2:17

NEHEMIAH 1:1–11

1 The words of Nehemiah son of Hacaliah:

News from Jerusalem

During the month of Chislev in the twentieth year, when I was in the fortress city of Susa, 2 Hanani, one of my brothers, arrived with men from Judah, and I questioned them about Jerusalem and the Jewish remnant that had survived the exile. 3 They said to me, "The remnant in the province, who survived the exile, are in great trouble and disgrace. Jerusalem's wall has been broken down, and its gates have been burned."

Nehemiah's Prayer

4 When I heard these words, I sat down and wept. I mourned for a number of days, fasting and praying before the God of the heavens. 5 I said,

> Lord, the God of the heavens, the great and awe-inspiring God who keeps his gracious covenant with those who love him and keep his commands, 6 let your eyes be open and your ears be attentive to hear your servant's prayer that I now pray to you day and night for your servants, the Israelites. I confess the sins we have committed against you. Both I and my father's family have sinned. 7 We have acted corruptly toward you and have not kept the commands, statutes, and ordinances you gave your servant Moses. 8 Please remember what you commanded your servant Moses: "If you are unfaithful, I will scatter you among the peoples. 9 But if you return to me and carefully observe my commands, even though your exiles were banished to the farthest horizon, I will gather them from there and bring them to the place where I chose to have my name dwell." 10 They are your servants and your people. You redeemed them by your great power and strong hand. 11 Please, Lord, let your ear be attentive to the prayer of your servant and to that of your servants who delight to revere your name. Give your servant success today, and grant him compassion in the presence of this man.

At the time, I was the king's cupbearer.

NEHEMIAH 2:11–18

Preparing to Rebuild the Walls

11 After I arrived in Jerusalem and had been there three days, 12 I got up at night and took a few men with me. I didn't tell anyone what my God had laid on my heart to do for Jerusalem. The only animal I took was the one I was riding. 13 I went out at night through the Valley Gate toward the Serpent's Well and the Dung Gate, and I inspected the walls of Jerusalem that had been broken down and its gates that had been destroyed by fire. 14 I went on to the Fountain Gate and the King's Pool, but farther down it became too narrow for my animal to go through. 15 So I went up at night by way of the valley and inspected the wall. Then heading back, I entered through the Valley Gate and returned. 16 The officials did not know where I had gone or what I was doing, for I had not yet told the Jews, priests, nobles, officials, or the rest of those who would be doing the work. 17 So I said to them, "You see the trouble we are in. Jerusalem lies in ruins and its gates have been burned. Come, let's rebuild Jerusalem's wall, so that we will no longer be a disgrace." 18 I told them how the gracious hand of my God had been on me, and what the king had said to me.

They said, "Let's start rebuilding," and their hands were strengthened to do this good work.

NEHEMIAH 4:11–21

Progress in Spite of Opposition

11 And our enemies said, "They won't realize it until we're among them and can kill them and stop the work." 12 When the Jews who lived nearby arrived, they said to us time and again, "Everywhere you turn, they attack us." 13 So I stationed people behind the lowest sections of the wall, at the vulnerable areas. I stationed them by families with their swords, spears, and bows. 14 After I made an inspection, I stood up and said to the nobles, the officials, and the rest of the people, "Don't be afraid of them. Remember the great and awe-inspiring Lord, and fight for your countrymen, your sons and daughters, your wives and homes."

15 When our enemies heard that we knew their scheme and that God had frustrated it, every one of us returned to his own work on the wall. 16 From that day on, half of my men did the work while the other half held spears, shields, bows, and armor. The officers supported all the people of Judah, 17 who were rebuilding the wall. The laborers who carried the loads worked with one hand and held a weapon with the other. 18 Each of the builders had his sword strapped around his waist while he was building, and the one who sounded the ram's horn was beside me. 19 Then I said to the nobles, the officials, and the rest of the people, "The work is enormous and spread out, and we are separated far from one another along the wall. 20 Wherever you hear the sound of the ram's horn, rally to us there. Our God will fight for us!" 21 So we continued the work, while half of the men were holding spears from daybreak until the stars came out.

JOHN 2:19–22

19 Jesus answered, "Destroy this temple, and I will raise it up in three days."

20 Therefore the Jews said, "This temple took forty-six years to build, and will you raise it up in three days?"

21 But he was speaking about the temple of his body. 22 So when he was raised from the dead, his disciples remembered that he had said this, and they believed the Scripture and the statement Jesus had made.

Back in 2014, when the She Reads Truth community was not quite two years old, Raechel and I felt called to something unexpected and, frankly, a little terrifying. Feeling a kinship to Nehemiah and his call to rebuild the city walls to establish a safe place for his people to gather and worship, we believed the Lord laid it on our hearts to build a Bible app for women to read God's Word together every day. As that app was being built, the community read the book of Nehemiah. And today, more than a decade later, we are still reading Scripture together and marveling at the fact that God is still faithful and His Word is still true.

When Nehemiah heard that Jerusalem's walls had been destroyed and its gates burned to the ground, he was devastated. As he wept for his home and his people, he did the one thing he knew to do: He sought the Lord. With prayer and fasting and confession, Nehemiah petitioned the Lord on behalf of Jerusalem. He declared God's goodness and recalled God's faithfulness. He spoke the Lord's promises back to Him, believing those promises to be true while also petitioning the Lord to act on them.

Nehemiah longed for his city to be restored, and he felt a fire in his bones to bring about that restoration with his own two hands. But before he put his hands to work, he bowed his knees in prayer. In his humility we see a truth confirmed throughout Scripture: Any sense of calling we have, even those directly related to our faith in Christ, rests on the strength, sovereignty, and grace found only in Him.

Any good work is God's work. He invites and equips us to participate in it—by faith in Him, not in ourselves.

In His own ministry, Jesus fulfilled all that Nehemiah pointed to. He wept over His people, sought God with tears and petitions, and preached God's goodness and faithfulness (Luke 19:41–42; Hebrews 5:7). He not only reminded the world of God's promises, but He became the *fulfillment* of those promises (Matthew 5:17; 2 Corinthians 1:20). On top of that, Jesus did away with the need for a physical temple, His work and His Spirit making way for a new temple where God would dwell—the living temple of the Church (Ephesians 2:19–22).

Any good work is God's work.

When you read Nehemiah's story, look for Jesus. Remember that God is building His kingdom right here and now—in Bible-reading communities and in conference rooms, at local schools and at neighborhood cookouts, and everywhere in between. Because of Jesus, you and I get to roll up our sleeves and take part in that good work. Speak God's promises back to Him and celebrate all the ways they are fulfilled in Christ.

What good, hard, worth-it, kingdom work lies before you today?

Esther

If you keep silent at this time,
relief and deliverance will come
to the Jewish people from another
place, but you and your father's
family will be destroyed.
Who knows, perhaps
you have come to your royal
position for such a time as this.

ESTHER 4:14

ESTHER 3:1–2, 8–11

Haman's Plan to Kill the Jews

1 After all this took place, King Ahasuerus honored Haman, son of Hammedatha the Agagite. He promoted him in rank and gave him a higher position than all the other officials. 2 The entire royal staff at the King's Gate bowed down and paid homage to Haman, because the king had commanded this to be done for him. But Mordecai would not bow down or pay homage.

. . .

8 Then Haman informed King Ahasuerus, "There is one ethnic group, scattered throughout the peoples in every province of your kingdom, keeping themselves separate. Their laws are different from everyone else's and they do not obey the king's laws. It is not in the king's best interest to tolerate them. 9 If the king approves, let an order be drawn up authorizing their destruction, and I will pay 375 tons of silver to the officials for deposit in the royal treasury."

10 The king removed his signet ring from his hand and gave it to Haman son of Hammedatha the Agagite, the enemy of the Jews. 11 Then the king told Haman, "The money and people are given to you to do with as you see fit."

ESTHER 4:1–3, 10–16

Mordecai Appeals to Esther

1 When Mordecai learned all that had occurred, he tore his clothes, put on sackcloth and ashes, went into the middle of the city, and cried loudly and bitterly. 2 He went only as far as the King's Gate, since the law prohibited anyone wearing sackcloth from entering the King's Gate. 3 There was great mourning among the Jewish people in every province where the king's command and edict reached. They fasted, wept, and lamented, and many lay in sackcloth and ashes.

. . .

10 Esther spoke to Hathach and commanded him to tell Mordecai, 11 "All the royal officials and the people of the royal provinces know that one law applies to every man or woman who approaches the king in the inner courtyard and who has not been summoned—the death penalty—unless the king extends the gold scepter, allowing that person to live. I have not been summoned to appear before the king for the last thirty days." 12 Esther's response was reported to Mordecai.

13 Mordecai told the messenger to reply to Esther, "Don't think that you will escape the fate of all the Jews because you are in the king's palace. 14 If you keep silent at this time, relief and deliverance will come to the Jewish people from another place, but you and your father's family will be destroyed. Who knows, perhaps you have come to your royal position for such a time as this."

15 Esther sent this reply to Mordecai: 16 "Go and assemble all the Jews who can be found in Susa and fast for me. Don't eat or drink for three days, night or day. I and my female servants will also fast in the same way. After that, I will go to the king even if it is against the law. If I perish, I perish."

ESTHER 8:1–8

Esther Intervenes for the Jews

1 That same day King Ahasuerus awarded Queen Esther the estate of Haman, the enemy of the Jews. Mordecai entered the king's presence because Esther had revealed her relationship to Mordecai. 2 The king removed his signet ring he had recovered from Haman and gave it to Mordecai, and Esther put him in charge of Haman's estate.

3 Then Esther addressed the king again. She fell at his feet, wept, and begged him to revoke the evil of Haman the Agagite and his plot he had devised against the Jews. 4 The king extended the gold scepter toward Esther, so she got up and stood before the king.

5 She said, "If it pleases the king and I have found favor with him, if the matter seems right to the king and I am pleasing in his eyes, let a royal edict be written. Let it revoke the documents the scheming Haman son of Hammedatha the Agagite wrote to destroy the Jews who are in all the king's provinces. 6 For how could I bear to see the disaster that would come on my people? How could I bear to see the destruction of my relatives?"

7 King Ahasuerus said to Esther the queen and to
Mordecai the Jew, "Look, I have given Haman's
estate to Esther, and he was hanged on the gallows
because he attacked the Jews. 8 Write in the king's
name whatever pleases you concerning the Jews,
and seal it with the royal signet ring. A document
written in the king's name and sealed with the
royal signet ring cannot be revoked."

ESTHER 9:1, 20–22b

Victories of the Jews

1 The king's command and law went into effect
on the thirteenth day of the twelfth month, the
month Adar. On the day when the Jews' enemies
had hoped to overpower them, just the opposite
happened. The Jews overpowered those who hated
them.

. . .

20 Mordecai recorded these events and sent letters
to all the Jews in all of King Ahasuerus's provinces,
both near and far. 21 He ordered them to celebrate
the fourteenth and fifteenth days of the month of
Adar every year. 22 That was the month when their
sorrow was turned into rejoicing and their mourning into a holiday. They were to be days of feasting,
rejoicing, and of sending gifts to one another and
to the poor.

GENESIS 50:19–20

Joseph's Kindness

19 But Joseph said to them, "Don't be afraid. Am
I in the place of God? 20 You planned evil against
me; God planned it for good to bring about the
present result—the survival of many people."

NEHEMIAH 9:27

National Confession of Sin

So you handed them over to their enemies,
who oppressed them.
In their time of distress, they cried out to you,
and you heard from heaven.
In your abundant compassion
you gave them deliverers, who rescued them
from the power of their enemies.

GALATIANS 4:4–7

Sons and Heirs

4 When the time came to completion, God sent
his Son, born of a woman, born under the law,
5 to redeem those under the law, so that we might
receive adoption as sons. 6 And because you are
sons, God sent the Spirit of his Son into our hearts,
crying, "*Abba*, Father!" 7 So you are no longer a
slave but a son, and if a son, then God has made
you an heir.

One day years ago, I texted my friend Raechel a photo of my four-year-old son in the ICU. He was lying unconscious in the hospital bed, his little body riddled with tubes, and the bed was surrounded by machines and IV pumps doing the complex work of keeping him alive. It was a dark and desperate situation.

I will never forget what she texted me in response: "It's a picture of God at work."

Esther's situation was dark and desperate too. An edict had gone out to destroy the Jewish people—Esther's people—and nothing could be done to stop it. When the sun rose the next day, Haman's scheme would play out just as he planned, and an entire people group would be gone forever.

But our God can work even in the darkness, and He was already reversing Israel's doom into delight. Instead of meeting sure destruction, "that was the month when their sorrow was turned into rejoicing and their mourning into a holiday" (Esther 9:22).

God's name is never mentioned in the book of Esther, but His hand is evident as He works through ordinary men and women to bring about this dramatic rescue of His people. Esther herself, a Jewish orphan girl turned Persian queen "for such a time as this," laid her life on the line to advocate for God's people before the king (Esther 4:14). And for no apparent reason other than a supernaturally softened heart, the king listened and granted her request. What should have been a day of destruction was a day of deliverance!

> **"It's a picture of God at work."**

A sudden reversal like this is not calculable or predictable. It wasn't ultimately the result of Esther and Mordecai's strategy or the king's change of heart, and it certainly wasn't coincidence. This unexpected turn of events was only unexpected because it came from outside the realm of human control. God Himself had acted and unraveled Haman's finely crafted plot against the Jews.

This story foreshadows another time when evil intentions were thwarted by God's goodness. Centuries after Esther, in the darkness of Good Friday, it looked like the Enemy had won. The Lord of Life died a cruel death, and it seemed He had become a prisoner of the grave forever. But on the third day, the greatest reversal of all time took place when the Son of God rose from the grave, overcoming our edict of death and giving us eternal life with Him. Because of Jesus, our sorrow has turned to rejoicing and our mourning to a holiday.

Is there an area of your life that feels dark and desperate? What would it change to see this thing as "a picture of God at work"? Because that's the truth. God is working. He is the God who acts, not according to human whims and wishes, but according to His good purposes and in His good time. He hasn't forgotten you—even when it's dark, even when you're surrounded. Hold on and wait for the Lord. "Be strong and take heart and wait for the LORD" (Psalm 27:14 NIV).

Job

But I know that my Redeemer
lives, and at the end he
will stand on the dust.

JOB 19:25

JOB 1:1–3, 8–22

Job and His Family

1 There was a man in the country of Uz named Job.
He was a man of complete integrity, who feared
God and turned away from evil. 2 He had seven
sons and three daughters. 3 His estate included
seven thousand sheep and goats, three thousand
camels, five hundred yoke of oxen, five hundred
female donkeys, and a very large number of servants. Job was the greatest man among all the
people of the east.

. . .

Satan's First Test of Job

8 Then the LORD said to Satan, "Have you considered my servant Job? No one else on earth is like
him, a man of perfect integrity, who fears God and
turns away from evil."

9 Satan answered the LORD, "Does Job fear God
for nothing? 10 Haven't you placed a hedge around
him, his household, and everything he owns? You
have blessed the work of his hands, and his possessions have increased in the land. 11 But stretch out
your hand and strike everything he owns, and he
will surely curse you to your face."

12 "Very well," the LORD told Satan, "everything he
owns is in your power. However, do not lay a hand
on Job himself." So Satan left the LORD's presence.

13 One day when Job's sons and daughters were
eating and drinking wine in their oldest brother's
house, 14 a messenger came to Job and reported,
"While the oxen were plowing and the donkeys
grazing nearby, 15 the Sabeans swooped down and
took them away. They struck down the servants
with the sword, and I alone have escaped to tell
you!"

16 He was still speaking when another messenger
came and reported, "God's fire fell from heaven.
It burned the sheep and the servants and devoured
them, and I alone have escaped to tell you!"

17 That messenger was still speaking when yet
another came and reported, "The Chaldeans
formed three bands, made a raid on the camels,
and took them away. They struck down the
servants with the sword, and I alone have escaped
to tell you!"

18 He was still speaking when another messenger
came and reported, "Your sons and daughters were
eating and drinking wine in their oldest brother's
house. 19 Suddenly a powerful wind swept in from
the desert and struck the four corners of the house.
It collapsed on the young people so that they died,
and I alone have escaped to tell you!"

20 Then Job stood up, tore his robe, and shaved
his head. He fell to the ground and worshiped,
21 saying:

> Naked I came from my mother's womb,
> and naked I will leave this life.
> The LORD gives, and the LORD takes away.
> Blessed be the name of the LORD.

22 Throughout all this Job did not sin or blame
God for anything.

JOB 19:23–27

Job's Reply to Bildad

23 I wish that my words were written down,
that they were recorded on a scroll
24 or were inscribed in stone forever
by an iron stylus and lead!
25 But I know that my Redeemer lives,
and at the end he will stand on the dust.
26 Even after my skin has been destroyed,
yet I will see God in my flesh.
27 I will see him myself;
my eyes will look at him, and not as a stranger.
My heart longs within me.

JOB 42:16–17

God Restores Job

16 Job lived 140 years after this and saw his children and their children to the fourth generation.
17 Then Job died, old and full of days.

JAMES 1:2–4

Trials and Maturity

2 Consider it a great joy, my brothers and sisters, whenever you experience various trials, 3 because you know that the testing of your faith produces endurance. 4 And let endurance have its full effect, so that you may be mature and complete, lacking nothing.

1 PETER 2:21–25

21 For you were called to this, because Christ also suffered for you, leaving you an example, that you should follow in his steps. 22 He did not commit sin, "and no deceit was found in his mouth;" 23 when he was insulted, he did not insult in return; when he suffered, he did not threaten but entrusted himself to the one who judges justly. 24 He himself bore our sins in his body on the tree; so that, having died to sins, we might live for righteousness. "By his wounds you have been healed." 25 For you "were like sheep going astray," but you have now returned to the Shepherd and Overseer of your souls.

REVELATION 1:12–18

John's Vision of the Risen Lord

12 Then I turned to see whose voice it was that spoke to me. When I turned I saw seven golden lampstands, 13 and among the lampstands was one like the Son of Man, dressed in a robe and with a golden sash wrapped around his chest. 14 The hair of his head was white as wool—white as snow—and his eyes like a fiery flame. 15 His feet were like fine bronze as it is fired in a furnace, and his voice like the sound of cascading waters. 16 He had seven stars in his right hand; a sharp double-edged sword came from his mouth, and his face was shining like the sun at full strength.

17 When I saw him, I fell at his feet like a dead man. He laid his right hand on me and said, "Don't be afraid. I am the First and the Last, 18 and the Living One. I was dead, but look—I am alive forever and ever, and I hold the keys of death and Hades.

Every Missouri farm girl like me knows what a cocklebur is. But in case you aren't a Missouri farm girl, let me explain: They are tiny, spiky black thistles that fuse themselves to you when you walk through the woods. They stick to your socks and boots, your pants and shirt, your dog and your children. It's enough to make even the best country girl dream of life in the big city.

But those little, spiky shells house a seed. The barbs cling to passersby and are spread far and wide. Sure, they inflict some minor "suffering" on their host, but it is not suffering without purpose. It is an ingenious method of perpetuating life.

The story of suffering in the book of Job never gets easier to read. Job was "a man of complete integrity, who feared God and turned away from evil" (Job 1:1). If a good man is hard to find, Job was that anomaly. He deserved an award. Instead, he lost his children, his fortune, and his health—he lost everything.

The phrase "everything happens for a reason" is born out of our desperation to look into Job-like suffering and see purpose. We all want our suffering to mean something. It's why we offer hollow platitudes in hospital rooms and funeral homes. We are like Job's friends, so desperate to find purpose in pain that we sometimes say stupid things. But Job's story doesn't give us the satisfactory explanation we crave. Sure, the things he lost were restored, but we are left wondering, *Why did Job have to suffer at all? What was the higher purpose?*

We don't get answers to all the "whys" and "whats" of suffering, in Job's life or our own. And so we look to the ultimate answer of "who" that echoes throughout Scripture. We look to Jesus.

We all want our suffering to mean something.

Jesus suffered more than we can know or comprehend. He was beaten, bloodied, humiliated, scorned, crucified, and killed (Matthew 27:27–31). Yes, Job was as righteous as a fallen man can be in this world, but he was ultimately a sinner, incapable of perfectly keeping God's holy standards. Not Jesus. He never sinned, not once. And yet, He suffered unimaginably. Jesus's sinlessness makes His suffering unbearable unless we look past the cross to what it accomplished.

Job's suffering was an answer to the Enemy's accusation. Jesus suffered to silence the Accuser forever (Job 1:9–11; 1 Corinthians 15:55). Job was wounded, seemingly to no higher end. Jesus was pierced for our transgressions, crushed for our sins (Isaiah 53:5). The book of Job ends without an explanation for his suffering. Jesus's life ended to fix creation's biggest problem: sin (1 Peter 3:18). Infinitely more miraculous than a forest full of cockleburs, Christ's work on the cross carried salvation across all time and for all who would repent and believe.

Jesus's suffering gave us life. His pain made a way for the redemptive ending I am so desperate for, and His unimaginable suffering was for our immeasurable relief. Thank you, Jesus.

Psalms

The Lord is gracious and
righteous; our God is
compassionate. The Lord guards
the inexperienced;
I was helpless, and he saved me.

PSALM 116:5–6

PSALM 116:1–19

Thanks to God for Deliverance

[1] I love the LORD because he has heard
my appeal for mercy.
[2] Because he has turned his ear to me,
I will call out to him as long as I live.

[3] The ropes of death were wrapped around me,
and the torments of Sheol overcame me;
I encountered trouble and sorrow.
[4] Then I called on the name of the LORD:
"LORD, save me!"

[5] The LORD is gracious and righteous;
our God is compassionate.
[6] The LORD guards the inexperienced;
I was helpless, and he saved me.
[7] Return to your rest, my soul,
for the LORD has been good to you.
[8] For you, LORD, rescued me from death,
my eyes from tears,
my feet from stumbling.
[9] I will walk before the LORD
in the land of the living.
[10] I believed, even when I said,
"I am severely oppressed."
[11] In my alarm I said,
"Everyone is a liar."

[12] How can I repay the LORD
for all the good he has done for me?
[13] I will take the cup of salvation
and call on the name of the LORD.
[14] I will fulfill my vows to the LORD
in the presence of all his people.

[15] The death of his faithful ones
is valuable in the LORD's sight.
[16] LORD, I am indeed your servant;
I am your servant, the son of your female servant.
You have loosened my bonds.

[17] I will offer you a thanksgiving sacrifice
and call on the name of the LORD.
[18] I will fulfill my vows to the LORD
in the presence of all his people,
[19] in the courts of the LORD's house—
within you, Jerusalem.
Hallelujah!

PSALM 145:17–21

Praising God's Greatness

[17] The LORD is righteous in all his ways
and faithful in all his acts.
[18] The LORD is near all who call out to him,
all who call out to him with integrity.
[19] He fulfills the desires of those who fear him;
he hears their cry for help and saves them.
[20] The LORD guards all those who love him,
but he destroys all the wicked.
[21] My mouth will declare the LORD's praise;
let every living thing
bless his holy name forever and ever.

COLOSSIANS 1:9–14

Prayer for Spiritual Growth

9 For this reason also, since the day we heard this, we haven't stopped praying
for you. We are asking that you may be filled with the knowledge of his will in
all wisdom and spiritual understanding, 10 so that you may walk worthy of the
Lord, fully pleasing to him: bearing fruit in every good work and growing in the
knowledge of God, 11 being strengthened with all power, according to his glorious might, so that you may have great endurance and patience, joyfully 12 giving
thanks to the Father, who has enabled you to share in the saints' inheritance in the
light. 13 He has rescued us from the domain of darkness and transferred us into
the kingdom of the Son he loves. 14 In him we have redemption, the forgiveness
of sins.

Prayer is a startling invitation—one that, after forty years of following Jesus, I still struggle to accept.

"Call to me and I will answer you and tell you great and incomprehensible things you do not know," the Lord says to His people in Jeremiah 33:3. The book of Hebrews urges the Christ follower to "approach the throne of grace with boldness" (Hebrews 4:16), and Paul tells the Philippians not to "worry about anything" but instead to petition God in prayer (Hebrews 4:6). Perhaps most astonishing of all, Jesus Himself instructs His disciples, "Whenever you pray, say, Father . . ." (Luke 11:2).

Call out to God. Go boldly to the throne. Ask instead of worry. Talk to God as your Father.

This is the invitation. But what do we say? How do we find the words to pray?

Prayer, like everything else in the Christian life, is a practice learned over time. And when it comes to learning the language of prayer, there is no better teacher than the psalms.

The book of Psalms was both the hymnbook and prayer book for the people of God even before the days of Jesus, and the church has been singing and shaping her own prayers with these writings ever since. From praising God, to calling out to Him with our deepest cares and concerns, to lifting up the needs of the whole world, the psalms show us that we can bring it all to Him.

Experiencing grief? The psalms of lament can guide your heartfelt cries to God. Want to express your gratitude? The psalms of thanksgiving can give you the words. Desperate to remember God's character or lay hold of His help in trouble? The psalms of trust show us what faith and hope in the Lord sounds like in hard times. The whole range of human emotion is present right there in the center of our Bibles, like a giant welcome mat inviting us to bring our whole selves to the Lord.

Four decades after my first prayer, I'm still learning how to talk to God. I'm a person accustomed to communicating with other people, after all, and prayer is wholly other. There is no hiding, no putting on airs, no manipulation. All attempts at deceit are futile. God created us with the capacity to feel the very emotions we try to conceal. He knows our needs before we ask (Matthew 6:8), and none of our circumstances are hidden from Him (Hebrews 4:13).

The book of Psalms was both the hymnbook and prayer book for the people of God.

There is nothing—not even our hearts—over which our God does not rule. And over time, I've realized how freeing that is. In prayer, I don't have to hide or make things sound better. Like the psalmists, I can be honest, and trust that God will receive me as His child no matter my mood or subject matter.

What emotions are you feeling today? Tell the Lord about it. Let the psalms draw you into a daily and ongoing conversation with Him, and may His Word teach you to use your own to express your heart to Him in prayer.

Proverbs

The fear of the LORD is the
beginning of knowledge;
fools despise wisdom
and discipline.

PROVERBS 1:7

PROVERBS 1:1–7

The Purpose of Proverbs

[1] The proverbs of Solomon son of David, king of Israel:
[2] For learning wisdom and discipline;
for understanding insightful sayings;
[3] for receiving prudent instruction
in righteousness, justice, and integrity;
[4] for teaching shrewdness to the inexperienced,
knowledge and discretion to a young man—
[5] let a wise person listen and increase learning,
and let a discerning person obtain guidance—
[6] for understanding a proverb or a parable,
the words of the wise, and their riddles.

[7] The fear of the LORD
is the beginning of knowledge;
fools despise wisdom and discipline.

PROVERBS 3:5–12

Trust the LORD

[5] Trust in the LORD with all your heart,
and do not rely on your own understanding;
[6] in all your ways know him,
and he will make your paths straight.
[7] Don't be wise in your own eyes;
fear the LORD and turn away from evil.
[8] This will be healing for your body
and strengthening for your bones.
[9] Honor the LORD with your possessions
and with the first produce of your entire harvest;
[10] then your barns will be completely filled,
and your vats will overflow with new wine.
[11] Do not despise the LORD's instruction, my son,
and do not loathe his discipline;
[12] for the LORD disciplines the one he loves,
just as a father disciplines the son in whom he delights.

MATTHEW 7:24–27

The Two Foundations

24 "Therefore, everyone who hears these words of mine and acts on them will be like a wise man who built his house on the rock. 25 The rain fell, the rivers rose, and the winds blew and pounded that house. Yet it didn't collapse, because its foundation was on the rock. 26 But everyone who hears these words of mine and doesn't act on them will be like a foolish man who built his house on the sand. 27 The rain fell, the rivers rose, the winds blew and pounded that house, and it collapsed. It collapsed with a great crash."

EPHESIANS 1:16–19

Prayer for Spiritual Insight

16 I never stop giving thanks for you as I remember you in my prayers. 17 I pray that the God of our Lord Jesus Christ, the glorious Father, would give you the Spirit of wisdom and revelation in the knowledge of him. 18 I pray that the eyes of your heart may be enlightened so that you may know what is the hope of his calling, what is the wealth of his glorious inheritance in the saints, 19 and what is the immeasurable greatness of his power toward us who believe, according to the mighty working of his strength.

JAMES 3:17

The Wisdom from Above

But the wisdom from above is first pure, then peace-loving, gentle, compliant, full of mercy and good fruits, unwavering, without pretense.

We have five blueberry bushes on the land behind our house—a fun surprise we discovered the summer after we moved in. Life was more chaotic than usual that year, with all of our available time spent visiting our youngest son in the hospital that had become his home. Berries came and went without much notice, and certainly without the baking of any cobblers.

But the next year all six of us were back under one roof, together again. Week after week, I watched as berries formed on those five bushes, turning from green to pink to red, then finally, a powdery dark blue. Now, a few delicious blueberry seasons later, here's what I've learned.

From afar, they look like any other green, leafy bush; only up close does the treasure reveal itself. And the process takes much longer than I expected. The berries don't ripen all at once, so the picking is truly that—plucking individual berries rather than clusters off the branch. (Though, when you do find a ripe cluster, it is sheer delight.) A perfect berry is most often surrounded by smaller, tougher, greener ones, still weeks from their own glory. Picking one before its time only results in disappointment for me and food for the birds. Another thing: You can pick in one spot for ages, convinced you've taken all that side of the blueberry bush has to give, but look from another angle and you'll see there's more to discover. Which reminds me: The best berries are often the hardest to reach.

The book of Proverbs—a collection of wise sayings and poems often attributed to King Solomon—reminds me of my beloved blueberry bushes. Cultivating wisdom takes time. It's not easy or straightforward. It doesn't happen all at once, and it cannot be forced. It's a slow, steady, beautiful harvest that comes to fruition as we walk with God and grow in our knowledge of Him. And just when you think you've mastered one lesson, a closer look reveals there is still more to glean.

The best berries are often the hardest to reach.

Scripture teaches that true wisdom is a fruit of our connection with God, our source and Creator. Proverbs 1:7 declares, "The fear of the LORD is the beginning of knowledge." Our role in cultivating wisdom is to stay connected to Him—to be patient, to pay attention, and to follow His instruction. The world will offer shortcuts and guarantees and call it wisdom. But only the wisdom from above is pure and peace-loving, gentle and unwavering, "full of mercy and good fruits" (James 3:17). Like freshly picked berries in the summertime, God's wisdom nourishes our souls. Like a house built on a rock, it is a refuge in life's storms.

In what areas of your life do you need to seek patience as God slowly develops wisdom in you? Take some extra time to settle into God's Word today, patiently seeking the wisdom that comes only from Him. He is the source of all wisdom, and He matures us in His time for His glory.

Ecclesiastes

When all has been heard, the
conclusion of the matter is this:
fear God and keep his
commands, because this
is for all humanity.

ECCLESIASTES 12:13

ECCLESIASTES 1:1–18

Everything Is Futile

1 The words of the Teacher, son of David, king in Jerusalem.

2 "Absolute futility," says the Teacher.
"Absolute futility. Everything is futile."
3 What does a person gain for all his efforts
that he labors at under the sun?
4 A generation goes and a generation comes,
but the earth remains forever.
5 The sun rises and the sun sets;
panting, it hurries back to the place
where it rises.
6 Gusting to the south,
turning to the north,
turning, turning, goes the wind,
and the wind returns in its cycles.
7 All the streams flow to the sea,
yet the sea is never full;
to the place where the streams flow,
there they flow again.
8 All things are wearisome,
more than anyone can say.
The eye is not satisfied by seeing
or the ear filled with hearing.
9 What has been is what will be,
and what has been done is what will be done;
there is nothing new under the sun.
10 Can one say about anything,
"Look, this is new"?
It has already existed in the ages before us.
11 There is no remembrance of those who
came before;
and of those who will come after
there will also be no remembrance
by those who follow them.

The Limitations of Wisdom

12 I, the Teacher, have been king over Israel in
Jerusalem. 13 I applied my mind to examine and
explore through wisdom all that is done under
heaven. God has given people this miserable task
to keep them occupied. 14 I have seen all the things
that are done under the sun and have found everything to be futile, a pursuit of the wind.

15 What is crooked cannot be straightened;
what is lacking cannot be counted.

16 I said to myself, "See, I have amassed wisdom
far beyond all those who were over Jerusalem
before me, and my mind has thoroughly grasped
wisdom and knowledge." 17 I applied my mind to
know wisdom and knowledge, madness and folly;
I learned that this too is a pursuit of the wind.

18 For with much wisdom is much sorrow;
as knowledge increases, grief increases.

ECCLESIASTES 12:9–14

The Teacher's Objectives and Conclusion

9 In addition to the Teacher being a wise man,
he constantly taught the people knowledge; he
weighed, explored, and arranged many proverbs.
10 The Teacher sought to find delightful sayings
and write words of truth accurately. 11 The sayings
of the wise are like cattle prods, and those from
masters of collections are like firmly embedded
nails. The sayings are given by one Shepherd.

12 But beyond these, my son, be warned: there is
no end to the making of many books, and much
study wearies the body. 13 When all has been heard,
the conclusion of the matter is this: fear God and
keep his commands, because this is for all humanity. 14 For God will bring every act to judgment,
including every hidden thing, whether good or
evil.

PROVERBS 2:1–6

Wisdom's Worth

1 My son, if you accept my words
and store up my commands within you,
2 listening closely to wisdom
and directing your heart to understanding;
3 furthermore, if you call out to insight
and lift your voice to understanding,
4 if you seek it like silver
and search for it like hidden treasure,
5 then you will understand the fear of the LORD
and discover the knowledge of God.
6 For the LORD gives wisdom;
from his mouth come knowledge and
understanding.

EPHESIANS 5:15–17

Consistency in the Christian Life

15 Pay careful attention, then, to how you walk—not
as unwise people but as wise— 16 making the most
of the time, because the days are evil. 17 So don't be
foolish, but understand what the Lord's will is.

Am I the only one in this house who knows how to load the washing machine?!" I bark my question loudly to everyone within earshot and no one in particular. Instead of listening for an answer, I groan and shovel another pile of sweaty jerseys, dirt-covered socks, and permanently stained baseball pants from the laundry basket to the machine. I'm annoyed, and I need them to know it. But underneath my irritated sighs, there is another feeling—a fleeting but familiar twinge of disappointment in my heart's bent toward temporary things.

This scene in my home reminds me of the word that echoes throughout the book of Ecclesiastes: futility. Looking for lasting meaning or satisfaction apart from God is futile—as futile as trying to keep all the clothes clean in a house filled with sports-loving kids and coffee-spilling adults. "'Absolute futility,' says the Teacher. 'Absolute futility. Everything is futile'" (Ecclesiastes 1:2).

The book of Ecclesiastes is attributed to King Solomon—the man who had everything. He was king. He had a palace. He had all the money and wisdom in the world. And yet even Solomon said he found all this effort to be fruitless, "a pursuit of the wind" (Ecclesiastes 1:14). Pursuing success by the world's standards, Solomon warned, ultimately amounts to chasing after a breeze—something you can't quite grasp in the end.

Do I really expect an empty washing machine to fill me up?

It feels silly to admit my laundry drama. I'm a grown woman, for crying out loud. Do I really expect an empty washing machine to fill me up? The honest answer is, yes, sometimes I do. Just like I sometimes tie my self-worth to the cleanliness of my home, I can also try to find eternal meaning in a thousand other things: the work I do or clothes I wear, the behavior of my children or affection of my husband, the size of my bank account or my waistline. It's exhausting, really. And I know Solomon is right: It's just chasing the wind.

As Ecclesiastes records Solomon's search for life's meaning, we're told this search is taking place "under the sun" (Ecclesiastes 1:3)—that is, here on our fallen earth. Solomon found what we, too, find if we tug on our meaning threads hard enough: Every earthly thing unravels. Nothing lasts. No manmade meaning can fill the human heart in a full and lasting way.

As hopeless as it sounds, this is good news because it points us to the only source of true meaning and fulfillment: Jesus. In the kingdom of God, life's meaning is not determined by a mortal king's earthly resources, but by the eternal King's perfect goodness, justice, and love. The world we see with our eyes is temporary and fraught with futility, but our life in Christ is everlasting and marked by unimaginable satisfaction.

It's true—life in a fallen world will disappoint us. Every earthly pursuit in this life will fail us, but we know the One who will one day undo all the fallenness and renew the world in glory. With Him, nothing is meaningless. With Him, we have eternal hope.

Where are you chasing the wind today? How can you chase Jesus instead?

Song of Songs

A huge torrent cannot extinguish
love; rivers cannot sweep it away.
If a man were to give all his
wealth for love,
it would be utterly scorned.

SONG OF SONGS 8:7

SONG OF SONGS 7:1–13

Man

1 How beautiful are your sandaled feet, princess!
The curves of your thighs are like jewelry,
the handiwork of a master.
2 Your navel is a rounded bowl;
it never lacks mixed wine.
Your belly is a mound of wheat
surrounded by lilies.
3 Your breasts are like two fawns,
twins of a gazelle.
4 Your neck is like a tower of ivory,
your eyes like pools in Heshbon
by Bath-rabbim's gate.
Your nose is like the tower of Lebanon
looking toward Damascus.
5 Your head crowns you like Mount Carmel,
the hair of your head like purple cloth—
a king could be held captive in your tresses.
6 How beautiful you are and how pleasant,
my love, with such delights!
7 Your stature is like a palm tree;
your breasts are clusters of fruit.
8 I said, "I will climb the palm tree
and take hold of its fruit."
May your breasts be like clusters of grapes,
and the fragrance of your breath like apricots.
9 Your mouth is like fine wine—

Woman

flowing smoothly for my love,
gliding past my lips and teeth!
10 I am my love's,
and his desire is for me.

11 Come, my love,
let's go to the field;
let's spend the night among the henna blossoms.
12 Let's go early to the vineyards;
let's see if the vine has budded,
if the blossom has opened,
if the pomegranates are in bloom.
There I will give you my caresses.
13 The mandrakes give off a fragrance,
and at our doors is every delicacy,
both new and old.
I have treasured them up for you, my love.

SONG OF SONGS 8:5–7

Young Women

5 Who is this coming up from the wilderness,
leaning on the one she loves?

Woman

I awakened you under the apricot tree.
There your mother conceived you;
there she conceived and gave you birth.
6 Set me as a seal on your heart,
as a seal on your arm.
For love is as strong as death;
jealousy is as unrelenting as Sheol.
Love's flames are fiery flames—
an almighty flame!
7 A huge torrent cannot extinguish love;
rivers cannot sweep it away.
If a man were to give all his wealth for love,
it would be utterly scorned.

GENESIS 2:24–25

Man and Woman in the Garden

24 This is why a man leaves his father and mother and bonds with his wife, and they become one flesh. 25 Both the man and his wife were naked, yet felt no shame.

ISAIAH 62:5

Zion's Restoration

For as a young man marries a young woman,
so your sons will marry you;
and as a groom rejoices over his bride,
so your God will rejoice over you.

1 CORINTHIANS 13:1–8

Love: The Superior Way

1 If I speak human or angelic tongues but do not have love, I am a noisy gong or a clanging cymbal. 2 If I have the gift of prophecy and understand all mysteries and all knowledge, and if I have all faith so that I can move mountains but do not have love, I am nothing. 3 And if I give away all my possessions, and if I give over my body in order to boast but do not have love, I gain nothing.

4 Love is patient, love is kind. Love does not envy, is not boastful, is not arrogant, 5 is not rude, is not self-seeking, is not irritable, and does not keep a record of wrongs. 6 Love finds no joy in unrighteousness but rejoices in the truth. 7 It bears all things, believes all things, hopes all things, endures all things.

8 Love never ends. But as for prophecies, they will come to an end; as for tongues, they will cease; as for knowledge, it will come to an end.

I once had a box of love letters that I kept way past their expiration date.

The letters were from a boy I knew when I was a teenager. We lived in different states, met at a church event, and "dated" long distance for a while, seeing each other only a handful of times. (This was back when high school kids didn't have email addresses and dinosaurs roamed the earth, so letter-writing was our primary means of communication.)

I kept those letters long after our young relationship ended, and thinking back on it, I'm not sure why. It wasn't because I was pining for the boy—I hardly knew him, after all. I think I kept them because of my feelings for feelings. I liked remembering the anticipation our distance created and the way my stomach did flips each time his handwriting appeared in my mailbox. I liked recalling the connection I felt as I read his letters, even though they were about normal, everyday things.

Love—even faint glimpses of it—forces us to feel. Romantic love awakens our senses, making us keenly aware of our built-in longing for intimacy and connection. Maybe this is one of the reasons God included Song of Songs in the Bible: to wake us up.

Song of Songs is a book of Israelite love poetry attributed to King Solomon, celebrating God's good gift of love between a woman and a man in the seasons before and throughout marriage. Solomon could hardly contain himself when it came to his beautiful bride in Song of Songs 4:1–3 and 6:7, comparing her hair to "a flock of goats," her brow to "a slice of pomegranate"—even rejoicing that she has all her teeth! We roll our eyes at the absurdity of these metaphors because we know Solomon's bride was human and imperfect. But at the same time, we get it. Whether we've experienced the thrill of romantic love firsthand or just blushed at the thought of it, we can imagine the electric feeling that comes from a stolen glance or a first kiss.

I kept the love letters because of my feelings for feelings.

Reading this poetry out loud makes me uncomfortable, like I'm eavesdropping on a private conversation. But you know what? It does not shock or embarrass God. He created us for intimacy, and marriage allows us to enjoy knowing another person on the most vulnerable level. Solomon is finally joining with his bride, and there's no need for embarrassment. The Bible celebrates this!

Love, relationships, and yes, even sex, remind us that we are made for connection. We are created by a God who loves us, and created us to love each other within the boundaries God has established for our flourishing. We misuse and abuse His gifts—and pain, tears, and shame result when we do—but the gifts themselves are good. Solomon is right to rejoice.

Earthly marriage is wonderful, but it ultimately points to only one love that truly fulfills our expectations: Christ's love for His Church. The Scriptures paint Jesus as a heavenly groom coming for His bride—His people—who He will never fail or forget. And if limited, flawed, earthly love can feel as strong as the words of Song of Songs, just imagine how strong Christ's love is for us!

Isaiah

Now this is what the LORD says—
the one who created you, Jacob,
and the one who formed you,
Israel—"Do not fear, for I have
redeemed you; I have called you
by your name; you are mine."

ISAIAH 43:1

ISAIAH 43:1–7, 14–21

Restoration of Israel

[1] Now this is what the LORD says—
the one who created you, Jacob,
and the one who formed you, Israel—
"Do not fear, for I have redeemed you;
I have called you by your name; you are mine.
[2] When you pass through the waters,
I will be with you,
and the rivers will not overwhelm you.
When you walk through the fire,
you will not be scorched,
and the flame will not burn you.
[3] For I am the LORD your God,
the Holy One of Israel, and your Savior.
I have given Egypt as a ransom for you,
Cush and Seba in your place.
[4] Because you are precious in my sight
and honored, and I love you,
I will give people in exchange for you
and nations instead of your life.
[5] Do not fear, for I am with you;
I will bring your descendants from the east,
and gather you from the west.
[6] I will say to the north, 'Give them up!'
and to the south, 'Do not hold them back!'
Bring my sons from far away,
and my daughters from the ends of the earth—
[7] everyone who bears my name
and is created for my glory.
I have formed them; indeed, I have made them."

. . .

God's Deliverance of Rebellious Israel

[14] This is what the LORD, your Redeemer, the Holy One of Israel says:

Because of you, I will send an army to
Babylon
and bring all of them as fugitives,
even the Chaldeans in the ships in which
they rejoice.
[15] I am the LORD, your Holy One,
the Creator of Israel, your King.

[16] This is what the LORD says—
who makes a way in the sea,
and a path through raging water,
[17] who brings out the chariot and horse,
the army and the mighty one together
(they lie down, they do not rise again;
they are extinguished, put out like a wick)—
[18] "Do not remember the past events;
pay no attention to things of old.
[19] Look, I am about to do something new;
even now it is coming. Do you not see it?
Indeed, I will make a way in the wilderness,
rivers in the desert.
[20] Wild animals—
jackals and ostriches—will honor me,
because I provide water in the wilderness,
and rivers in the desert,
to give drink to my chosen people.
[21] The people I formed for myself
will declare my praise."

1 PETER 2:9–10

The Living Stone and a Holy People

9 But you are "a chosen race, a royal priesthood,
a holy nation, a people for his possession, so that
you may proclaim the praises" of the one who
called you out of darkness into his marvelous light.
10 Once you were not a people, but now you are
God's people; you had not received mercy, but now
you have received mercy.

PSALM 46:1–7

God Our Refuge

1 God is our refuge and strength,
a helper who is always found
in times of trouble.
2 Therefore we will not be afraid,
though the earth trembles
and the mountains topple
into the depths of the seas,
3 though its water roars and foams
and the mountains quake with its turmoil.*Selah*

4 There is a river—
its streams delight the city of God,
the holy dwelling place of the Most High.
5 God is within her; she will not be toppled.
God will help her when the morning dawns.
6 Nations rage, kingdoms topple;
the earth melts when he lifts his voice.
7 The LORD of Armies is with us;
the God of Jacob is our stronghold.*Selah*

When I read Isaiah 43, I am instantly transported to a small church in a small town in Alabama thirty years ago. I am in the choir room, standing around the piano with the other members of the youth choir while Mrs. Becky, our church organist and choir director, plays from the familiar sheet music. We look from our open choir folders to Mrs. Becky's face and back again as she directs our singing with emphatic head nods, eyebrow raises, and an occasional gesture of her right hand when it breaks free from the keys. The hymn is titled simply "Isaiah 43," and the lyrics are straight from the prophet:

"Do not fear, for I have redeemed you;
I have called you by your name; you are mine.
When you pass through the waters,
I will be with you" (Isaiah 43:1b–2a).

I was a teenager when I learned these verses, and though I believed them, my life experience had not yet tested them. I hadn't yet known the relentless waves of grief, or been nearly dragged under by a current of utter despair. I had seen a measure of pain and uncertainty in my young life, but not yet to the point that I couldn't catch my breath. And so I confidently belted out the refrain:

"For I am the Lord your God,
the Holy One of Israel, and your Savior . . .
Do not fear . . ." (Isaiah 43:3a, 5a).

Sometimes we have to sing what we're still learning to understand.

Israel could not have understood the fullness of the promises God made to them here in the center of their story. For generations they had turned from Him, living in disobedience, pain, and destruction. And for generations, He had called them back to Himself through the Prophets—this time through the prophet Isaiah.

In chapter 43, we get a glimpse of the lavish promise that came with this invitation. To comfort His people in exile, God promised them His presence and His provision, His love and His very name. Though the full weight of it would unfold over time, culminating in the person and work of Jesus hundreds of years later, the promise was already true. The merciful, powerful, and redeeming God who invited Israel into restored relationship with Him then is the same God who invites us into restored relationship with Him now.

That hymn still gets stuck in my head any time I read Isaiah 43. But I sing it differently now, thirty years and a lot of miles from the stained-glass church where I first learned the words. It's not because they are more true now than they were then, it's just that I've caught a bigger glimpse of the God who writes the story. I have seen Him do what He says He will do, both in the pages of Scripture and of my own life.

Sometimes we have to sing what we're still learning to understand.

Where is He teaching you to trust Him more deeply today?

Jeremiah

"Instead, this is the covenant I
will make with the house of Israel
after those days"
—the LORD's declaration.
"I will put my teaching within
them and write it on their hearts.
I will be their God,
and they will be my people."

JEREMIAH 31:33

JEREMIAH 31:7–14, 31–34

God's People Brought Home

7 For this is what the LORD says:

Sing with joy for Jacob;
shout for the foremost of the nations!
Proclaim, praise, and say,
"LORD, save your people,
the remnant of Israel!"
8 Watch! I am going to bring them from
the northern land.
I will gather them from remote regions
of the earth—
the blind and the lame will be with them,
along with those who are pregnant and
those about to give birth.
They will return here as a great assembly!
9 They will come weeping,
but I will bring them back with consolation.
I will lead them to wadis filled with water,
by a smooth way where they will not stumble,
for I am Israel's Father,
and Ephraim is my firstborn.
10 Nations, hear the word of the LORD,
and tell it among the far off coasts and islands!
Say, "The one who scattered Israel will
gather him.
He will watch over him as a shepherd
guards his flock,
11 for the LORD has ransomed Jacob
and redeemed him from the power of one
stronger than he."
12 They will come and shout for joy on
the heights of Zion;
they will be radiant with joy
because of the LORD's goodness,
because of the grain, the new wine, the
fresh oil,
and because of the young of the flocks
and herds.
Their life will be like an irrigated garden,
and they will no longer grow weak from
hunger.
13 Then the young women will rejoice
with dancing,
while young and old men rejoice together.
I will turn their mourning into joy,
give them consolation,
and bring happiness out of grief.
14 I will refresh the priests with an
abundance,
and my people will be satisfied with my
goodness.
This is the LORD's declaration.

. . .

The New Covenant

31 "Look, the days are coming"—this is the LORD's
declaration—"when I will make a new covenant
with the house of Israel and with the house of
Judah. 32 This one will not be like the covenant
I made with their ancestors on the day I took
them by the hand to lead them out of the land of
Egypt—my covenant that they broke even though
I am their master"—the LORD's declaration.
33 "Instead, this is the covenant I will make with
the house of Israel after those days"—the LORD's
declaration. "I will put my teaching within them
and write it on their hearts. I will be their God,
and they will be my people. 34 No longer will one
teach his neighbor or his brother, saying, 'Know
the LORD,' for they will all know me, from the least
to the greatest of them"—this is the LORD's declaration. "For I will forgive their iniquity and never
again remember their sin."

LUKE 22:19–20

The First Lord's Supper

[19] And he took bread, gave thanks, broke it, gave it to them, and said, "This is my body, which is given for you. Do this in remembrance of me."

[20] In the same way he also took the cup after supper and said, "This cup is the new covenant in my blood, which is poured out for you."

HEBREWS 8:6

A Heavenly Priesthood

But Jesus has now obtained a superior ministry, and to that degree he is the mediator of a better covenant, which has been established on better promises.

HEBREWS 10:11–18

The Perfect Sacrifice

[11] Every priest stands day after day ministering and offering the same sacrifices time after time, which can never take away sins. [12] But this man, after offering one sacrifice for sins forever, sat down at the right hand of God. [13] He is now waiting until his enemies are made his footstool. [14] For by one offering he has perfected forever those who are sanctified. [15] The Holy Spirit also testifies to us about this. For after he says:

> [16] "This is the covenant I will make with them
> after those days,"

the Lord says,

> "I will put my laws on their hearts
> and write them on their minds,"

[17] and "I will never again remember

> their sins" and their lawless acts.

[18] Now where there is forgiveness of these, there is no longer an offering for sin.

Is it hard for you to imagine things will ever look much different than they do right now?

I doubt any Israelite in Egypt could have imagined their exodus across the dry sea floor. The disciples huddled together in Jerusalem could not have foreseen the power of Pentecost. And when we were slaves to our sin, we could not have comprehended true freedom (Romans 6:17; John 8:36). It seems God is always moving us toward something more than we dare to ask, imagine, or hope for (Ephesians 3:20).

Those who served and worshiped under the Old Testament covenant surely could not have grasped that a day would come when the law would not be written on slabs of stone, but instead on the hearts and minds of God's beloved children (Jeremiah 31:33). Yet, this is the very thing the prophet Jeremiah declared—a shocking message, given the state of God's people at the time.

Jeremiah's job was to warn Israel of the impending consequences should they continue violating their current covenant with God. They were persistently cruel, unjust, and idolatrous, and God would not ignore it. But God's people did not heed Jeremiah's warning, and their consequences came: the destruction of Jerusalem, plus a season of exile.

It is in this dark context that the unimaginable promise of a new covenant dawns. Even though God's people faced short-term consequences for their actions, a day was coming when God would finally solve the problem underlying their waywardness—their hearts. While all the Old Covenant participants were marked as God's people on a ritual level, only some truly knew Him on the heart level. But Jeremiah's words hold out hope: Some day, in the New Covenant, all covenant participants would "know the LORD" (Jeremiah 31:34). How? Rather than experiencing God's law by way of a tablet or scroll, it would be written on their hearts from the start. They'd *want* to follow it.

It is in this dark context that the unimaginable promise of a new covenant dawns.

Just imagine being in their situation and hearing this promise from the Lord: *It won't always be this way. A time will come when the way things are will be referred to as "the old way."* This covenant would bring a new era with it—one when "the blood of bulls and goats" from ongoing sacrifices were no longer required because Christ's blood is sufficient to atone once and for all (Hebrews 10:4). One where the curtain of the temple would be torn in two, making access to God something for everyone, rather than just a few (Matthew 27:51).

As followers of Jesus, we are the beneficiaries of Jeremiah's promise—we are people of the new covenant! In Christ, the first covenant is "obsolete . . . ready to vanish away" (Hebrews 8:13). And it's better than our wildest hopes: God's law is written on our hearts and minds. We are forgiven and loved, and one day we will be in our forever home with Him.

Maybe you can't quite picture it. Perhaps your heart doesn't dare believe it, but that won't stop the Lord from delivering it.

Lamentations

Because of the LORD's faithful love we do not perish, for his mercies never end. They are new every morning; great is your faithfulness!

LAMENTATIONS 3:22–23

LAMENTATIONS 1:12–16

ל *Lamed*

12 Is this nothing to you, all you who pass by?
Look and see!
Is there any pain like mine,
which was dealt out to me,
which the Lord made me suffer
on the day of his burning anger?

מ *Mem*

13 He sent fire from on high into my bones;
he made it descend.
He spread a net for my feet
and turned me back.
He made me desolate,
sick all day long.

נ *Nun*

14 My transgressions have been formed into a yoke,
fastened together by his hand;
they have been placed on my neck,
and the Lord has broken my strength.
He has handed me over
to those I cannot withstand.

ס *Samek*

15 The Lord has rejected
all the mighty men within me.
He has summoned an army against me
to crush my young warriors.
The Lord has trampled Virgin Daughter Judah
like grapes in a winepress.

ע *Ayin*

16 I weep because of these things;
my eyes flow with tears.
For there is no one nearby to comfort me,
no one to keep me alive.
My children are desolate
because the enemy has prevailed.

LAMENTATIONS 3:16–24

ו *Waw*

16 He ground my teeth with gravel
and made me cower in the dust.
17 I have been deprived of peace;
I have forgotten what prosperity is.
18 Then I thought, "My future is lost,
as well as my hope from the Lord."

ז *Zayin*

19 Remember my affliction and my homelessness,
the wormwood and the poison.
20 I continually remember them
and have become depressed.
21 Yet I call this to mind,
and therefore I have hope:

ח *Cheth*

22 Because of the Lord's faithful love
we do not perish,
for his mercies never end.
23 They are new every morning;
great is your faithfulness!
24 I say, "The Lord is my portion,
therefore I will put my hope in him."

PSALM 36:5–9

Human Wickedness and God's Love

5 LORD, your faithful love reaches to heaven,
your faithfulness to the clouds.
6 Your righteousness is like the highest mountains,
your judgments like the deepest sea.
LORD, you preserve people and animals.
7 How priceless your faithful love is, God!
People take refuge in the shadow of your wings.
8 They are filled from the abundance of your house.
You let them drink from your refreshing stream.
9 For the wellspring of life is with you.
By means of your light we see light.

ISAIAH 53:1–5

The Servant's Suffering and Exaltation

1 Who has believed what we have heard?
And to whom has the arm of the LORD been revealed?
2 He grew up before him like a young plant
and like a root out of dry ground.
He didn't have an impressive form
or majesty that we should look at him,
no appearance that we should desire him.
3 He was despised and rejected by men,
a man of suffering who knew what sickness was.
He was like someone people turned away from;
he was despised, and we didn't value him.

4 Yet he himself bore our sicknesses,
and he carried our pains;
but we in turn regarded him stricken,
struck down by God, and afflicted.
5 But he was pierced because of our rebellion,
crushed because of our iniquities;
punishment for our peace was on him,
and we are healed by his wounds.

HEBREWS 13:8

Jesus Christ is the same yesterday, today,
and forever.

As we wound our way through the sunlit woods, the path became holy ground. Our conversation turned to the upcoming anniversary of her beloved boy's death. Pain and dread cut through my friend like a knife. Words stuck in her throat and tears fell as she doubled over in grief. I stopped and placed my hand on her back, yearning to bring comfort where no comfort could be found. There we stood in the middle of the path, undone before the Lord and each other. Only the trees stood sentinel with us, our hearts crying out, "God, where are you? We can't bear this pain! Why have you forsaken us?"

Can we really talk to God like this?

The book of Lamentations answers with a resounding *yes*, revealing that God doesn't merely allow such soul-wrenching wrestling—He invites it. Lamentations records Jeremiah's laments over the destruction of Jerusalem and Judah's captivity in Babylon. He weeps over the state of God's people.

Through Jeremiah's words, God welcomes us to meet Him in the midst of our suffering. Instead of offering a set of techniques, easy answers, or inspiring slogans for facing pain and grief, this book gives voice to our pain through lament. It also includes an extended expression of hope in God's faithful love, declaring that even in the darkness, God's love and mercy know no end. This declaration reorients our focus to God's faithfulness, affirming that He can sustain us through the unimaginable.

Only the trees stood sentinel with us.

We know the truth: Jesus came to shoulder our sorrows and save us from sin and death. One day He will wipe away every tear. "Death will be no more; grief, crying, and pain will be no more" (Revelation 21:4). But until that glorious day, we still walk in this fallen world, carrying the weight of sadness, anger, disappointment, anxiety, and fear. And we aren't alone—all creation joins us as we groan for God to heal and restore every person, place, and thing (Romans 8:22).

Lament is good and right. Scripture instructs us to pour out our hearts before God (Psalm 62:8). Even Jesus wept—not only over the state of His people, but over the reality of death (Luke 19:41–44; John 11:33–36). In lament, God offers us a release valve as we express our emotions, doubts, and distress, both individually and communally.

Why do we resist His invitation? Maybe we think it's sinful to admit struggle, or we assume that acceptable faith should always appear unshakable. But make no mistake: Expressing both praise and pain to God is worship. Whether we are joyfully raising our hands or sorrowfully turning our tear-streaked faces toward Him, we are engaging in genuine relationship with our Creator.

As you walk through seasons of lament, remember: Jesus stands sentinel with you. He has wrestled death itself and understands pain. What anguish do you need to release to Him today?

Ezekiel

"I will give you a new heart and
put a new spirit within you;
I will remove your heart of stone
and give you a heart of flesh."

EZEKIEL 36:26

EZEKIEL 36:24–28

Restoration of Israel's People

24 "For I will take you from the nations and gather
you from all the countries, and will bring you into
your own land. 25 I will also sprinkle clean water
on you, and you will be clean. I will cleanse you
from all your impurities and all your idols. 26 I will
give you a new heart and put a new spirit within
you; I will remove your heart of stone and give you
a heart of flesh. 27 I will place my Spirit within you
and cause you to follow my statutes and carefully
observe my ordinances. 28 You will live in the land
that I gave your ancestors; you will be my people,
and I will be your God."

EZEKIEL 37:1–14

The Valley of Dry Bones

1 The hand of the LORD was on me, and he brought
me out by his Spirit and set me down in the middle
of the valley; it was full of bones. 2 He led me all
around them. There were a great many of them on
the surface of the valley, and they were very dry.
3 Then he said to me, "Son of man, can these bones
live?"

I replied, "Lord GOD, only you know."

4 He said to me, "Prophesy concerning these bones
and say to them: Dry bones, hear the word of the
LORD! 5 This is what the Lord GOD says to these
bones: I will cause breath to enter you, and you
will live. 6 I will put tendons on you, make flesh
grow on you, and cover you with skin. I will put
breath in you so that you come to life. Then you
will know that I am the LORD."

7 So I prophesied as I had been commanded.
While I was prophesying, there was a noise, a rat-
tling sound, and the bones came together, bone to
bone. 8 As I looked, tendons appeared on them,
flesh grew, and skin covered them, but there was
no breath in them. 9 He said to me, "Prophesy to
the breath, prophesy, son of man. Say to it: This is
what the Lord GOD says: Breath, come from the
four winds and breathe into these slain so that they
may live!" 10 So I prophesied as he commanded
me; the breath entered them, and they came to life
and stood on their feet, a vast army.

11 Then he said to me, "Son of man, these bones
are the whole house of Israel. Look how they say,
'Our bones are dried up, and our hope has perished; we are cut off.' 12 Therefore, prophesy and
say to them, 'This is what the Lord GOD says: I am
going to open your graves and bring you up from
them, my people, and lead you into the land of
Israel. 13 You will know that I am the LORD, my
people, when I open your graves and bring you up
from them. 14 I will put my Spirit in you, and you
will live, and I will settle you in your own land.
Then you will know that I am the LORD. I have
spoken, and I will do it. This is the declaration of
the LORD.'"

GALATIANS 2:20–21

Freedom from the Law

20 I have been crucified with Christ, and I no longer live, but Christ lives in me. The life I now live in the body, I live by faith in the Son of God, who loved me and gave himself for me. 21 I do not set aside the grace of God, for if righteousness comes through the law, then Christ died for nothing.

ROMANS 6:4–7

The New Life in Christ

4 Therefore we were buried with him by baptism into death, in order that, just as Christ was raised from the dead by the glory of the Father, so we too may walk in newness of life. 5 For if we have been united with him in the likeness of his death, we will certainly also be in the likeness of his resurrection. 6 For we know that our old self was crucified with him so that the body ruled by sin might be rendered powerless so that we may no longer be enslaved to sin, 7 since a person who has died is freed from sin.

2 CORINTHIANS 3:3

Living Letters

You show that you are Christ's letter, delivered by us, not written with ink but with the Spirit of the living God—not on tablets of stone but on tablets of human hearts.

1 PETER 2:24–25

24 He himself bore our sins in his body on the tree; so that, having died to sins, we might live for righteousness. "By his wounds you have been healed." 25 For you "were like sheep going astray," but you have now returned to the Shepherd and Overseer of your souls.

I'll admit it: I'm a plant lady. I have at least twenty houseplants of varying styles and personalities trailing about the house, reaching for patches of sunlight. They all survived a blistering California summer, but once winter came, I accidentally left one overnight in the backyard and it froze to the core. Cold and crispy, the shriveled leaves turned black. I was pretty sure she was a goner.

Then a wondrous thing happened. After a few weeks of gentle watering and a dash of foolish hope, I saw a brand new leaf unfurl at the tip—bright, green, beautiful. I couldn't have been more surprised. Despite my neglect, this proud little leaf burst into existence almost overnight.

J. R. R. Tolkien called this a "eucatastrophe"[6]—a sudden, joyous turn of events. When all hope seems lost, something changes the story's end. Death in reverse. Hope restored. What comes after is nothing like what came before. There was an old way of doing things, and now there is a new way. Now, when I look at this little fiddle leaf fig, I don't see an ordinary houseplant—I see the power of death-reversing, hope-restoring life at work.

Our regenerated life in Christ is similar, only far better. "Christ was raised from the dead by the glory of the Father, so we too may walk in newness of life" (Romans 6:4). As each bud draws its life from the whole plant, so we draw our new life from Christ's glory.

God has given us new hearts, new minds, new eyes to bear witness to His miracles. Unlike those in the Old Testament, we live in an age full of firsthand stories that speak to how the resurrection shapes our present lives. Many of these appear in Scripture, and others are happening around us—even within us! Dusty, dry bones are brought back to life.

Despite my neglect, this proud little leaf burst into existence almost overnight.

Ezekiel, one of Israel's prophets, had a vision of this promised New Covenant reality in the valley—a picture of what it looks like for we who were dead in sin to be raised to new life in Christ, His Spirit breathed into us (Ezekiel 37). It also reminds us that God will raise our bodies one day, ushering us into the resurrected reality that Ezekiel's prophecy pointed toward when God promised: "I am going to open your graves and bring you up from them" (Ezekiel 37:12).

The gospel is the ultimate eucatastrophe! God has raised Christ from the grave, reversing death and restoring hope, and He will raise us too. In the meantime, we are freed from our "old self" (Romans 6:6–7), the version of ourselves that is unbridled and inclined to sin. We are healed and restored and have the privilege of partnering with Jesus in healing and restoring others. And we have the joy of walking with Him as our daily companion and friend.

If you are in Christ, you have been given a new heart, new mind, and new eyes to bear witness to His miracles. What do you see when you look around? Where have you seen dry bones brought back to life?

Daniel

For his dominion is an everlasting dominion, and his kingdom is from generation to generation.

DANIEL 4:34b

DANIEL 2:44–45

[Nebuchadnezzar's First Dream Interpreted]

44 "In the days of those kings, the God of the heavens will set up a kingdom that will never be destroyed, and this kingdom will not be left to another people. It will crush all these kingdoms and bring them to an end, but will itself endure forever. 45 You saw a stone break off from the mountain without a hand touching it, and it crushed the iron, bronze, fired clay, silver, and gold. The great God has told the king what will happen in the future. The dream is certain, and its interpretation reliable."

DANIEL 4:24–37

[Nebuchadnezzar's Second Dream Interpreted]

24 "This is the interpretation, Your Majesty, and this is the decree of the Most High that has been issued against my lord the king: 25 You will be driven away from people to live with the wild animals. You will feed on grass like cattle and be drenched with dew from the sky for seven periods of time, until you acknowledge that the Most High is ruler over human kingdoms, and he gives them to anyone he wants. 26 As for the command to leave the tree's stump with its roots, your kingdom will be restored to you as soon as you acknowledge that Heaven rules. 27 Therefore, may my advice seem good to you my king. Separate yourself from your sins by doing what is right, and from your injustices by showing mercy to the needy. Perhaps there will be an extension of your prosperity."

The Sentence Executed

28 All this happened to King Nebuchadnezzar. 29 At the end of twelve months, as he was walking on the roof of the royal palace in Babylon, 30 the king exclaimed, "Is this not Babylon the Great that I have built to be a royal residence by my vast power and for my majestic glory?"

31 While the words were still in the king's mouth, a voice came from heaven: "King Nebuchadnezzar, to you it is declared that the kingdom has departed from you. 32 You will be driven away from people to live with the wild animals, and you will feed on grass like cattle for seven periods of time, until you acknowledge that the Most High is ruler over human kingdoms, and he gives them to anyone he wants."

33 At that moment the message against Nebuchadnezzar was fulfilled. He was driven away from people. He ate grass like cattle, and his body was drenched with dew from the sky, until his hair grew like eagles' feathers and his nails like birds' claws.

Nebuchadnezzar's Praise

34 But at the end of those days, I, Nebuchadnezzar, looked up to heaven, and my sanity returned to me. Then I praised the Most High and honored and glorified him who lives forever:

> For his dominion is an everlasting dominion,
> and his kingdom is from generation to
> generation.
> 35 All the inhabitants of the earth are
> counted as nothing,
> and he does what he wants with the army
> of heaven
> and the inhabitants of the earth.
> There is no one who can block his hand
> or say to him, "What have you done?"

36 At that time my sanity returned to me, and my majesty and splendor returned to me for the glory of my kingdom. My advisers and my nobles sought me out, I was reestablished over my kingdom, and even more greatness came to me. 37 Now I, Nebuchadnezzar, praise, exalt, and glorify the King of the heavens, because all his works are true and his ways are just. He is able to humble those who walk in pride.

PSALM 145:10–13

Praising God's Greatness

10 All you have made will thank you, LORD;
the faithful will bless you.
11 They will speak of the glory of your kingdom
and will declare your might,
12 informing all people of your mighty acts
and of the glorious splendor of your kingdom.
13 Your kingdom is an everlasting kingdom;
your rule is for all generations.
The LORD is faithful in all his words
and gracious in all his actions.

REVELATION 11:15

The Seventh Trumpet

The seventh angel blew his trumpet, and there were loud voices in heaven saying,

> The kingdom of the world has become
> the kingdom
> of our Lord and of his Christ,
> and he will reign forever and ever.

I come from a board game family. Mystery games, settlement games, strategy games, card games—we love them all. But there are games we return to again and again, where everyone joins in and everyone has fun. (Note: If you ever join in a Williams family game night, have ear plugs handy. The decibel level may surprise you.)

I adore group game nights, with one notable exception: rule disputes. If even one person insists on playing by a different set of rules, disaster ensues. And if anyone in your group is the least bit competitive (in our case, all of us), it doesn't take long until arguing over the rules actually *becomes* the game.

The kingdom of God—or, the kingdom of Heaven, as it's also referred to in Scripture—has a set of rules that are both set and kept by God Himself. These rules are an outflow of God's character; they are reflective of who He is. God is good, merciful, just, righteous, and loving, so God's kingdom is ruled by goodness, mercy, righteousness, and love. And like God, His kingdom has no end.

In the time of the prophet Daniel, Nebuchadnezzar was king of the most powerful kingdom in the world. And while there were times it seemed he was inclined to acknowledge the God who rules all the world's kingdoms, the king could never quite let go of his pride. "Your God is indeed God of gods, Lord of kings," he said to Daniel (Daniel 2:47). But then he promptly constructed a ninety-foot-high gold statue and commanded everyone in his vast kingdom to worship it instead.

If even one person insists on playing by a different set of rules, disaster ensues.

This push and pull continued with the prideful Nebuchadnezzar until God delivered an ultimatum through Daniel: "You will be driven away from people to live with the wild animals. You will feed on grass like cattle . . . until you acknowledge that the Most High is ruler over human kingdoms" (Daniel 4:25). To have his kingdom restored, Nebuchadnezzar would have to do something his pride would abhor: "acknowledge that Heaven rules" (Daniel 4:26).

At this point in the story I'm rooting for ole King Neb to come around. Instead he exclaims, "Is this not Babylon the Great that I have built to be a royal residence by my vast power and for my majestic glory?" (Daniel 4:30). Nope.

The first rule of God's kingdom is that God is indeed God (Exodus 20:1–3). So when Nebuchadnezzar puts himself in Yahweh's place, it's game over.

Nebuchadnezzar's punishment was intense and unusual, perhaps to match the depth of his pride. But when he came out of this period of exile, he declared what had been true of God all along:

"For his dominion is an everlasting dominion,
and his kingdom is from generation to generation" (Daniel 4:34)

Where in your life do you need to acknowledge that heaven rules? What mini-kingdoms of your own making do you need to set aside in order to embrace the reign of your good, merciful, just, righteous, and loving God? He stands ready to hear your confession: He alone is God, and He alone is King.

Hosea

"For I desire faithful love and not sacrifice, the knowledge of God rather than burnt offerings."

HOSEA 6:6

HOSEA 1:1–11

[1] The word of the LORD that came to Hosea son of Beeri during the reigns of Uzziah, Jotham, Ahaz, and Hezekiah, kings of Judah, and of Jeroboam son of Jehoash, king of Israel.

Hosea's Marriage and Children

[2] When the LORD first spoke to Hosea, he said this to him:

Go and marry a woman of promiscuity,
and have children of promiscuity,
for the land is committing blatant acts of promiscuity
by abandoning the LORD.

[3] So he went and married Gomer daughter of Diblaim, and she conceived and bore him a son.
[4] Then the LORD said to him:

Name him Jezreel, for in a little while
I will bring the bloodshed of Jezreel
on the house of Jehu
and put an end to the kingdom of the house of Israel.
[5] On that day I will break the bow of Israel
in Jezreel Valley.

[6] She conceived again and gave birth to a daughter, and the LORD said to him:

Name her Lo-ruhamah,
for I will no longer have compassion
on the house of Israel.
I will certainly take them away.
[7] But I will have compassion on the house of Judah,
and I will deliver them by the LORD their God.
I will not deliver them by bow, sword, or war,
or by horses and cavalry.

[8] After Gomer had weaned Lo-ruhamah, she conceived and gave birth to a son. [9] Then the LORD
said:

Name him Lo-ammi,
for you are not my people,
and I will not be your God.
[10] Yet the number of the Israelites
will be like the sand of the sea,
which cannot be measured or counted.
And in the place where they were told:
You are not my people,
they will be called: Sons of the living God.
[11] And the Judeans and the Israelites
will be gathered together.
They will appoint for themselves a single ruler
and go up from the land.
For the day of Jezreel will be great.

HOSEA 4:1–3

God's Case Against Israel

[1] Hear the word of the LORD, people of Israel,
for the LORD has a case
against the inhabitants of the land:
There is no truth, no faithful love,
and no knowledge of God in the land!
[2] Cursing, lying, murder, stealing,
and adultery are rampant;
one act of bloodshed follows another.
[3] For this reason the land mourns,
and everyone who lives in it languishes,
along with the wild animals and the birds of the sky;
even the fish of the sea disappear.

HOSEA 6:1–10

A Call to Repentance

[1] Come, let's return to the LORD.
For he has torn us,
and he will heal us;
he has wounded us,
and he will bind up our wounds.
[2] He will revive us after two days,
and on the third day he will raise us up
so we can live in his presence.
[3] Let's strive to know the LORD.
His appearance is as sure as the dawn.
He will come to us like the rain,
like the spring showers that water the land.

The LORD's First Lament

[4] What am I going to do with you, Ephraim?
What am I going to do with you, Judah?
Your love is like the morning mist
and like the early dew that vanishes.

[5] This is why I have used the prophets
to cut them down;
I have killed them with the words from my mouth.
My judgment strikes like lightning.
[6] For I desire faithful love and not sacrifice,
the knowledge of God rather than burnt offerings.

[7] But they, like Adam, have violated the covenant;
there they have betrayed me.

[8] Gilead is a city of evildoers,
tracked with bloody footprints.
[9] Like raiders who wait in ambush for someone,
a band of priests murders on the road to Shechem.
They commit atrocities.
[10] I have seen something horrible in the house
of Israel:
Ephraim's promiscuity is there; Israel is defiled.

MATTHEW 9:10–13

The Call of Matthew

[10] While he was reclining at the table in the house,
many tax collectors and sinners came to eat with
Jesus and his disciples. [11] When the Pharisees saw
this, they asked his disciples, "Why does your
teacher eat with tax collectors and sinners?"

[12] Now when he heard this, he said, "It is not those
who are well who need a doctor, but those who
are sick. [13] Go and learn what this means: 'I desire
mercy and not sacrifice.' For I didn't come to call
the righteous, but sinners."

TITUS 3:1–7

Christian Living Among Outsiders

[1] Remind them to submit to rulers and authorities, to obey, to be ready for every good work,
[2] to slander no one, to avoid fighting, and to be
kind, always showing gentleness to all people. [3] For
we too were once foolish, disobedient, deceived,
enslaved by various passions and pleasures, living
in malice and envy, hateful, detesting one another.

[4] But when the kindness of God our Savior and
his love for mankind appeared, [5] he saved us—not
by works of righteousness that we had done, but
according to his mercy—through the washing of
regeneration and renewal by the Holy Spirit. [6] He
poured out his Spirit on us abundantly through
Jesus Christ our Savior [7] so that, having been justified by his grace, we may become heirs with the
hope of eternal life.

When my husband and I got married, an older family friend pulled him aside a day before the ceremony. The words he spoke were not merely advice; they were a mandate. "Be faithful to your wife," he said. "You aren't immune to infidelity; don't give yourself the opportunity."

Not a year goes by when we don't remember his advice, praying God's grace on the promise we made all those years ago.

At heart, I am Hosea's wife, Gomer—the wanderer. I am a woman who sabotages love in spite of what I know to be true. I did it when I was younger, looking for love in the places it wasn't. And I do it now, looking for love in the praise and approval of others. I hear the call of my false loves every day. And every day, I hear the Lord—the true Lover of my soul—calling me back.

Here's what God said to the prophet Hosea when Israel was going her adulterous way:

Go and marry a woman of promiscuity,
and have children of promiscuity,
for the land is committing blatant acts of promiscuity
by abandoning the L*ORD* *(Hosea 1:2).*

The word *promiscuity* here is a heavy word. Some versions translate it as "wife of whoredom," "wife of harlotry," or even "prostitute." The woman God was calling Hosea to pursue was not just double-minded; she was actively and consistently deceitful and disloyal. She was all of us, without God.

I hear the call of my false loves every day.

Israel was violating her covenant with God, and God was ready to get her attention. Hosea was to show Israel her sin, literally, by taking an unfaithful wife and being faithful to her.

God's judgment on His unfaithful people was more than clear. They were not fit to be His people. They were not fit to be His, period. And yet . . .

Yet the number of the Israelites
will be like the sand of the sea,
which cannot be measured or counted.
And in the place where they were told:
You are not my people,
they will be called: Sons of the living God (Hosea 1:10).

The Lord, the perfect and faithful One, declared He would extend mercy and grace to Israel: "I will deliver them by the LORD their God. I will not deliver them by bow, sword, or war, or by horses and cavalry" (Hosea 1:7). This would be no worldly rescue. This would be the promised salvation of God's people, a promise established from the first sin of the first marriage in the first book of the Bible (Genesis 3:15).

Sin's consequences are real and painful, and we are right to warn each other to be on guard. Hosea reminds us that our rescue comes not by our own merit, but by God's merciful grace ultimately displayed in the person and work of Jesus. Christ is the perfectly faithful Groom who came for His Bride, the Church, and He will never leave her, no matter how many times she wanders.

That includes you. You may run after false loves, but Christ runs after you. Praise the Lord, His faithfulness is greater than our sin.

Joel

Tear your hearts, not just your clothes, and return to the Lord your God. For he is gracious and compassionate, slow to anger, abounding in faithful love, and he relents from sending disaster.

JOEL 2:13

JOEL 2:12–17

God's Call for Repentance

12 Even now—
this is the LORD's declaration—
turn to me with all your heart,
with fasting, weeping, and mourning.
13 Tear your hearts,
not just your clothes,
and return to the LORD your God.
For he is gracious and compassionate,
slow to anger, abounding in faithful love,
and he relents from sending disaster.
14 Who knows? He may turn and relent
and leave a blessing behind him,
so you can offer a grain offering and a drink offering
to the LORD your God.

15 Blow the ram's horn in Zion!
Announce a sacred fast;
proclaim a solemn assembly.
16 Gather the people;
sanctify the congregation;
assemble the aged;
gather the infants,
even babies nursing at the breast.
Let the groom leave his bedroom,
and the bride her honeymoon chamber.
17 Let the priests, the LORD's ministers,
weep between the portico and the altar.
Let them say,
"Have pity on your people, LORD,
and do not make your inheritance a disgrace,
an object of scorn among the nations.
Why should it be said among the peoples,
'Where is their God?'"

ISAIAH 55:1–13

Come to the LORD

[1] "Come, everyone who is thirsty,
come to the water;
and you without silver,
come, buy, and eat!
Come, buy wine and milk
without silver and without cost!
[2] Why do you spend silver on what is not food,
and your wages on what does not satisfy?
Listen carefully to me, and eat what is good,
and you will enjoy the choicest of foods.
[3] Pay attention and come to me;
listen, so that you will live.
I will make a permanent covenant with you
on the basis of the faithful kindnesses of David.
[4] Since I have made him a witness to the peoples,
a leader and commander for the peoples,
[5] so you will summon a nation you do not know,
and nations who do not know you will run to you.
For the LORD your God,
even the Holy One of Israel,
has glorified you."

[6] Seek the LORD while he may be found;
call to him while he is near.
[7] Let the wicked one abandon his way
and the sinful one his thoughts;
let him return to the LORD,
so he may have compassion on him,
and to our God, for he will freely forgive.

[8] "For my thoughts are not your thoughts,
and your ways are not my ways."
This is the LORD's declaration.
[9] "For as heaven is higher than earth,
so my ways are higher than your ways,
and my thoughts than your thoughts.
[10] For just as rain and snow fall from heaven
and do not return there
without saturating the earth
and making it germinate and sprout,
and providing seed to sow
and food to eat,
[11] so my word that comes from my mouth
will not return to me empty,
but it will accomplish what I please
and will prosper in what I send it to do."
[12] You will indeed go out with joy
and be peacefully guided;
the mountains and the hills will break into
singing before you,
and all the trees of the field will clap their hands.
[13] Instead of the thornbush, a cypress will come up,
and instead of the brier, a myrtle will come up;
this will stand as a monument for the LORD,
an everlasting sign that will not be destroyed.

ACTS 3:19–20

[19] Therefore repent and turn back, so that your sins
may be wiped out, [20] that seasons of refreshing may
come from the presence of the Lord, and that he
may send Jesus, who has been appointed for you
as the Messiah.

JAMES 4:1–10

Proud or Humble

[1] What is the source of wars and fights among you?
Don't they come from your passions that wage
war within you? [2] You desire and do not have. You
murder and covet and cannot obtain. You fight
and wage war. You do not have because you do not
ask. [3] You ask and don't receive because you ask
with wrong motives, so that you may spend it on
your pleasures.

[4] You adulterous people! Don't you know that
friendship with the world is hostility toward God?
So whoever wants to be the friend of the world
becomes the enemy of God. [5] Or do you think it's
without reason that the Scripture says: The spirit
he made to dwell in us envies intensely?

[6] But he gives greater grace. Therefore he says:

> "God resists the proud
> but gives grace to the humble."

[7] Therefore, submit to God. Resist the devil, and
he will flee from you. [8] Draw near to God, and he
will draw near to you. Cleanse your hands, sinners,
and purify your hearts, you double-minded. [9] Be
miserable and mourn and weep. Let your laughter
be turned to mourning and your joy to gloom.
[10] Humble yourselves before the Lord, and he will
exalt you.

Have you ever done something that was deplorable—something you felt desperate to take back as soon as it was done? Even the memory of it can grind you down and make your fingers ache with regret.

Along with the other Old Testament prophets, the book of Joel shows us what expending our energy to pursue sin results in: a locust-eaten wasteland of emptiness and shame. When Joel witnesses God's people receiving the miserable consequences of their actions, his assessment is bleak: "Indeed, human joy has dried up" (Joel 1:12).

Plagues, wrath, and judgment descend upon God's people, Judah. It is a time of national crisis for them, and it is utterly devastating. When I read the words of Joel, I know deep in my bones that I can't shoulder the weight of such miserable punishment. I can't take my sins back any more than Judah could.

Russian composer Igor Stravinksy once said, "Sins cannot be undone, only forgiven."[7] He's right. We can't unsay and undo the shameful things we've done, desperate though we may be to do so. But the book of Joel gives us hope. While it's true that judgment for our sins is a sure and unstoppable force (Joel 1:1–2:17), somehow, God's forgiveness, compassion, restoration, and restitution are even more powerful (Joel 2:26–27; 3:1–20).

I can't take my sins back any more than Judah could.

So how do we go from the fear of coming judgment to the comfort of God's forgiveness?

We obey the voice of God as He says, "turn to me with all your heart, with fasting, weeping, and mourning. Tear your hearts, not just your clothes, and return to the LORD your God. For he is gracious and compassionate, slow to anger, abounding in faithful love, and he relents from sending disaster" (Joel 2:12–13).

In short, we repent—for real, not just for show. We remember the gospel—that God levies judgment against us because of our sin, and then takes that punishment on His own shoulders in the person of Christ. And we remember the power we have in God's Spirit—the indwelling presence of the Lord Himself, empowering us to follow Him from the inside out (Joel 2:28). We may not be able to undo our sins; what's done is done. But when we acknowledge and repent of our sins, Christ's blood covers them and our debt is paid. What's done is done.

What sins are eating away at you? Where is God graciously opening your eyes to your sin through conviction? Repent now. For real, not just for show. No matter how many times you stumble, you can return to Him with your whole heart, crying out to Him with deep thankfulness.

Amos

But let justice flow like water, and righteousness, like an unfailing stream.

AMOS 5:24

AMOS 5:4–24

Seek God and Live

[4] For the LORD says to the house of Israel:

Seek me and live!
[5] Do not seek Bethel
or go to Gilgal
or journey to Beer-sheba,
for Gilgal will certainly go into exile,
and Bethel will come to nothing.
[6] Seek the LORD and live,
or he will spread like fire
throughout the house of Joseph;
it will consume everything
with no one at Bethel to extinguish it.
[7] Those who turn justice into wormwood
also throw righteousness to the ground.

[8] The one who made the Pleiades and Orion,
who turns darkness into dawn
and darkens day into night,
who summons the water of the sea
and pours it out over the surface of the
earth—
the LORD is his name.
[9] He brings destruction on the strong,
and it falls on the fortress.

[10] They hate the one who convicts the guilty
at the city gate,
and they despise the one who speaks with
integrity.
[11] Therefore, because you trample on the poor
and exact a grain tax from him,
you will never live in the houses of cut stone
you have built;
you will never drink the wine
from the lush vineyards
you have planted.
[12] For I know your crimes are many
and your sins innumerable.
They oppress the righteous, take a bribe,
and deprive the poor of justice at the city
gates.
[13] Therefore, those who have insight will
keep silent
at such a time,
for the days are evil.

[14] Pursue good and not evil
so that you may live,
and the LORD, the God of Armies,
will be with you
as you have claimed.
[15] Hate evil and love good;
establish justice at the city gate.
Perhaps the LORD, the God of Armies,
will be gracious
to the remnant of Joseph.

[16] Therefore the LORD, the God of Armies, the
Lord, says:

There will be wailing in all the public squares;
they will cry out in anguish in all the streets.
The farmer will be called on to mourn,
and professional mourners to wail.
[17] There will be wailing in all the vineyards,
for I will pass among you.
The LORD has spoken.

The Day of the LORD

[18] Woe to you who long for the day of the LORD!
What will the day of the LORD be for you?
It will be darkness and not light.
[19] It will be like a man who flees from a lion
only to have a bear confront him.
He goes home and rests his hand against the wall
only to have a snake bite him.
[20] Won't the day of the LORD
be darkness rather than light,
even gloom without any brightness in it?
[21] I hate, I despise, your feasts!
I can't stand the stench
of your solemn assemblies.
[22] Even if you offer me
your burnt offerings and grain offerings,
I will not accept them;
I will have no regard
for your fellowship offerings of fattened cattle.
[23] Take away from me the noise of your songs!
I will not listen to the music of your harps.
[24] But let justice flow like water,
and righteousness, like an unfailing stream.

PSALM 147:1–11

God Restores Jerusalem

1 Hallelujah!
How good it is to sing to our God,
for praise is pleasant and lovely.

2 The LORD rebuilds Jerusalem;
he gathers Israel's exiled people.
3 He heals the brokenhearted
and bandages their wounds.
4 He counts the number of the stars;
he gives names to all of them.
5 Our Lord is great, vast in power;
his understanding is infinite.
6 The LORD helps the oppressed
but brings the wicked to the ground.

7 Sing to the LORD with thanksgiving;
play the lyre to our God,
8 who covers the sky with clouds,
prepares rain for the earth,
and causes grass to grow on the hills.
9 He provides the animals with their food,
and the young ravens what they cry for.

10 He is not impressed by the strength of a horse;
he does not value the power of a warrior.
11 The LORD values those who fear him,
those who put their hope in his faithful love.

JEREMIAH 22:3

This is what the LORD says: Administer justice and righteousness. Rescue the victim of robbery from his oppressor. Don't exploit or brutalize the resident alien, the fatherless, or the widow. Don't shed innocent blood in this place.

PHILIPPIANS 4:8–9

Practical Counsel

8 Finally brothers and sisters, whatever is true, whatever is honorable, whatever is just, whatever is pure, whatever is lovely, whatever is commendable—if there is any moral excellence and if there is anything praiseworthy—dwell on these things.
9 Do what you have learned and received and heard from me, and seen in me, and the God of peace will be with you.

The first time I visited the National Museum of African American History and Culture, I wept. The museum beautifully and evocatively captures both the lament and celebration of current and historical moments—from the galleries filled with artifacts and interactive exhibits, to the comfort of the restaurant's multi-regional soul food cooking, to the spaces thoughtfully designed for reflection and contemplation.

One of these spaces—called the Contemplative Court—is a large room with a wide, round opening at the top. A waterfall pours from this opening all the way down into a pool bordered by long, high-back marble benches. Each wall in the Contemplative Court, coppery bronze and overlaid with glass, bears a quote from a key historical figure. On one wall is a famous quote from Martin Luther King Jr., inspired by the book of Amos and communicating his determination to keep fighting for change until "justice run[s] down like water, and righteousness like a mighty stream" (Amos 5:24 NKJV). Whenever I visit the Contemplative Court, I make sure to sit on the bench facing that wall so that the quote appears behind the waterfall. The sight and sound of streaming water create a powerful experience, intensifying my longing for the reality of those words.

The book of Amos reveals God's view of justice and righteousness, primarily through Israel's failure to practice them. They have exploited the poor for economic benefit. They have ignored and mistreated the most vulnerable members of their communities. And they have committed idolatry and other sinful actions. Amos's imagery and sharp tone carry strong emotion, revealing God's heart of righteousness and justice for all people.

While God's judgment warns punishment, it is also a prompt to return to Him. He shouts in Amos 5:4, "Seek me and live!"

That's the call that rings throughout the centuries to us today. The book of Amos invites us to sit in the tension of the brokenness we have experienced and even perpetuated. But it's not for guilt's sake. God's imperative to "let justice flow like water, and righteousness, like an unfailing stream" (Amos 5:24) is an invitation to life! In a world heavy with sin, those who pursue God and His ways experience the freedom, joy, and abundance that only He can give.

Your forgiveness does not rely on your own righteousness.

Don't be afraid to lament the ways you've turned from God. Have you stopped pursuing good, or shrugged away justice? Confess your sin and lean into Him even more. Your forgiveness does not rely on your own righteousness, but on that of another. Jesus Christ is the one who proclaims "liberty to the captives and freedom to the prisoners," who "heals the brokenhearted and bandages their wounds" (Isaiah 61:1; Psalm 147:3). He alone is our hope. Seek God and live!

Obadiah

Saviors will ascend Mount Zion
to rule over the hill country
of Esau, and the kingdom
will be the LORD's.

OBADIAH 1:21

OBADIAH 15–21

Judgment of the Nations

15 For the day of the LORD is near,
against all the nations.
As you have done, it will be done to you;
what you deserve will return on your own head.
16 As you have drunk on my holy mountain,
so all the nations will drink continually.
They will drink and gulp down
and be as though they had never been.
17 But there will be a deliverance on Mount Zion,
and it will be holy;
the house of Jacob will dispossess
those who dispossessed them.
18 Then the house of Jacob will be a blazing fire,
and the house of Joseph, a burning flame,
but the house of Esau will be stubble;
Jacob will set them on fire and consume Edom.
Therefore no survivor will remain
of the house of Esau,
for the LORD has spoken.

Future Blessing for Israel

19 People from the Negev will possess
the hill country of Esau;
those from the Judean foothills will possess
the land of the Philistines.
They will possess
the territories of Ephraim and Samaria,
while Benjamin will possess Gilead.
20 The exiles of the Israelites who are in Halah
and who are among the Canaanites as far as Zarephath
as well as the exiles of Jerusalem who are in Sepharad
will possess the cities of the Negev.
21 Saviors will ascend Mount Zion
to rule over the hill country of Esau,
and the kingdom will be the LORD's.

GENESIS 27:41–42

Esau's Anger

41 Esau held a grudge against Jacob because of the
blessing his father had given him. And Esau determined in his heart: "The days of mourning for my
father are approaching; then I will kill my brother
Jacob."

42 When the words of her older son Esau were
reported to Rebekah, she summoned her younger
son Jacob and said to him, "Listen, your brother
Esau is consoling himself by planning to kill you."

EZEKIEL 25:12–14

Judgment Against Edom

12 "This is what the Lord God says: Because Edom
acted vengefully against the house of Judah and
incurred grievous guilt by taking revenge on them,
13 therefore this is what the Lord God says: I will
stretch out my hand against Edom and cut off
both people and animals from it. I will make it a
wasteland; they will fall by the sword from Teman
to Dedan. 14 I will take my vengeance on Edom
through my people Israel, and they will deal with
Edom according to my anger and wrath. So they
will know my vengeance. This is the declaration of
the Lord God."

MICAH 4:7

The LORD's Rule from Restored Zion

"I will make the lame into a remnant,
those far removed into a strong nation.
Then the LORD will reign over them in Mount Zion
from this time on and forever."

MATTHEW 21:1–10

The Triumphal Entry

1 When they approached Jerusalem and came to
Bethphage at the Mount of Olives, Jesus then sent
two disciples, 2 telling them, "Go into the village
ahead of you. At once you will find a donkey tied
there with her colt. Untie them and bring them to
me. 3 If anyone says anything to you, say that the
Lord needs them, and he will send them at once."

4 This took place so that what was spoken through
the prophet might be fulfilled:

> 5 "Tell Daughter Zion,
> 'See, your King is coming to you,
> gentle, and mounted on a donkey,
> and on a colt,
> the foal of a donkey.'"

6 The disciples went and did just as Jesus directed
them. 7 They brought the donkey and the colt;
then they laid their clothes on them, and he sat
on them. 8 A very large crowd spread their clothes
on the road; others were cutting branches from
the trees and spreading them on the road. 9 Then
the crowds who went ahead of him and those who
followed shouted:

> "'*Hosanna*' to the Son of David!"
> "Blessed is he who comes in the name
> of the Lord!"
> "'*Hosanna*' in the highest heaven!"

10 When he entered Jerusalem, the whole city was
in an uproar, saying, "Who is this?"

ACTS 2:29–36

Peter's Sermon

29 "Brothers and sisters, I can confidently speak to
you about the patriarch David: He is both dead
and buried, and his tomb is with us to this day.
30 Since he was a prophet, he knew that God had
sworn an oath to him to seat one of his descendants on his throne. 31 Seeing what was to come, he
spoke concerning the resurrection of the Messiah:
'He was not abandoned in Hades, and his flesh did
not experience decay.'"

32 "God has raised this Jesus; we are all witnesses of
this. 33 Therefore, since he has been exalted to the
right hand of God and has received from the Father
the promised Holy Spirit, he has poured out what
you both see and hear. 34 For it was not David who
ascended into the heavens, but he himself says:

> 'The Lord declared to my Lord,
> "Sit at my right hand
> 35 until I make your enemies your footstool."'

36 "Therefore let all the house of Israel know with
certainty that God has made this Jesus, whom you
crucified, both Lord and Messiah."

I am reading Obadiah from the front porch swing just before dark. It's raining, and I wonder how long it will last. As I open the news app on my phone to check the weather section, my eyes can't avoid the string of headlines—different from the day before but somehow the same.

Another leader has fallen. Another politician has lied. Another CEO has embezzled. The list goes on and on.

At this point we're all familiar with that sinking feeling of witnessing an influential person become blinded by their own power and wield it in hurtful, selfish ways. Maybe they thought no one was watching their deeds done in the dark, or maybe they assumed they were too powerful to be called out. Either way, the dominoes of destruction fall, and we wonder, *Does God see what's happening here? Does He care?*

The book of Obadiah gives us an answer. And it is a resounding *yes*.

The string of books in the Old Testament called the Minor Prophets proclaim God's judgment on many nations, but the tiny book of Obadiah calls out only one—Edom. Edom is the nation descended from Esau, son of Isaac and twin brother of Jacob. And though Edom's sins were surely many, Obadiah focuses on one sin that seems to be the root of all their others: pride.

Edom felt—and acted—untouchable, invincible. They mocked their neighbors in distress; they lorded their power over others; they failed to offer justice and compassion. And while they did hold a privileged position among their neighboring nations, they were not beyond the reach of the sovereign Lord of all nations.

Though you seem to soar like an eagle
and make your nest among the stars,
even from there I will bring you down.
This is the LORD's declaration (Obadiah 4).

History books, Scripture included, are riddled with rulers and nations like Edom who failed to wield their power wisely. King Saul was lauded as a wise and good king at the start of his reign, but he later turned his back on God, endangering his people and losing his throne (1 Samuel 13). King David was beloved by his people, but his moral failure had disastrous consequences and his own son led a rebellion against him (2 Samuel 11–18). King Herod was so drunk on power that he ordered a massacre of children in his kingdom (Matthew 2:16). God saw it all, and God sees it all. And He promises to set right every unjust thing.

God saw it all, and God sees it all.

From ancient Edom to first-century Bethlehem to the news app on my front porch swing, we see a timeless truth: There is only one God worthy of our trust, one King worthy of our worship. Jesus lived a perfect life of justice, compassion, and righteousness, then took the punishment for our injustice, pride, and sin upon Himself. The very One who came to bring justice to the nations also brings peace to our hearts.

Humans will fail and nations will fall, but the kingdom will be the Lord's. You can set all your hope and trust on Him.

Jonah

I knew that you are a gracious
and compassionate God,
slow to anger, abounding in
faithful love, and one who
relents from sending disaster.

JONAH 4:2b

JONAH 1:1–4, 14–17

Jonah's Flight

1 The word of the LORD came to Jonah son of Amittai: 2 "Get up! Go to the great city of Nineveh and preach against it because their evil has come up before me." 3 Jonah got up to flee to Tarshish from the LORD's presence. He went down to Joppa and found a ship going to Tarshish. He paid the fare and went down into it to go with them to Tarshish from the LORD's presence.

4 But the LORD threw a great wind onto the sea, and such a great storm arose on the sea that the ship threatened to break apart.

. . .

14 So they called out to the LORD, "Please, LORD, don't let us perish because of this man's life, and don't charge us with innocent blood! For you, LORD, have done just as you pleased." 15 Then they picked up Jonah and threw him into the sea, and the sea stopped its raging. 16 The men were seized by great fear of the LORD, and they offered a sacrifice to the LORD and made vows.

17 The LORD appointed a great fish to swallow Jonah, and Jonah was in the belly of the fish three days and three nights.

JONAH 2:1–2, 7–10

Jonah's Prayer

1 Jonah prayed to the LORD his God from the belly of the fish:

> 2 I called to the LORD in my distress,
> and he answered me.
> I cried out for help from deep inside Sheol;
> you heard my voice.

. . .

> 7 As my life was fading away,
> I remembered the LORD,
> and my prayer came to you,
> to your holy temple.
> 8 Those who cherish worthless idols
> abandon their faithful love,
> 9 but as for me, I will sacrifice to you
> with a voice of thanksgiving.
> I will fulfill what I have vowed.
> Salvation belongs to the LORD.

10 Then the LORD commanded the fish, and it vomited Jonah onto dry land.

JONAH 3:1–10

Jonah's Preaching

1 The word of the LORD came to Jonah a second time: 2 "Get up! Go to the great city of Nineveh and preach the message that I tell you." 3 Jonah got up and went to Nineveh according to the LORD's command.

Now Nineveh was an extremely great city, a three-day walk. 4 Jonah set out on the first day of his walk in the city and proclaimed, "In forty days Nineveh will be demolished!" 5 Then the people of Nineveh believed God. They proclaimed a fast and dressed in sackcloth—from the greatest of them to the least.

6 When word reached the king of Nineveh, he got up from his throne, took off his royal robe, covered himself with sackcloth, and sat in ashes. 7 Then he issued a decree in Nineveh:

> By order of the king and his nobles: No person or animal, herd or flock, is to taste anything at all. They must not eat or drink water. 8 Furthermore, both people and animals must be covered with sackcloth, and everyone must call out earnestly to God. Each must turn from his evil ways and from his wrongdoing. 9 Who knows? God may turn and relent; he may turn from his burning anger so that we will not perish.

10 God saw their actions—that they had turned from their evil ways—so God relented from the disaster he had threatened them with. And he did not do it.

JONAH 4:1–4

Jonah's Anger

1 Jonah was greatly displeased and became furious. 2 He prayed to the LORD, "Please, LORD, isn't this what I said while I was still in my own country? That's why I fled toward Tarshish in the first place. I knew that you are a gracious and compassionate God, slow to anger, abounding in faithful love, and one who relents from sending disaster. 3 And now, LORD, take my life from me, for it is better for me to die than to live."

4 The LORD asked, "Is it right for you to be angry?"

MATTHEW 12:38–41

The Sign of Jonah

38 Then some of the scribes and Pharisees said to him, "Teacher, we want to see a sign from you."

39 He answered them, "An evil and adulterous generation demands a sign, but no sign will be given to it except the sign of the prophet Jonah. 40 For as Jonah was in the belly of the huge fish three days and three nights, so the Son of Man will be in the heart of the earth three days and three nights. 41 The men of Nineveh will stand up at the judgment with this generation and condemn it, because they repented at Jonah's preaching; and look—something greater than Jonah is here."

LUKE 15:8–10

The Parable of the Lost Coin

8 "Or what woman who has ten silver coins, if she loses one coin, does not light a lamp, sweep the house, and search carefully until she finds it? 9 When she finds it, she calls her friends and neighbors together, saying, 'Rejoice with me, because I have found the silver coin I lost!' 10 I tell you, in the same way, there is joy in the presence of God's angels over one sinner who repents."

ACTS 1:8

The Holy Spirit Promised

"But you will receive power when the Holy Spirit has come on you, and you will be my witnesses in Jerusalem, in all Judea and Samaria, and to the ends of the earth."

ROMANS 5:6–8

The Justified Are Reconciled

6 For while we were still helpless, at the right time, Christ died for the ungodly. 7 For rarely will someone die for a just person—though for a good person perhaps someone might even dare to die. 8 But God proves his own love for us in that while we were still sinners, Christ died for us.

If there was ever a reluctant preacher, Jonah was it. The prophet didn't just ignore a direct order from God to preach to the city of Nineveh—he headed in the opposite direction. Now, I'm not sure how thoroughly he thought through this particular plan, but it did not end well for him. All his running earned him a near-shipwreck and a three-day and three-night stay in the belly of a great fish. And he still had to go preach to the city of Nineveh anyway.

Willing or not, it was worth it. In fact, the repentance of the Ninevites hearts may be one of the greatest revivals ever recorded. Jonah preached a seven-word sermon (Jonah 3:4), and everyone in the city fasted and repented, even the livestock! The story is a remarkable display of God's mercy and His desire to extend that mercy to those who do not know Him. The Ninevites were not God's people. They were outsiders, but through their story, God demonstrated His steadfast intention to pursue and redeem all the nations of the world.

In Matthew 12, Jesus references this famed story when pressed by the religious elite to prove the legitimacy of His God-given authority. In turn, He rebukes those leaders, telling them they are slaves to the spirit of the age, members of an evil and adulterous generation (Matthew 12:38–39). When I read these verses, I feel the tension there and wonder, *Shouldn't these religious leaders, the ones who were most familiar with the promises and faithfulness of God, be able to recognize the Son of God standing in front of them?* Imagine them there, demanding that the Son of God demonstrate His authority!

Jesus's rebuke of the scribes and Pharisees is an opportunity to turn their hearts back toward the truth. In reminding them of Nineveh's repentance, Jesus assures them, "something greater than Jonah is here" (Matthew 12:41). This was true on every level. While Jonah's mission was marked by reluctance and rebellion, Jesus's entire earthly ministry was built on obedience and submission to the will of the Father. While God rerouted an unwilling Jonah by way of three days in the belly of a fish, Jesus willingly spent three days in the belly of the earth (Matthew 12:40). While Jonah hoped to see the Ninevites destroyed for their sin, Jesus didn't come to condemn sinners (John 3:17). Rather, "God relented from the disaster" (Jonah 3:10), sparing the Ninevites in the same way He spares everyone who repents and trusts Him for eternal life.

I don't want to be so proud of where the Lord has brought me that I forget where I once was.

I don't want to be so proud of where the Lord has brought me that I forget where I once was and who I would be without Jesus. I want to love my neighbor and see them with the compassionate eyes of Christ. I want to walk in repentance and extend to others the same mercy that God extends to me.

Is your heart soft and receptive to the work of God in the world today? Are you eager to see the people around you—even your enemies—encounter the life-changing mercy of Jesus?

Micah

Mankind, he has told each of you what is good and what it is the LORD requires of you: to act justly, to love faithfulness, and to walk humbly with your God.

MICAH 6:8

MICAH 1:1–2, 8–9

[1] The word of the LORD that came to Micah the Moreshite—what he saw regarding Samaria and Jerusalem in the days of Jotham, Ahaz, and Hezekiah, kings of Judah.

Coming Judgment on Israel

[2] Listen, all you peoples;
pay attention, earth and everyone in it!
The Lord GOD will be a witness against you,
the Lord, from his holy temple.

. . .

Micah's Lament

[8] Because of this I will lament and wail;
I will walk barefoot and naked.
I will howl like the jackals
and mourn like ostriches.
[9] For her wound is incurable
and has reached even Judah;
it has approached my people's city gate,
as far as Jerusalem.

MICAH 3:1, 8

Unjust Leaders Judged

[1] Then I said, "Now listen, leaders of Jacob,
you rulers of the house of Israel.
Aren't you supposed to know what is just?

. . .

[8] As for me, however, I am filled with power
by the Spirit of the LORD,
with justice and courage,
to proclaim to Jacob his rebellion
and to Israel his sin.

MICAH 5:2–5a, 10–14

From Defeated Ruler to Conquering King

[2] Bethlehem Ephrathah,
you are small among the clans of Judah;
one will come from you
to be ruler over Israel for me.
His origin is from antiquity,
from ancient times.
[3] Therefore, Israel will be abandoned
until the time
when she who is in labor has given birth;
then the rest of the ruler's brothers will return
to the people of Israel.
[4] He will stand and shepherd them
in the strength of the LORD,
in the majestic name of the LORD his God.
They will live securely,
for then his greatness will extend
to the ends of the earth.
[5] He will be their peace.

. . .

The Glorious Purified Remnant

[10] In that day—
this is the LORD's declaration—
I will remove your horses from you
and wreck your chariots.
[11] I will remove the cities of your land
and tear down all your fortresses.
[12] I will remove sorceries from your hands,
and you will not have any more fortune-tellers.
[13] I will remove your carved images
and sacred pillars from you
so that you will no longer worship
the work of your hands.
[14] I will pull up the Asherah poles from
among you
and demolish your cities.

MICAH 6:1–8

God's Lawsuit against Judah

[1] Now listen to what the LORD is saying:

Rise, plead your case before the mountains,
and let the hills hear your complaint.
[2] Listen to the LORD's lawsuit,
you mountains and enduring foundations
of the earth,
because the LORD has a case against his
people,
and he will argue it against Israel.
[3] My people, what have I done to you,
or how have I wearied you?
Testify against me!
[4] Indeed, I brought you up from the land
of Egypt

and redeemed you from that place of slavery.
I sent Moses, Aaron, and Miriam ahead of you.
5 My people,
remember what King Balak of Moab proposed,
what Balaam son of Beor answered him,
and what happened from the Acacia
Grove to Gilgal
so that you may acknowledge
the LORD's righteous acts.

6 What should I bring before the LORD
when I come to bow before God on high?
Should I come before him with burnt
offerings,
with year-old calves?
7 Would the LORD be pleased with
thousands of rams
or with ten thousand streams of oil?
Should I give my firstborn for my
transgression,
the offspring of my body for my own sin?

8 Mankind, he has told each of you
what is good
and what it is the LORD requires of you:
to act justly,
to love faithfulness,
and to walk humbly with your God.

MICAH 7:7–9, 18–19

Zion's Vindication

7 But I will look to the LORD;
I will wait for the God of my salvation.
My God will hear me.

8 Do not rejoice over me, my enemy!
Though I have fallen, I will stand up;
though I sit in darkness,
the LORD will be my light.
9 Because I have sinned against him,
I must endure the LORD's fury
until he champions my cause
and establishes justice for me.
He will bring me into the light;
I will see his salvation.

. . .

Micah's Prayer Answered

18 Who is a God like you,
forgiving iniquity and passing over rebellion
for the remnant of his inheritance?
He does not hold on to his anger forever
because he delights in faithful love.
19 He will again have compassion on us;
he will vanquish our iniquities.
You will cast all our sins
into the depths of the sea.

DEUTERONOMY 10:12–13

What God Requires

12 And now, Israel, what does the LORD your God
ask of you except to fear the LORD your God by
walking in all his ways, to love him, and to worship
the LORD your God with all your heart and all your
soul? 13 Keep the LORD's commands and statutes I
am giving you today, for your own good.

ISAIAH 58:6–8

True Fasting

6 "Isn't this the fast I choose:
To break the chains of wickedness,
to untie the ropes of the yoke,
to set the oppressed free,
and to tear off every yoke?
7 Is it not to share your bread with the hungry,
to bring the poor and homeless into your house,
to clothe the naked when you see him,
and not to ignore your own flesh and blood?
8 Then your light will appear like the dawn,
and your recovery will come quickly.
Your righteousness will go before you,
and the LORD's glory will be your rear guard."

MATTHEW 23:23–24

Religious Hypocrites Denounced

23 "Woe to you, scribes and Pharisees, hypocrites!
You pay a tenth of mint, dill, and cumin, and yet
you have neglected the more important matters of
the law—justice, mercy, and faithfulness. These
things should have been done without neglecting
the others. 24 Blind guides! You strain out a gnat,
but gulp down a camel!"

When I was a high school senior, I wrote out my life plan: Go to a Christian college, get engaged to my high school sweetheart during my freshman year, get married after sophomore year, purchase a home before graduation, and begin filling that home with children by age twenty-four. We would have a dog, a yard, close friendships, a savings plan, and a real estate strategy that would set us up nicely for retirement.

A few years ago, I found the handwritten plan in an old box and read it to my husband, awestruck at how much of it had come to fruition. But what the younger me couldn't have predicted was all the life that came in between those milestones. Young marriage was hard. We'd buried a baby, trusted friends had betrayed us, and the market had done what the market does. Those ten years hadn't exactly thwarted our plan, but living adult life had moved us from people who put their hope in benchmarks, to those who put their hope in Christ.

The book of Micah was written to Judah in a time when their hope was in anything but God. Micah prophesies that the Messiah will come out of Bethlehem to shepherd His people. "In that day," He will remove their horses, chariots, fortresses, cities, fortune-tellers, and sacred pillars, so that they "will no longer worship to the work of your hands" (Micah 5:10–13). In other words, He'd remove all the stuff they trusted to shepherd them safely through the future—all the stuff they considered proof that their relationship with God was fine.

Living life had moved us from people who put their hope in benchmarks, to those who put their hope in Christ.

Imagine a modern reading: *In that day, I will do away with your false hopes—your cars, houses, degrees, financial investments, security systems, and family plans—so that you will not worship or rely on anything but me. I will be your Hope.*

Now, cars, homes, families, and investments aren't bad things. They are often wonderful things! It's when we put our ultimate hope in them that we will be put to shame. They are gifts from a good Father, but they cannot shepherd us safely into our ultimate future and they are not proof that we're genuinely devoted to God.

So what *is* proof of genuine devotion? What *does* God see as a life well-lived? "What should I bring before the LORD when I come to bow before God on high" (Micah 6:6)?

"Mankind, he has told each of you what is good and what it is the LORD requires of you: to act justly, to love faithfulness, and to walk humbly with your God" (Micah 6:8). Are we just in all our dealings? Are we faithful to God and His Word? In the good and the hard, are we walking with the Lord, humbly trusting that His presence is enough?

If not, it's not too late! Remember that the Shepherd from Bethlehem came, and He delights to shepherd you into that kind of life.

He will stand and shepherd them in the strength of the LORD,
in the majestic name of the LORD his God.
They will live securely, for then his greatness will extend
to the ends of the earth. He will be their peace (Micah 5:4–5a).

Nahum

The LORD is good, a stronghold in a day of distress; he cares for those who take refuge in him.

NAHUM 1:7

NAHUM 1:1–15

1 The pronouncement concerning Nineveh. The book of the vision of Nahum the Elkoshite.

God's Vengeance

2 The LORD is a jealous and avenging God;
the LORD takes vengeance
and is fierce in wrath.
The LORD takes vengeance against his foes;
he is furious with his enemies.
3 The LORD is slow to anger but great in power;
the LORD will never leave the guilty unpunished.
His path is in the whirlwind and storm,
and clouds are the dust beneath his feet.
4 He rebukes the sea and dries it up,
and he makes all the rivers run dry.
Bashan and Carmel wither;
even the flower of Lebanon withers.
5 The mountains quake before him,
and the hills melt;
the earth trembles at his presence—
the world and all who live in it.
6 Who can withstand his indignation?
Who can endure his burning anger?
His wrath is poured out like fire;
even rocks are shattered before him.

Destruction of Nineveh

7 The LORD is good,
a stronghold in a day of distress;
he cares for those who take refuge in him.
8 But he will completely destroy Nineveh
with an overwhelming flood,
and he will chase his enemies into darkness.

9 Whatever you plot against the LORD,
he will bring it to complete destruction;
oppression will not rise up a second time.
10 For they will be consumed
like entangled thorns,
like the drink of a drunkard
and like straw that is fully dry.
11 One has gone out from you,
who plots evil against the LORD,
and is a wicked counselor.

Promise of Judah's Deliverance

12 This is what the LORD says:

Though they are strong and numerous,
they will still be mowed down,
and he will pass away.
Though I have punished you,
I will punish you no longer.
13 For I will now break off his yoke from you
and tear off your shackles.

The Assyrian King's Demise

14 The LORD has issued an order concerning you:

There will be no offspring
to carry on your name.
I will eliminate the carved idol and cast image
from the house of your gods;
I will prepare your grave,
for you are contemptible.

15 Look to the mountains—
the feet of the herald,
who proclaims peace.
Celebrate your festivals, Judah;
fulfill your vows.
For the wicked one will never again
march through you;
he will be entirely wiped out.

2 SAMUEL 22:1–4

David's Song of Thanksgiving

1 David spoke the words of this song to the LORD
on the day the LORD rescued him from the grasp
of all his enemies and from the grasp of Saul. 2 He
said:

The LORD is my rock, my fortress, and
my deliverer,
3 my God, my rock where I seek refuge.
My shield, the horn of my salvation, my
stronghold, my refuge,
and my Savior, you save me from violence.
4 I called to the LORD, who is worthy of
praise,
and I was saved from my enemies.

LUKE 1:72–75

Zechariah's Prophecy

72 He has dealt mercifully with our ancestors
and remembered his holy covenant—
73 the oath that he swore to our father Abraham,
to grant that we,
74 having been rescued
from the hand of our enemies,
would serve him without fear
75 in holiness and righteousness
in his presence all our days.

God is great, God is good, let us thank Him for our food."

I don't remember when I was first taught this prayer, but I do remember cheerfully chanting it as a child before mealtimes. And I'm glad I did, because this simple prayer instilled in me two essential truths about God.

God is great. He is powerful, sovereign, and holy. We see this on full display in the opening verses of Nahum, a book that tells the other half of Jonah's story. Back in the book of Jonah, we read about Nineveh, and how God responded with forgiveness and grace when its people turned toward God and away from their evil deeds.

But in the years after that deliverance, Nineveh—a city in the brutal, domineering nation of Assyria—had turned back to its sin. God's redemptive work in their city was forgotten. In 2 Kings 19:10–11, their king Sennacherib mocked the living God and His promises with a taunt: "Don't let your God, on whom you rely, deceive you . . . Will you be rescued?"

In Nahum 1, the prophet shares God's response to the actions of this unrepentant people: Judgment will come to the cruel and arrogant Nineveh. Our great God is just—slow to anger but righteous in dealing with sin, oppression, and plots against Him (Nahum 1:3, 9).

I sometimes feel whispers of Sennacherib's taunt slipping into my thoughts as I read the Minor Prophets. The descriptions of the greatness of God remind me of my own rebellion, my own sinful nature. And so I wonder, *Is this God I claim to rely on really to be trusted? Will I really be rescued?* But the declaration of Nahum 1:7 drowns out those whispers:

The Lord is good,
a stronghold in a day of distress;
he cares for those who take refuge in him.

This verse reminds us that God's greatness is entwined with another essential truth.

God is good. He is close to His people, a stronghold in days of distress. He is compassionate and gracious, abounding in mercy and kindness (Psalm 86:15). He is faithful even when we are not (2 Timothy 2:13). Through the work of Jesus, God invites us to know Him and belong to Him—extending the invitation even while we were sinners, rescuing us from suffering, despair, and the punishments our sins deserve (Romans 5:8).

This is our God, both great and good.

This is our God, both great and good. While passages like the judgment of Nineveh in Nahum show us the devastating consequences of sin, they also paint a picture of a God who is fully just, fully loving, and fully good in His response to wayward hearts and repentant ones.

If you feel yourself tempted toward arrogance or self-sufficiency today, remember God's greatness. He is mighty in power—to a measure you cannot be. Trying to attain His level of greatness only leads to destruction. And if you are tempted toward despair and distress as you feel the weight of your sin, remember God's goodness. Run toward Him as your refuge, and He will receive you and protect you every time.

Habakkuk

Yet I will celebrate in the Lord;
I will rejoice in the God of my
salvation! The Lord my Lord is
my strength; he makes my feet
like those of a deer and enables
me to walk on mountain heights!

HABAKKUK 3:18–19

HABAKKUK 3:1–19

Habakkuk's Third Prayer

[1] A prayer of the prophet Habakkuk. According to *Shigionoth*.

[2] LORD, I have heard the report about you;
LORD, I stand in awe of your deeds.
Revive your work in these years;
make it known in these years.
In your wrath remember mercy!

[3] God comes from Teman,
the Holy One from Mount Paran. *Selah*
His splendor covers the heavens,
and the earth is full of his praise.
[4] His brilliance is like light;
rays are flashing from his hand.
This is where his power is hidden.
[5] Plague goes before him,
and pestilence follows in his steps.
[6] He stands and shakes the earth;
he looks and startles the nations.
The age-old mountains break apart;
the ancient hills sink down.
His pathways are ancient.
[7] I see the tents of Cushan in distress;
the tent curtains of the land of Midian tremble.
[8] Are you angry at the rivers, LORD?
Is your wrath against the rivers?
Or is your fury against the sea
when you ride on your horses,
your victorious chariot?
[9] You took the sheath from your bow;
the arrows are ready to be used with an
oath. *Selah*
You split the earth with rivers.
[10] The mountains see you and shudder;
a downpour of water sweeps by.
The deep roars with its voice
and lifts its waves high.
[11] Sun and moon stand still in their lofty
residence,
at the flash of your flying arrows,
at the brightness of your shining spear.
[12] You march across the earth with indignation;
you trample down the nations in wrath.
[13] You come out to save your people,
to save your anointed.
You crush the leader of the house of the
wicked
and strip him from foot to neck. *Selah*
[14] You pierce his head
with his own spears;
his warriors storm out to scatter us,
gloating as if ready to secretly devour the
weak.
[15] You tread the sea with your horses,
stirring up the vast water.

Habakkuk's Confidence in God Expressed

[16] I heard, and I trembled within;
my lips quivered at the sound.
Rottenness entered my bones;
I trembled where I stood.
Now I must quietly wait for the day of distress
to come against the people invading us.
[17] Though the fig tree does not bud
and there is no fruit on the vines,
though the olive crop fails
and the fields produce no food,
though the flocks disappear from the pen
and there are no herds in the stalls,
[18] yet I will celebrate in the LORD;
I will rejoice in the God of my salvation!
[19] The LORD my Lord is my strength;
he makes my feet like those of a deer
and enables me to walk on mountain heights!

For the choir director: on stringed instruments.

ISAIAH 40:25–31

God's People Comforted

25 "To whom will you compare me,
or who is my equal?" asks the Holy One.
26 Look up and see!
Who created these?
He brings out the stars by number;
he calls all of them by name.
Because of his great power and strength,
not one of them is missing.

27 Jacob, why do you say,
and Israel, why do you assert,
"My way is hidden from the LORD,
and my claim is ignored by my God"?
28 Do you not know?
Have you not heard?
The LORD is the everlasting God,
the Creator of the whole earth.
He never becomes faint or weary;
there is no limit to his understanding.
29 He gives strength to the faint
and strengthens the powerless.
30 Youths may become faint and weary,
and young men stumble and fall,
31 but those who trust in the LORD
will renew their strength;
they will soar on wings like eagles;
they will run and not become weary,
they will walk and not faint.

HEBREWS 4:16

Our Great High Priest

Therefore, let us approach the throne of grace with boldness, so that we may receive mercy and find grace to help us in time of need.

It wasn't until I was in college studying grammar and literature that I realized something: The word "wait" is an action verb. Something is happening, something is in motion—even when the word itself implies the opposite. To wait on someone means to serve them by being actively present, even without words. Waiting in line? Active. Waiting for rain? Also active. Waiting on a tough situation to resolve, a difficult season to pass, or a deep longing of your heart to come to fruition? All active, and painfully so.

In the book of Habakkuk, waiting abounds. The people of God are waiting for an answer, and God is waiting until the time is right. Neither wait is wrong, and neither wait is without action.

The prophet Habakkuk watches as the people of God fall headlong into a shockingly terrible condition, both ethically and spiritually. Moral deterioration eats away at everything he sees—especially the rich citizens and the spiritual leaders—and Habakkuk wonders how long God will wait to address the internal corruption among His people. *How long will this injustice go unseen and undealt with, God?*

God answers him, and Habakkuk learns that the Lord already has a plan. In a move of poetic justice, the oppressors will now be oppressed. To call their corruption to account, God's chosen "insider" nation will now be overrun by outsiders. And these are not just any outsiders, but the Babylonians (or Chaldeans), known to be especially "bitter," "fierce," and "terrifying" enemies of God's people (Habakkuk 1:6–7). Did Habakkuk long for God to address His people's sin? Of course. But facing the cruelty and oppression of the Babylonians—whose corruption goes even deeper than that of God's people—leaves Habakkuk and the people of Judah waiting and begging, imploring God to hear, answer, and save them. There they stand, wondering all over again: *How long, Lord?*

"How long will this injustice go unseen and undealt with, God?"

Habakkuk had to wait for God to address Judah's sin. After that, he watched and waited through their difficult season of discipline. Meanwhile, God also waited. He waited for the perfect, predetermined time to discipline sin. And He waited for the perfect time to alleviate His people's afflictions. At every point in the journey, God was not worried about being too early or too late. He was present, even when He may have seemed silent. His waiting was good, even when it felt painful to Judah at the time.

Are you waiting for something today? I am, too. We all have something we cry out to God about, asking: *How long, Lord? How long will you wait to deal with injustice in this situation I'm facing? How long will you allow my affliction to last?*

I can't answer how long it will be. But I know God will move at the perfect time, and I know He hears your pleas. In the meantime, remember: Wait is a verb. God is at work in your waiting, and you are at work in it, too.

Zephaniah

The Lord your God is among you, a warrior who saves. He will rejoice over you with gladness. He will be quiet in his love. He will delight in you with singing.

ZEPHANIAH 3:17

ZEPHANIAH 2:1–3

A Call to Repentance

[1] Gather yourselves together;
gather together, undesirable nation,
[2] before the decree takes effect
and the day passes like chaff,
before the burning of the LORD's anger overtakes you,
before the day of the LORD's anger overtakes you.
[3] Seek the LORD, all you humble of the earth,
who carry out what he commands.
Seek righteousness, seek humility;
perhaps you will be concealed
on the day of the LORD's anger.

ZEPHANIAH 3:1–5, 9–20

Woe to Oppressive Jerusalem

[1] Woe to the city that is rebellious and defiled,
the oppressive city!
[2] She has not obeyed;
she has not accepted discipline.
She has not trusted in the LORD;
she has not drawn near to her God.
[3] The princes within her are roaring lions;
her judges are wolves of the night,
which leave nothing for the morning.
[4] Her prophets are reckless—
treacherous men.
Her priests profane the sanctuary;
they do violence to instruction.
[5] The righteous LORD is in her;
he does no wrong.
He applies his justice morning by morning;
he does not fail at dawn,
yet the one who does wrong knows no shame.

. . .

Final Restoration Promised

[9] For I will then restore
pure speech to the peoples
so that all of them may call
on the name of the LORD
and serve him with a single purpose.
[10] From beyond the rivers of Cush
my supplicants, my dispersed people,
will bring an offering to me.
[11] On that day you will not be put to shame
because of everything you have done
in rebelling against me.
For then I will remove
from among you your jubilant, arrogant people,
and you will never again be haughty
on my holy mountain.
[12] I will leave
a meek and humble people among you,
and they will take refuge in the name of the LORD.
[13] The remnant of Israel will no longer
do wrong or tell lies;
a deceitful tongue will not be found
in their mouths.
They will pasture and lie down,
with nothing to make them afraid.

[14] Sing for joy, Daughter Zion;
shout loudly, Israel!
Be glad and celebrate with all your heart,
Daughter Jerusalem!
[15] The LORD has removed your punishment;
he has turned back your enemy.
The King of Israel, the LORD, is among you
you need no longer fear harm.
[16] On that day it will be said to Jerusalem:
"Do not fear;
Zion, do not let your hands grow weak.
[17] The LORD your God is among you,
a warrior who saves.
He will rejoice over you with gladness.
He will be quiet in his love.
He will delight in you with singing."

[18] I will gather those who have been driven
from the appointed festivals;
they will be a tribute from you
and a reproach on her.
[19] Yes, at that time
I will deal with all who oppress you.
I will save the lame and gather the outcasts;
I will make those who were disgraced
throughout the earth
receive praise and fame.
[20] At that time I will bring you back,
yes, at the time I will gather you.
I will give you fame and praise
among all the peoples of the earth,
when I restore your fortunes before your eyes.
The LORD has spoken.

ISAIAH 30:18–21

The Lord's Mercy to Israel

18 Therefore the Lord is waiting to
show you mercy,
and is rising up to show you compassion,
for the Lord is a just God.
All who wait patiently for him are happy.

19 For people will live on Zion in Jerusalem. You will never weep again; he will show favor to you at the sound of your outcry; as soon as he hears, he will answer you. 20 The Lord will give you meager bread and water during oppression, but your Teacher will not hide any longer. Your eyes will see your Teacher, 21 and whenever you turn to the right or to the left, your ears will hear this command behind you: "This is the way. Walk in it."

COLOSSIANS 3:1–4

The Life of the New Man

1 So if you have been raised with Christ, seek the things above, where Christ is, seated at the right hand of God. 2 Set your minds on things above, not on earthly things. 3 For you died, and your life is hidden with Christ in God. 4 When Christ, who is your life, appears, then you also will appear with him in glory.

HEBREWS 11:27–28

Living By Faith

27 By faith he left Egypt behind, not being afraid of the king's anger, for Moses persevered as one who sees him who is invisible. 28 By faith he instituted the Passover and the sprinkling of the blood, so that the destroyer of the firstborn might not touch the Israelites.

I never knew how I was supposed to feel about "The Day of the Lord." On one hand, *Yay! Lord, hasten your day!* On the other hand, *Why does it feel so . . . ominous?*

The truth is, it's both. We aren't wrong to feel a heaviness when we hear the phrase. The New Testament reminds us: "The day of the Lord will come just like a thief in the night," bringing "sudden destruction" on those who walk in darkness (1 Thessalonians 5:2–3). It's right to sense a holy fear and even a solemnity. And at the same time, it's not wrong for hope to flutter in the souls of the righteous at the thought of the Lord taking His promised action in a final sweep of justice.

In Zechariah's prophecies, God's rebuke of His people centers on their inversion of justice and injustice. The prophets were reckless, not wise. The priests were profane, not holy. And when God confronted them, their response was not repentance, but increased corruption. These evildoers were not only walking in darkness, they were proud of it. So, God declared a coming reckoning when these night-dwellers would be held accountable and swept away entirely.

But how can we possibly endure this "night" of judgment and make it to the "day" on the other side? Aren't we guilty of similar things? Scripture says that when the great reckoning comes, it will sweep through the nations like a fiery storm. How can any of us stand?

When God confronted them, their response was not repentance, but increased corruption.

The answer is Christ, the warrior who saves. Just as the blood of the unblemished lambs protected Israel's firstborns from impending death at the first passover (Exodus 12), the blood of Jesus, the "Lamb of God" will protect us from destruction on the Day of the Lord (John 1:29; Zephaniah 2:3). Those hidden in Him will be safe from harm (Colossians 3:3).

When that Day comes, He will redeem and restore everything—not only our bodies, but our relationships, our disappointments, and even the world we live in. On that Day, "God's dwelling [will be] with humanity, and he will live with them . . . Death will be no more; grief, crying, and pain will be no more, because the previous things [will] have passed away" (Revelation 21:3–4).

The God of Zephaniah is a terrible force to those who oppose Him. But for those who seek Him, there is hope! God "applies his justice morning by morning; he does not fail at dawn" (Zephaniah 3:5). To those who love and serve Him, He is a tender and loving warrior who saves. "He will rejoice over you with gladness. He will be quiet in his love. He will delight in you with singing" (Zephaniah 3:17). It makes my soul flutter, in both trembling and joy.

Lord, hasten your Day.

Haggai

“The final glory of this house
will be greater than the first,”
says the LORD of Armies.
“I will provide peace in this
place”—this is the declaration
of the LORD of Armies.

—HAGGAI 2:9

HAGGAI 2:1–9

Encouragement and Promise

[1] On the twenty-first day of the seventh month, the word of the Lord came
through the prophet Haggai: [2] "Speak to Zerubbabel son of Shealtiel, governor of
Judah, to the high priest Joshua son of Jehozadak, and to the remnant of the people: [3] 'Who is left among you who saw this house in its former glory? How does
it look to you now? Doesn't it seem to you like nothing by comparison? [4] Even so,
be strong, Zerubbabel—this is the Lord's declaration. Be strong, Joshua son of
Jehozadak, high priest. Be strong, all you people of the land—this is the Lord's
declaration. Work! For I am with you—the declaration of the Lord of Armies.
[5] This is the promise I made to you when you came out of Egypt, and my Spirit is
present among you; don't be afraid.'"

[6] For the Lord of Armies says this: "Once more, in a little while, I am going to
shake the heavens and the earth, the sea and the dry land. [7] I will shake all the
nations so that the treasures of all the nations will come, and I will fill this house
with glory," says the Lord of Armies. [8] "The silver and gold belong to me"—this
is the declaration of the Lord of Armies. [9] "The final glory of this house will
be greater than the first," says the Lord of Armies. "I will provide peace in this
place"—this is the declaration of the Lord of Armies.

JOHN 2:13–22

Cleansing the Temple

13 The Jewish Passover was near, and so Jesus went up to Jerusalem. 14 In the temple he found people selling oxen, sheep, and doves, and he also found the money changers sitting there. 15 After making a whip out of cords, he drove everyone out of the temple with their sheep and oxen. He also poured out the money changers' coins and overturned the tables. 16 He told those who were selling doves, "Get these things out of here! Stop turning my Father's house into a marketplace!"

17 And his disciples remembered that it is written: "Zeal for your house will consume me."

18 So the Jews replied to him, "What sign will you show us for doing these things?"

19 Jesus answered, "Destroy this temple, and I will raise it up in three days."

20 Therefore the Jews said, "This temple took forty-six years to build, and will you raise it up in three days?"

21 But he was speaking about the temple of his body. 22 So when he was raised from the dead, his disciples remembered that he had said this, and they believed the Scripture and the statement Jesus had made.

2 CORINTHIANS 4:1–6, 16–18

The Light of the Gospel

1 Therefore, since we have this ministry because we were shown mercy, we do not give up. 2 Instead, we have renounced secret and shameful things, not acting deceitfully or distorting the word of God, but commending ourselves before God to everyone's conscience by an open display of the truth. 3 But if our gospel is veiled, it is veiled to those who are perishing. 4 In their case, the god of this age has blinded the minds of the unbelievers to keep them from seeing the light of the gospel of the glory of Christ, who is the image of God. 5 For we are not proclaiming ourselves but Jesus Christ as Lord, and ourselves as your servants for Jesus's sake. 6 For God who said, "Let light shine out of darkness," has shone in our hearts to give the light of the knowledge of God's glory in the face of Jesus Christ.

. . .

16 Therefore we do not give up. Even though our outer person is being destroyed, our inner person is being renewed day by day. 17 For our momentary light affliction is producing for us an absolutely incomparable eternal weight of glory. 18 So we do not focus on what is seen, but on what is unseen. For what is seen is temporary, but what is unseen is eternal.

HEBREWS 6:16–18

Inheriting the Promise

16 For people swear by something greater than themselves, and for them a confirming oath ends every dispute. 17 Because God wanted to show his unchangeable purpose even more clearly to the heirs of the promise, he guaranteed it with an oath, 18 so that through two unchangeable things, in which it is impossible for God to lie, we who have fled for refuge might have strong encouragement to seize the hope set before us.

I've always been skeptical when it comes to promises—and maybe I have a right to be. People have not always kept their promises to me, and I've not always kept mine to them either. Even with best intentions, so many of our promises to each other fall short. This is why nothing is more precious to me than God's promises to His people. He has shown me over and over that His promises never fail. He is a God of His Word, and His Word can be trusted.

When all that the scattered Israelites could see with their eyes was their ruined temple, God, through the prophet Haggai, made them a big promise: "Once more, in a little while, I am going to shake the heavens and the earth, the sea and the dry land. I will shake all the nations so that the treasures of all the nations will come, and I will fill this house with glory . . . The final glory of this house will be greater than the first . . . I will provide peace in this place" (Haggai 2:6–9).

Peace? In this place? How could this be?

It must have seemed impossible. And yet God did what He said He would do—in His perfect timing and in His perfect way. Not only would God restore the temple, but Jesus Himself would become the temple (John 2:19–21). Peace Himself would become their place! And God continues to build His temple even now in the building of His Church, each of us a living stone filled by the Holy Spirit (1 Peter 2:4–5).

God kept His promise to His people, and He keeps His promises to us, too. Everywhere we see destruction in our lives, we will one day see restoration (Acts 3:21). Where we feel only brokenness, we will one day experience wholeness (1 Thessalonians 5:23–24). The grief we know so intimately now will one day be replaced with deep, lasting peace (Revelation 21:4). At this very moment, Jesus is working to make all things new. It won't be long now.

He is a God of His Word, and His Word can be trusted.

Death will die. Tears will dry. All brokenness will mend. And where we currently see rubble, we will see a world rebuilt on the bedrock promises of God. And there will be peace.

When? In the words of the Lord Himself, "in a little while" (Haggai 2:6). On the radar screen of eternity, the time between now and the realization of His promises is just a blip. And as we wait, He tells us, "My Spirit is present among you; don't be afraid" (Haggai 2:5; see also Romans 8:10). These words are also a promise. Based solely on the evidence of their present circumstances, the Israelites had reason to believe God had abandoned them. Yet through Haggai, God reminded them to lift their eyes from the broken things and fix their gaze on Him.

The call is the same for us. Lift your eyes from the brokenness in and around you today, and look to the God who makes things right. Trust His promises. He is a God of His Word.

Zechariah

"I will put this third through the fire; I will refine them as silver is refined and test them as gold is tested. They will call on my name, and I will answer them. I will say, 'They are my people,' and they will say, 'The Lord is our God.'"

ZECHARIAH 13:9

ZECHARIAH 2:10–11

10 "Daughter Zion, shout for joy and be glad, for I am coming to dwell among
you"—this is the LORD's declaration. 11 "Many nations will join themselves to the
LORD on that day and become my people. I will dwell among you, and you will
know that the LORD of Armies has sent me to you."

ZECHARIAH 13:1–9

God's People Cleansed

1 "On that day a fountain will be opened for the house of David and for the
residents of Jerusalem, to wash away sin and impurity. 2 On that day"—this is the
declaration of the LORD of Armies—"I will remove the names of the idols from
the land, and they will no longer be remembered. I will banish the prophets and
the unclean spirit from the land. 3 If a man still prophesies, his father and his
mother who bore him will say to him, 'You cannot remain alive because you have
spoken a lie in the name of the LORD.' When he prophesies, his father and his
mother who bore him will pierce him through. 4 On that day every prophet will
be ashamed of his vision when he prophesies; they will not put on a hairy cloak
in order to deceive. 5 He will say, 'I am not a prophet; I work the land, for a man
purchased me as a servant since my youth.' 6 If someone asks him, 'What are these
wounds on your chest?'—then he will answer, 'I received the wounds in the house
of my friends.'

7 Sword, awake against my shepherd,
against the man who is my associate—
  this is the declaration of the LORD of Armies.
Strike the shepherd, and the sheep will be scattered;
I will turn my hand against the little ones.
8 In the whole land—
  this is the LORD's declaration—
two-thirds will be cut off and die,
but a third will be left in it.
9 I will put this third through the fire;
I will refine them as silver is refined
and test them as gold is tested.
They will call on my name,
and I will answer them.
I will say, 'They are my people,'
and they will say, 'The LORD is our God.'"

PSALM 35:27–28

Prayer for Victory

27 Let those who want my vindication
shout for joy and be glad;
let them continually say,
"The Lord be exalted.
He takes pleasure in his servant's well-being."
28 And my tongue will proclaim your righteousness,
your praise all day long.

1 PETER 1:3–9, 13–21

A Living Hope

3 Blessed be the God and Father of our Lord Jesus
Christ. Because of his great mercy he has given us
new birth into a living hope through the resurrection of Jesus Christ from the dead 4 and into
an inheritance that is imperishable, undefiled,
and unfading, kept in heaven for you. 5 You are
being guarded by God's power through faith for
a salvation that is ready to be revealed in the last
time. 6 You rejoice in this, even though now for
a short time, if necessary, you suffer grief in various trials 7 so that the proven character of your
faith—more valuable than gold which, though
perishable, is refined by fire—may result in praise,
glory, and honor at the revelation of Jesus Christ.
8 Though you have not seen him, you love him;
though not seeing him now, you believe in him,
and you rejoice with inexpressible and glorious joy,
9 because you are receiving the goal of your faith,
the salvation of your souls.

...

A Call to Holy Living

13 Therefore, with your minds ready for action, be
sober-minded and set your hope completely on
the grace to be brought to you at the revelation
of Jesus Christ. 14 As obedient children, do not be
conformed to the desires of your former ignorance.
15 But as the one who called you is holy, you also
are to be holy in all your conduct; 16 for it is written, "Be holy, because I am holy." 17 If you appeal
to the Father who judges impartially according
to each one's work, you are to conduct yourselves
in reverence during your time living as strangers.
18 For you know that you were redeemed from
your empty way of life inherited from your ancestors, not with perishable things like silver or gold,
19 but with the precious blood of Christ, like that
of an unblemished and spotless lamb. 20 He was
foreknown before the foundation of the world but
was revealed in these last times for you. 21 Through
him you believe in God, who raised him from the
dead and gave him glory, so that your faith and
hope are in God.

Apparently I didn't pay attention during the geology portion of high school science, because I was a full-grown adult when I learned that gold doesn't start as gold, it starts as ore. The material that most of us picture when we hear the word—the stuff of gold jewelry or gold bars, for example—does not exist in that form anywhere on earth. The ore must be mined and the impurities separated out so that the precious metal remains. And one of the oldest and most reliable methods for refining gold? Fire.

Fire is powerful, and it can even be scary. But the flames that consume can also refine. It all depends on what you are made of (Matthew 3:12). Jesus assures those who follow Him that they won't be like chaff that the wind blows away. They are like silver and gold, not consumed by the fire, but instead, refined and purified from what God finds unpleasing, unholy, and unwelcome in your heart (Isaiah 43:2). In other words, the metaphorical fires in our lives can actually leave us better than they found us. In God's hands, the heat from the flames can mold us into someone who looks more like Jesus.

But sometimes we don't *feel* like metal. Sometimes we feel empty and frail—like chaff lying discarded on the ground, just waiting to be whisked away by the wind. That's how I imagine God's people felt as they received Zechariah's prophecy. Exile was finally over and they were home in their beloved Jerusalem. But they were spent. The temple was still in ruins and the walls were a mess. How would they ever complete the work of rebuilding it?

The flames that consume can also refine.

The prophet Zechariah urged God's people not to forget His promises. Even as they stood among the rubble of their former lives, the prophet proclaimed a series of visions including a restored temple, a coming glorious king, and a world where everything is set right. God promised, "They will call on my name and I will answer them. I will say, 'They are my people,' and they will say, 'The LORD is our God'" (Zechariah 13:9).

This was good news! Their weary hearts needed the reminder that God had not forgotten them or the covenant promises He had made. The majority—two thirds—of those who received this prophecy from Zechariah would not choose to walk faithfully with God or live within His covenant. Instead, they would continue to live in unbelief and refuse to repent of their sin. Tragically, these would "be cut off and die" (Zechariah 13:8–9). But those who remained faithful would be placed in God's good and refining fire so that He might make them pure.

Are you able to view the fire you walk through as a good and refining gift from God? Pay attention to Zechariah's message and remember: Even through fire—especially through fire—our vision should be fixed on Christ alone.

This isn't a time to lose hope. It is time to hope all the more. God is doing the good work of purification.

Malachi

"But for you who fear my name,
the sun of righteousness will rise
with healing in its wings, and
you will go out and playfully
jump like calves from the stall."

MALACHI 4:2

MALACHI 1:1–5

The Lord's Love for Israel

1 A pronouncement:

The word of the Lord to Israel through Malachi.

2 "I have loved you," says the Lord.

Yet you ask, "How have you loved us?"

"Wasn't Esau Jacob's brother?" This is the Lord's
declaration. "Even so, I loved Jacob, 3 but I hated
Esau. I turned his mountains into a wasteland, and
gave his inheritance to the desert jackals."

4 Though Edom says, "We have been devastated,
but we will rebuild the ruins," the Lord of Armies
says this: "They may build, but I will demolish.
They will be called a wicked country and the people the Lord has cursed forever. 5 Your own eyes
will see this, and you yourselves will say, 'The Lord
is great, even beyond the borders of Israel.'

MALACHI 3:13–18

The Righteous and the Wicked

13 "Your words against me are harsh," says the Lord.

Yet you ask, "What have we spoken against you?"

14 You have said, "It is useless to serve God. What
have we gained by keeping his requirements and
walking mournfully before the Lord of Armies?
15 So now we consider the arrogant to be fortunate.
Not only do those who commit wickedness prosper, they even test God and escape."

16 At that time those who feared the Lord spoke to
one another. The Lord took notice and listened.
So a book of remembrance was written before him
for those who feared the Lord and had high regard
for his name. 17 "They will be mine," says the Lord
of Armies, "my own possession on the day I am
preparing. I will have compassion on them as a
man has compassion on his son who serves him.
18 So you will again see the difference between the
righteous and the wicked, between one who serves
God and one who does not serve him."

MALACHI 4:1–3

The Day of the Lord

1 "For look, the day is coming, burning like a
furnace, when all the arrogant and everyone who
commits wickedness will become stubble. The
coming day will consume them," says the Lord of
Armies, "not leaving them root or branches. 2 But
for you who fear my name, the sun of righteousness will rise with healing in its wings, and you
will go out and playfully jump like calves from the
stall. 3 You will trample the wicked, for they will be
ashes under the soles of your feet on the day I am
preparing," says the Lord of Armies.

HEBREWS 1:1–9

The Nature of the Son

1 Long ago God spoke to our ancestors by the prophets at different times and
in different ways. 2 In these last days, he has spoken to us by his Son. God has
appointed him heir of all things and made the universe through him. 3 The Son
is the radiance of God's glory and the exact expression of his nature, sustaining all
things by his powerful word. After making purification for sins, he sat down at the
right hand of the Majesty on high. 4 So he became superior to the angels, just as
the name he inherited is more excellent than theirs.

The Son Superior to Angels

5 For to which of the angels did he ever say,

> "You are my Son;
> today I have become your Father,"

or again,

> "I will be his Father,
> and he will be my Son"?

6 Again, when he brings his firstborn into the world, he says,

> "And let all God's angels worship him."

7 And about the angels he says:

> "He makes his angels winds,
> and his servants a fiery flame,"

8 but to the Son:

> "Your throne, God,
> is forever and ever,
> and the scepter of your kingdom
> is a scepter of justice.
> 9 You have loved righteousness
> and hated lawlessness;
> this is why God, your God,
> has anointed you
> with the oil of joy
> beyond your companions."

Have you ever been faithfully loved and pursued by a friend, only to respond with resistance? For me, that friend was my cousin Jeni. As we grew up, Jeni watched me pay lip service to God only to turn around and worship boys and popularity. Jeni also saw me give up the charade of being a Christian altogether during my freshman year of college as I tried to find healing in all the wrong places. I was running from God—and in order to do that, I had to run from Jeni too.

I mean that literally. We lived in the same dorm, and when I heard Jeni's footsteps padding down the hallway, I'd bolt out of sight. I knew what was coming: another invitation to a college ministry retreat. *No thank you, Jeni. Keep on walking.*

But she persisted. She basically knocked my door down until I finally said yes just to get her off my back. And you know what? That retreat was when the gospel clicked for me, and my life began to change. I'm a Christian today because Jeni kept holding out God's love to me no matter how often I swatted it away.

The book of Malachi is the last book of the Old Testament. God's opening words show His persistent posture toward His people for generations: "I have loved you" (Malachi 1:2). Nothing could be truer. Israel had gone through the motions with God, all the while worshiping everything but Him. Yet throughout their countless cycles of turning away from Him and returning to Him again, God held out His love to them, knocking on their door and welcoming them back into His covenant and care.

You'd think the love of a God like this would change their hearts forever—that they would finally open the door wide to God's invitation and never close it again. But that's not what happened. As He called them again to covenant living, Israel smirked and resisted God all over again.

This time, when God heard Israel's scoffing, what did He do? Did He fold up the Old Testament and say, "That's it. You're on your own"? He didn't. He leaned in closer. He warned them again of the consequences of their continued actions, yes. But He also promised to keep knocking. One day His Son would come like the "sun of righteousness" with healing in His wings, able to "turn the hearts" of God's people toward Himself and one another (Malachi 4:2, 6). In just a little while, Jesus would come to be the Light and Lamp of the world—the greatest expression of God's love knocking our door down (John 8:12; Revelation 21:23; 3:20).

I was running from God—and in order to do that, I had to run from her too.

Jesus was and is the full and final proof that no matter how often they swat it away, God's people—including you and me—are loved, have been loved, and will always be loved by Him. Forever.

Run as you may, friend, your God has loved you all the way. Don't resist His love. Receive it, and let it change you.

Matthew

From then on Jesus began to preach, "Repent, because the kingdom of heaven has come near."

MATTHEW 4:17

MATTHEW 3:1–3

The Herald of the Messiah

1 In those days John the Baptist came, preaching
in the wilderness of Judea 2 and saying, "Repent,
because the kingdom of heaven has come near!"
3 For he is the one spoken of through the prophet
Isaiah, who said:

> "A voice of one crying out in the wilderness:
> Prepare the way for the Lord;
> make his paths straight!"

MATTHEW 4:12–25

Ministry in Galilee

12 When he heard that John had been arrested,
he withdrew into Galilee. 13 He left Nazareth and
went to live in Capernaum by the sea, in the region
of Zebulun and Naphtali. 14 This was to fulfill what
was spoken through the prophet Isaiah:

> 15 "Land of Zebulun and land of Naphtali,
> along the road by the sea, beyond the Jordan,
> Galilee of the Gentiles.
> 16 The people who live in darkness
> have seen a great light,
> and for those living in the land of the
> shadow of death,
> a light has dawned."

17 From then on Jesus began to preach, "Repent,
because the kingdom of heaven has come near."

The First Disciples

18 As he was walking along the Sea of Galilee, he
saw two brothers, Simon (who is called Peter),
and his brother Andrew. They were casting a net
into the sea—for they were fishermen. 19 "Follow
me," he told them, "and I will make you fish for
people." 20 Immediately they left their nets and
followed him.

21 Going on from there, he saw two other brothers, James the son of Zebedee, and his brother
John. They were in a boat with Zebedee their
father, preparing their nets, and he called them.
22 Immediately they left the boat and their father
and followed him.

Teaching, Preaching, and Healing

23 Now Jesus began to go all over Galilee, teaching
in their synagogues, preaching the good news of
the kingdom, and healing every disease and sickness among the people. 24 Then the news about
him spread throughout Syria. So they brought
to him all those who were afflicted, those suffering from various diseases and intense pains, the
demon-possessed, the epileptics, and the paralyt-
ics. And he healed them. 25 Large crowds followed
him from Galilee, the Decapolis, Jerusalem, Judea,
and beyond the Jordan.

ISAIAH 61:1–7

Messiah's Jubilee

[1] The Spirit of the Lord GOD is on me,
because the LORD has anointed me
to bring good news to the poor.
He has sent me to heal the brokenhearted,
to proclaim liberty to the captives
and freedom to the prisoners;
[2] to proclaim the year of the LORD's favor,
and the day of our God's vengeance;
to comfort all who mourn,
[3] to provide for those who mourn in Zion;
to give them a crown of beauty instead of ashes,
festive oil instead of mourning,
and splendid clothes instead of despair.
And they will be called righteous trees,
planted by the LORD
to glorify him.
[4] They will rebuild the ancient ruins;
they will restore the former devastations;
they will renew the ruined cities,
the devastations of many generations.
[5] Strangers will stand and feed your flocks,
and foreigners will be your plowmen and vinedressers.

[6] But you will be called the LORD's priests;
they will speak of you as ministers of our God;
you will eat the wealth of the nations,
and you will boast in their riches.
[7] In place of your shame, you will have a double portion;
in place of disgrace, they will rejoice over their share.
So they will possess double in their land,
and eternal joy will be theirs.

JOEL 2:12–13

God's Call for Repentance

[12] Even now—
this is the LORD's declaration—
turn to me with all your heart,
with fasting, weeping, and mourning.
[13] Tear your hearts,
not just your clothes,
and return to the LORD your God.
For he is gracious and compassionate,
slow to anger, abounding in faithful love,
and he relents from sending disaster.

ROMANS 2:1–4

God's Righteous Judgment

[1] Therefore, every one of you who judges is without
excuse. For when you judge another, you condemn
yourself, since you, the judge, do the same things.
[2] Now we know that God's judgment on those
who do such things is based on the truth. [3] Do you
think—anyone of you who judges those who do
such things yet do the same—that you will escape
God's judgment? [4] Or do you despise the riches of
his kindness, restraint, and patience, not recogniz-
ing that God's kindness is intended to lead you to
repentance?

A lot of things haven't gone like I wanted them to. I think I meant to stay slimmer, make more money, and be a world-famous flautist by now. As I was growing up, the world was constantly telling me to stand up for myself, get what was mine, and hurt who I needed to hurt in order to make myself feel good. And man, it's tempting to shake your flute at people and demand your own way. You may not have a flute to wield, but you get the idea. Sometimes, I just want to give a giant tuba toot when someone tells me I can't get my security deposit back.

We want to organize our lives according to the kingdom of the world—a world where we demand what we think is owed to us and where the highest good is money and power. But what if the kingdom of the world is passing away? What if the only lasting kingdom is God's upside-down economy? Then everything the world holds dear is dust and ashes and we must look to His kingdom for our hope.

The kingdom of God is the theme of Matthew's Gospel, which sits at the hingepoint between the Old and New Testaments. The Prophets had told of this coming kingdom, and now here it was in the flesh—in the person of Jesus. The Son of God announced it Himself, declaring, "Repent, because the kingdom of heaven has come near" (Matthew 4:17).

It's tempting to shake your flute at people and demand your own way.

So, what is the nature of God's kingdom? Scripture gives us a beautifully rich, wide range of descriptions. His kingdom is vast, and "its prosperity will never end;" the zeal of the Lord will accomplish it (Isaiah 9:7). His kingdom brings freedom to captives and healing to the brokenhearted (Isaiah 61:1). It is a comfort and provision to all who mourn (Isaiah 61:2–3). He will replace shame with a double portion of blessing (Isaiah 61:7). It is all of this and more—and we are invited in (Matthew 5:3).

The kingdom of God is personal and offers profound relief from all the heartbreak of living in a fallen world. Jesus entered our suffering and took it on Himself so that this kingdom could be fully known and suffering would one day be no more. Sure, there was a time when I was honestly heartbroken about my flute-related failures, yet there is hope and healing in the kingdom of heaven for even these disappointments. I can put my angry tuba away and stop fighting for myself because God will make all things right.

This promise of healing for our deepest wounds and most agonizing heartbreaks is the hope the world is longing for. Our most awful pain will be fully healed in the kingdom of heaven. And this is not just a future hope—the kingdom is here! In the person of Jesus, the kingdom of God came to us, and it will come in full at His return. Jesus has brought—and will bring!—true comfort, blessing, and hope. He brings good news to the poor, He heals the brokenhearted, He brings liberty to captives, and He comforts all who mourn (Isaiah 61:1–2). Thanks be to our God for the utter goodness of His kingdom.

Mark

“For even the Son of Man
did not come to be served,
but to serve, and to give his
life as a ransom for many.”

MARK 10:45

MARK 9:33–37

Who Is the Greatest?

33 They came to Capernaum. When he was in the
house, he asked them, "What were you arguing
about on the way?" 34 But they were silent, because
on the way they had been arguing with one another
about who was the greatest. 35 Sitting down, he
called the Twelve and said to them, "If anyone
wants to be first, he must be last and servant of
all." 36 He took a child, had him stand among
them, and taking him in his arms, he said to them,
37 "Whoever welcomes one little child such as this
in my name welcomes me. And whoever welcomes
me does not welcome me, but him who sent me."

MARK 10:35–45

Suffering and Service

35 James and John, the sons of Zebedee, approached
him and said, "Teacher, we want you to do whatever we ask you."

36 "What do you want me to do for you?" he asked
them.

37 They answered him, "Allow us to sit at your right
and at your left in your glory."

38 Jesus said to them, "You don't know what you're
asking. Are you able to drink the cup I drink or to
be baptized with the baptism I am baptized with?"

39 "We are able," they told him.

Jesus said to them, "You will drink the cup I drink,
and you will be baptized with the baptism I am
baptized with. 40 But to sit at my right or left is not
mine to give; instead, it is for those for whom it has
been prepared."

41 When the ten disciples heard this, they began to
be indignant with James and John. 42 Jesus called
them over and said to them, "You know that those
who are regarded as rulers of the Gentiles lord
it over them, and those in high positions act as
tyrants over them. 43 But it is not so among you.
On the contrary, whoever wants to become great
among you will be your servant, 44 and whoever
wants to be first among you will be a slave to all.
45 For even the Son of Man did not come to be
served, but to serve, and to give his life as a ransom
for many."

ISAIAH 52:13–15

The Servant's Suffering and Exaltation

13 "See, my servant will be successful;
he will be raised and lifted up and greatly exalted.
14 Just as many were appalled at you—
his appearance was so disfigured
that he did not look like a man,
and his form did not resemble a human being—
15 so he will sprinkle many nations.
Kings will shut their mouths because of him,
for they will see what had not been told them,
and they will understand what they had not heard."

JOHN 13:12–17

The Meaning of Foot Washing

12 When Jesus had washed their feet and put on his
outer clothing, he reclined again and said to them,
"Do you know what I have done for you? 13 You
call me Teacher and Lord—and you are speaking
rightly, since that is what I am. 14 So if I, your Lord
and Teacher, have washed your feet, you also ought
to wash one another's feet. 15 For I have given you
an example, that you also should do just as I have
done for you.

16 "Truly I tell you, a servant is not greater than his
master, and a messenger is not greater than the one
who sent him. 17 If you know these things, you are
blessed if you do them."

PHILIPPIANS 2:5–11

Christ's Humility and Exaltation

5 Adopt the same attitude as that of Christ Jesus,

6 who, existing in the form of God,
did not consider equality with God
as something to be exploited.
7 Instead he emptied himself
by assuming the form of a servant,
taking on the likeness of humanity.
And when he had come as a man,
8 he humbled himself by becoming obedient
to the point of death—
even to death on a cross.
9 For this reason God highly exalted him
and gave him the name
that is above every name,
10 so that at the name of Jesus
every knee will bow—
in heaven and on earth
and under the earth—
11 and every tongue will confess
that Jesus Christ is Lord,
to the glory of God the Father.

I have decided that hospital hallways are some of the most hallowed places on earth.

It's among them that I've seen surgeons stoop low to investigate the design of a building-brick castle on the rollaway table across my son's bed. I've watched nurses create a makeshift hair salon out of an office chair and wash pan so he could have his hair washed with shampoo and water like a real, honest-to-goodness shower. I've been in the room when the maintenance crew has emptied the sharps container and biohazard can with smiles on their faces, gushing over my boy's handsome pinstripe pajamas. I've witnessed therapists creating scavenger hunts for snacks around the nurses' station because they know food is his love language.

I've spent days and weeks and months in hospital hallways, and I have seen my small-in-stature son treated like an absolute king. It's the upside-down kingdom in technicolor.

I think of these moments as I read the Gospel of Mark. The disciples were learning what it meant to follow Jesus, and it's safe to say it took them a while to catch on. They witnessed Him heal the sick, teach crowds, perform miracles—a few of them even saw Jesus transfigured on a mountain in the presence of Moses and Elijah! And yet, they got distracted time and again by their own egos.

Whether they were arguing over who was the greatest or asking Jesus for a place of honor in heaven, Jesus's response was the same: "If anyone wants to be first, he must be last," and, "whoever wants to become great among you will be your servant" (Mark 9:35; 10:43). In other words: "You're looking for greatness in all the wrong places." They were looking at the top instead of the bottom, looking for the powerful instead of the meek.

They were looking at the top instead of the bottom, looking for the powerful instead of the meek.

The posture of Jesus's ministry was clear from the moment of His birth, when He emptied Himself of the benefits of His divinity and took on humanity to dwell among us (Philippians 2:6–7). A carpenter's son, He lived in obscurity for thirty years. When He did enter the public eye, it was as one who healed and served and taught others, not as one who sought to gather power or wealth or acclaim. Refusing to defend Himself before His accusers, He was executed for crimes He did not commit.

And God called this success. "See, my servant will be successful; he will be raised and lifted up and greatly exalted" (Isaiah 52:13). God raised Jesus from the grave and exalted Him above every name—King of Kings, Lord of lords (Philippians 2:9).

This is our Savior. He is the God who washes feet, who heals lepers with the touch of His hand, who climbs the hill to Calvary with our cross upon His back. To follow Him means to stoop low, to look people in the eyes, to take out the trash and wash hair and treat the least like royalty. "For even the Son of Man did not come to be served, but to serve, and to give his life as a ransom for many" (Mark 10:45).

How can you serve in the merciful name of Jesus today?

Luke

"For the Son of Man has come to seek and to save the lost."

LUKE 19:10

LUKE 5:12–16

A Man Cleansed

12 While he was in one of the towns, a man was there who had leprosy all over him. He saw Jesus, fell facedown, and begged him, "Lord, if you are willing, you can make me clean."

13 Reaching out his hand, Jesus touched him, saying, "I am willing; be made clean," and immediately the leprosy left him. 14 Then he ordered him to tell no one: "But go and show yourself to the priest, and offer what Moses commanded for your cleansing as a testimony to them."

15 But the news about him spread even more, and large crowds would come together to hear him and to be healed of their sicknesses. 16 Yet he often withdrew to deserted places and prayed.

LUKE 15:1–7

The Parable of the Lost Sheep

1 All the tax collectors and sinners were approaching to listen to him. 2 And the Pharisees and scribes were complaining, "This man welcomes sinners and eats with them."

3 So he told them this parable: 4 "What man among you, who has a hundred sheep and loses one of them, does not leave the ninety-nine in the open field and go after the lost one until he finds it? 5 When he has found it, he joyfully puts it on his shoulders, 6 and coming home, he calls his friends and neighbors together, saying to them, 'Rejoice with me, because I have found my lost sheep!' 7 I tell you, in the same way, there will be more joy in heaven over one sinner who repents than over ninety-nine righteous people who don't need repentance."

LUKE 19:1–10

Jesus Visits Zacchaeus

1 He entered Jericho and was passing through. 2 There was a man named Zacchaeus who was a chief tax collector, and he was rich. 3 He was trying to see who Jesus was, but he was not able because of the crowd, since he was a short man. 4 So running ahead, he climbed up a sycamore tree to see Jesus, since he was about to pass that way. 5 When Jesus came to the place, he looked up and said to him, "Zacchaeus, hurry and come down because today it is necessary for me to stay at your house."

6 So he quickly came down and welcomed him joyfully. 7 All who saw it began to complain, "He's gone to stay with a sinful man."

8 But Zacchaeus stood there and said to the Lord, "Look, I'll give half of my possessions to the poor, Lord. And if I have extorted anything from anyone, I'll pay back four times as much."

9 "Today salvation has come to this house," Jesus told him, "because he too is a son of Abraham. 10 For the Son of Man has come to seek and to save the lost."

JEREMIAH 50:6–7

6 "My people were lost sheep;
their shepherds led them astray,
guiding them the wrong way in the mountains.
They wandered from mountain to hill;
they forgot their resting place.
7 Whoever found them devoured them.
Their adversaries said, 'We're not guilty;
instead, they have sinned against the LORD,
their righteous grazing land,
the hope of their ancestors, the LORD.'"

EZEKIEL 34:11–16

The Shepherds and God's Flock

11 "For this is what the Lord GOD says: See,
I myself will search for my flock and look for them.
12 As a shepherd looks for his sheep on the day he
is among his scattered flock, so I will look for my
flock. I will rescue them from all the places where
they have been scattered on a day of clouds and
total darkness. 13 I will bring them out from the
peoples, gather them from the countries, and bring
them to their own soil. I will shepherd them on the
mountains of Israel, in the ravines, and in all the
inhabited places of the land. 14 I will tend them in
good pasture, and their grazing place will be on
Israel's lofty mountains. There they will lie down in
a good grazing place; they will feed in rich pasture
on the mountains of Israel. 15 I will tend my flock
and let them lie down. This is the declaration of
the Lord GOD. 16 I will seek the lost, bring back
the strays, bandage the injured, and strengthen
the weak, but I will destroy the fat and the strong.
I will shepherd them with justice."

MARK 6:34

When [Jesus] went ashore, he saw a large crowd and had compassion on them, because they were like sheep without a shepherd. Then he began to teach them many things.

There are a handful of core people in my life who are indispensable to me. I would never give up on them, even though they are sometimes the ones who can bug me or hurt me the most. I also have peripheral friends and acquaintances. As seasons of life change, approaches to life change, or even if a friendship becomes a little draining, I tend to let those relationships run their course and fizzle out.

Jesus, on the other hand, saw *everyone* as indispensable—even the ones who drained Him, bugged Him, and hurt Him the most. Many times it would have been completely understandable for Him to let an opportunity for connection go by on account of how in-demand He was, but Jesus didn't turn people away. In fact, He sought them out.

Luke's Gospel has a unique focus on Jesus as a friend of sinners. He highlights Jesus's concern for including the outsider and seeking the lost. And the lost were everywhere! Jesus gave the widow her son back, delivered a demon-possessed man from bondage, and touched the untouchable leper, healing him. As word got out, the crowds began following Jesus, and "He welcomed them, spoke to them about the kingdom of God, and healed those who needed healing" (Luke 9:11). The Pharisees and Scribes, however, would have none of it and were overheard indicting, "This man welcomes sinners and eats with them" (Luke 15:2).

He sends out search parties to find us.

It was around this time that Jesus spotted Zacchaeus the tax collector up in a tree, straining to catch a glimpse of this healing rabbi who had everyone talking. No one would have held it against Jesus if He had pretended He didn't notice the man. Zacchaeus was, after all, a cheater and a crook who was literally draining the pockets of the people of Israel. But he was indispensable to Jesus. "Zacchaeus, hurry and come down because today it is necessary for me to stay at your house" (Luke 19:5). This really gave the Pharisees something to talk about!

Right then and there, after Jesus called his name but before they even went to his house, Zacchaeus turned his heart toward the one who seeks and saves. "Today salvation has come to this house," Jesus told him, "because he too is a son of Abraham" (Luke 19:9).

Jesus is the Good Shepherd, and we are all lost sheep. He sends out search parties to find us, and heaven rejoices when we are found. Even those we don't agree with. Even the people who make us tired. And yes, even the ones who've hurt us.

Jesus said it Himself: "For the Son of Man has come to seek and to save the lost" (Luke 19:10). I was one of them. I bet you were, too. And now, Jesus invites us to take the good news to those who don't yet know Him. Let's join the search party, shall we? We've got sheep to find!

John

In the beginning was the Word,
and the Word was with God,
and the Word was God.

JOHN 1:1

JOHN 1:1–14

Prologue

1 In the beginning was the Word, and the Word was with God, and the Word was God. 2 He was with God in the beginning. 3 All things were created through him, and apart from him not one thing was created that has been created. 4 In him was life, and that life was the light of men. 5 That light shines in the darkness, and yet the darkness did not overcome it.

6 There was a man sent from God whose name was John. 7 He came as a witness to testify about the light, so that all might believe through him. 8 He was not the light, but he came to testify about the light. 9 The true light that gives light to everyone was coming into the world.

10 He was in the world, and the world was created through him, and yet the world did not recognize him. 11 He came to his own, and his own people did not receive him. 12 But to all who did receive him, he gave them the right to be children of God, to those who believe in his name, 13 who were born, not of natural descent, or of the will of the flesh, or of the will of man, but of God.

14 The Word became flesh and dwelt among us. We observed his glory, the glory as the one and only Son from the Father, full of grace and truth.

JOHN 3:14–21

Jesus and Nicodemus

14 "Just as Moses lifted up the snake in the wilderness, so the Son of Man must be lifted up, 15 so that everyone who believes in him may have eternal life. 16 For God loved the world in this way: He gave his one and only Son, so that everyone who believes in him will not perish but have eternal life. 17 For God did not send his Son into the world to condemn the world, but to save the world through him. 18 Anyone who believes in him is not condemned, but anyone who does not believe is already condemned, because he has not believed in the name of the one and only Son of God. 19 This is the judgment: The light has come into the world, and people loved darkness rather than the light because their deeds were evil. 20 For everyone who does evil hates the light and avoids it, so that his deeds may not be exposed. 21 But anyone who lives by the truth comes to the light, so that his works may be shown to be accomplished by God."

JOHN 5:19–23

Honoring the Father and the Son

19 Jesus replied, "Truly I tell you, the Son is not able to do anything on his own, but only what he sees the Father doing. For whatever the Father does, the Son likewise does these things. 20 For the Father loves the Son and shows him everything he is doing, and he will show him greater works than these so that you will be amazed. 21 And just as the Father raises the dead and gives them life, so the Son also gives life to whom he wants. 22 The Father, in fact, judges no one but has given all judgment to the Son, 23 so that all people may honor the Son just as they honor the Father. Anyone who does not honor the Son does not honor the Father who sent him."

GENESIS 1:1–5

The Creation

1 In the beginning God created the heavens and
the earth.

2 Now the earth was formless and empty, darkness
covered the surface of the watery depths, and the
Spirit of God was hovering over the surface of the
waters. 3 Then God said, "Let there be light," and
there was light. 4 God saw that the light was good,
and God separated the light from the darkness.
5 God called the light "day," and the darkness he
called "night." There was an evening, and there was
a morning: one day.

REVELATION 1:4–8

Prologue

4 John: To the seven churches in Asia. Grace and
peace to you from the one who is, who was, and
who is to come, and from the seven spirits before
his throne, 5 and from Jesus Christ, the faithful
witness, the firstborn from the dead and the ruler
of the kings of the earth.

To him who loves us and has set us free from our
sins by his blood, 6 and made us a kingdom, priests
to his God and Father—to him be glory and
dominion forever and ever. Amen.

7 "Look, he is coming with the clouds,"
and "every eye will see him,
even those who pierced him.
And all the tribes" of the earth
"will mourn over him."
So it is to be. Amen.

8 "I am the Alpha and the Omega," says the Lord
God, "the one who is, who was, and who is to
come, the Almighty."

My college roommate knew a family growing up who had four sons. The four sons were named Matthew, Mark, Luke . . . and Roy. Roy, as luck would have it, was a family name.

It's one of my favorite anecdotes to share when a conversation turns to "unconventional name" stories. But today it got me thinking, *What if the canon of Scripture only contained Matthew, Mark, and Luke?* (Sorry, Roy.) Would three Gospels be enough? What would we be missing if John had not given us his Gospel account?

For starters, John's Gospel is roughly ninety percent new content that we wouldn't otherwise have. Rather than highlighting miracles, parables, and sermons like the other guys, John zeroes in on the identity of Jesus—specifically that He is the Son of God. In fact, John's opening line spells it out: "In the beginning was the Word, and the Word was with God, and the Word was God" (John 1:1).

From there, John recounts a series of Jesus's interactions with the people who declared, doubted, or denied that He was God. It's an honest look at humans reconciling with the reality of God in the flesh, right there with them. Nicodemus, Mary Magdalene, the woman at the well, and even Judas—people were getting it right and wrong and everything in between. And Jesus—who is, in fact, God—was so kind and patient.

My favorite example of this is Peter's restoration. Jesus loved Peter. He knew all that was and would be of Peter's life, and still, Jesus chose Peter to walk closely with Him. He washed Peter's feet and predicted that Peter would deny Him (John 13).

That very night, while Jesus was on trial for His life, Peter indeed denied knowing Him at all (John 18). It always hurts to read this part of the story, but it makes the ending of John's Gospel all the sweeter. In the final chapter, after the resurrected Jesus cooks breakfast for His disciples, He pulls Peter aside. In this holy moment, Jesus doesn't say, "Thanks for nothing, Peter!" or, "I knew you would bail when things got hard." He simply asks, "Simon, son of John, do you love me more than these?" (John 21:15). Peter responds emphatically, "Lord, you know everything; you know that I love you" (John 21:17). And Jesus responds by inviting him again: *Follow me.*

It's an honest look at humans reconciling with the reality of God in the flesh, right there with them.

Peter's restoration and so many other true stories of our Savior in John's Gospel demonstrate the unmistakable truth that Jesus is God, and He loves us even when we get it wrong. He knows all that was and will be about us, and yet He calls us to walk closely with Him. God sees our denials coming, and He pursues us, restores us, and invites us again to follow Him.

Where would we be without Jesus?

Acts

"But you will receive power when the Holy Spirit has come upon you, and you will be my witnesses in Jerusalem, in all Judea and Samaria, and to the ends of the earth."

ACTS 1:8

ACTS 1:4–11

The Holy Spirit Promised

4 While he was with them, he commanded them not to leave Jerusalem, but to wait for the Father's promise. "Which," he said, "you have heard me speak about; 5 for John baptized with water, but you will be baptized with the Holy Spirit in a few days."

6 So when they had come together, they asked him, "Lord, are you restoring the kingdom to Israel at this time?"

7 He said to them, "It is not for you to know times or periods that the Father has set by his own authority. 8 But you will receive power when the Holy Spirit has come on you, and you will be my witnesses in Jerusalem, in all Judea and Samaria, and to the ends of the earth."

The Ascension

9 After he had said this, he was taken up as they were watching, and a cloud took him out of their sight. 10 While he was going, they were gazing into heaven, and suddenly two men in white clothes stood by them. 11 They said, "Men of Galilee, why do you stand looking up into heaven? This same Jesus, who has been taken from you into heaven, will come in the same way that you have seen him going into heaven."

ACTS 2:1–4

Pentecost

1 When the day of Pentecost had arrived, they were all together in one place. 2 Suddenly a sound like that of a violent rushing wind came from heaven, and it filled the whole house where they were staying. 3 They saw tongues like flames of fire that separated and rested on each one of them. 4 Then they were all filled with the Holy Spirit and began to speak in different tongues, as the Spirit enabled them.

JOEL 2:28–32

God's Promise of His Spirit

28 "After this
I will pour out my Spirit on all humanity;
then your sons and your daughters will prophesy,
your old men will have dreams,
and your young men will see visions.
29 I will even pour out my Spirit
on the male and female slaves in those days.
30 I will display wonders
in the heavens and on the earth:
blood, fire, and columns of smoke.
31 The sun will be turned to darkness
and the moon to blood
before the great and terrible day of the LORD
comes.
32 Then everyone who calls
on the name of the LORD will be saved,
for there will be an escape
for those on Mount Zion and in Jerusalem,
as the LORD promised,
among the survivors the LORD calls."

JOHN 14:15–17, 25–26

Another Counselor Promised

15 "If you love me, you will keep my commands.
16 And I will ask the Father, and he will give you
another Counselor to be with you forever. 17 He is
the Spirit of truth. The world is unable to receive
him because it doesn't see him or know him. But
you do know him, because he remains with you
and will be in you."

...

The Father, the Son, and the Holy Spirit

25 "I have spoken these things to you while I
remain with you. 26 But the Counselor, the Holy
Spirit, whom the Father will send in my name, will
teach you all things and remind you of everything
I have told you."

There is a saying I love: "I want to be where my feet are." It's harder than it sounds, isn't it?

We long to be fully present right where we are. With our friends or family, at a meeting or dinner party, in a boardroom or hospital room, we want to make the most of the time we have in the relationships and places God puts us. Just yesterday, I wanted to be at my nephew's graduation, my twins' baseball doubleheader, home caring for my sick child, and helping my mom clean out her upstairs closet—all in one afternoon. But that's impossible. I can only be where my feet are, and my feet can only be in one place at a time.

In the days leading to His crucifixion, Jesus told His disciples something that must have felt impossible. "It is for your benefit that I go away, because if I don't go away the Counselor will not come to you" (John 16:7). How can that be? What could be better than walking with the living, breathing Messiah? The disciples did not understand that Jesus's death would give way to His resurrection, and His resurrection would secure the very thing they longed for—His presence with them forever.

My feet can only be in one place at a time.

After He rose from the dead and before He ascended to the Father, the resurrected Jesus instructed His disciples to stay in Jerusalem and "wait for the Father's promise" (Acts 1:4). And on the day of Pentecost, that promise arrived. The Holy Spirit was poured out on the disciples, filling them with the power and presence of the same Jesus they walked with just days before.

The Spirit—the Counselor and Comforter—had come to be with them forever.

While Jesus lived and ministered here on earth, He had to be where His feet were. He was human, after all. The book of Acts is the record of how the promised Holy Spirit filled the disciples, empowering them to continue Jesus's ministry not only in Jerusalem, but "in all Judea and Samaria, and to the ends of the earth" (Acts 1:8). Chapter after chapter in Acts, we see the Spirit move among the Church across geographical and cultural boundaries to heal the sick, raise the dead, free the oppressed, and baptize thousands upon thousands into new, eternal life in Christ. By the sending of His Spirit, Jesus's mission and message was unleashed to bring salvation to the whole world through the faith and feet of ordinary people like you and me.

The promise is for us, too. When we repent and believe that Jesus is the Christ, we receive the gift of that same Spirit. He is the Spirit of God alive in us, interceding for us in our trials, comforting us in our grief, and empowering us as ambassadors of the gospel to a hurting world.

Like it or not, you can only be where your feet are. But wherever your feet are, Jesus is there.

Romans

For all have sinned and fall short of the glory of God; they are justified freely by his grace through the redemption that is in Christ Jesus.

ROMANS 3:23–24

ROMANS 3:21–26

The Righteousness of God Through Faith

21 But now, apart from the law, the righteousness of God has been revealed, attested by the Law and the Prophets. 22 The righteousness of God is through faith in Jesus Christ, since there is no distinction. 23 For all have sinned and fall short of the glory of God; 24 they are justified freely by his grace through the redemption that is in Christ Jesus. 25 God presented him as the mercy seat by his blood, through faith, to demonstrate his righteousness, because in his restraint God passed over the sins previously committed. 26 God presented him to demonstrate his righteousness at the present time, so that he would be just and justify the one who has faith in Jesus.

ROMANS 5:1–11

Faith Triumphs

1 Therefore, since we have been justified by faith, we have peace with God through our Lord Jesus Christ. 2 We have also obtained access through him by faith into this grace in which we stand, and we boast in the hope of the glory of God. 3 And not only that, but we also boast in our afflictions, because we know that affliction produces endurance, 4 endurance produces proven character, and proven character produces hope. 5 This hope will not disappoint us, because God's love has been poured out in our hearts through the Holy Spirit who was given to us.

The Justified Are Reconciled

6 For while we were still helpless, at the right time, Christ died for the ungodly. 7 For rarely will someone die for a just person—though for a good person perhaps someone might even dare to die. 8 But God proves his own love for us in that while we were still sinners, Christ died for us. 9 How much more then, since we have now been justified by his blood, will we be saved through him from wrath. 10 For if, while we were enemies, we were reconciled to God through the death of his Son, then how much more, having been reconciled, will we be saved by his life. 11 And not only that, but we also boast in God through our Lord Jesus Christ, through whom we have now received this reconciliation.

JEREMIAH 9:23–24

Boast in the LORD

23 "This is what the LORD says:

The wise person should not boast in his
wisdom;
the strong should not boast in his strength;
the wealthy should not boast in his wealth.
24 But the one who boasts should boast
in this:
that he understands and knows me—
that I am the LORD, showing faithful love,
justice, and righteousness on the earth,
for I delight in these things.
This is the LORD's declaration."

PSALM 14:1–3

A Portrait of Sinners

1 The fool says in his heart, "There's no God."
They are corrupt; they do vile deeds.
There is no one who does good.
2 The LORD looks down from heaven on the
human race
to see if there is one who is wise,
one who seeks God.
3 All have turned away;
all alike have become corrupt.
There is no one who does good,
not even one.

1 CORINTHIANS 1:26–31

Boasting Only in the Lord

26 Brothers and sisters, consider your calling:
Not many were wise from a human perspective,
not many powerful, not many of noble birth.
27 Instead, God has chosen what is foolish in the
world to shame the wise, and God has chosen what
is weak in the world to shame the strong. 28 God
has chosen what is insignificant and despised in the
world—what is viewed as nothing—to bring to
nothing what is viewed as something, 29 so that no
one may boast in his presence. 30 It is from him that
you are in Christ Jesus, who became wisdom from
God for us—our righteousness, sanctification, and
redemption— 31 in order that, as it is written: "Let
the one who boasts, boast in the Lord."

I am naturally and annoyingly good at a surprising number of things. It's just how God made me.

So you can imagine my shock and dismay when I approached our "learn to surf" experience on vacation with an excessive amount of beginner's confidence, only to be chewed up and spit out by the unrelenting waves off the coast of Portugal. Now, I want to be clear, it wasn't for a lack of effort. My friends and I had prepared. We had done six weeks of prepare-to-surf workouts and hundreds of burpees between us. But the girl for whom many things come easily . . . well, let's just say she had the clearest sinuses in Cascais that day.

It can be frustrating to face the reality of our limitations. Whether it's watching your teenagers surf effortlessly past you while the instructor is still helping you get on your board, or wanting to sketch as beautifully and naturally as your friend, or any number of things that your body does or fails to do despite your biggest dreams and best efforts. There are things we simply cannot accomplish in our own effort, even with all of the burpees in the world.

In a similar but much more tragic way, there is one dire and universal limitation we all share. No natural ability can skirt it, no amount of effort will evade it. We all, as Paul writes to the Romans, have sinned and failed to meet God's standards, and the price for that sin is death (Romans 3:23; 6:23). The debt we owed was our actual lives. Helpless to save ourselves, "at the right time, Christ died for the ungodly" (Romans 5:6). He saw us in our most helpless, debt-ridden, sinuses cleared, hair amok, over-confident, exhausted-by-effort state, and He loved us enough to justify us by His blood. He paid the debt with His actual life.

There are things we simply cannot accomplish in our own effort, even with all the burpees in the world.

When it comes to all the ways we're limited as humans, by and large, we'll be just fine. Not a great surfer? Don't worry, it probably won't come up often. Not much of a cook? Take a bag of groceries to someone who is! But our souls—born under a curse, they're prone to wander and condemned to eternal separation from God. It doesn't matter how naturally good at things you are or how hard you try. There is nothing any of us can do about it. Not a thing. And so we cry, "Help! Save us!" And He did. And He does.

This is the gospel. It's the worst news and the best news in one breath. "For all have sinned and fall short of the glory of God; they are justified freely by his grace through the redemption that is in Christ Jesus" (Romans 3:23–24). He did for us what we couldn't do for ourselves. He met us in our limitations—before we were even aware of them—and did what we could not do, simply because He loves us.

Hear that today. He loves you to death and back. It doesn't mean you won't be limited in all kinds of ways on this side of glory. But it does mean glory for all us overconfident try-ers who couldn't do it on our own. Find rest in His work today, and give thanks.

1 Corinthians

God is faithful; you were called
by him into fellowship with his
Son, Jesus Christ our Lord.

1 CORINTHIANS 1:9

1 CORINTHIANS 1:4–11

Thanksgiving

4 I always thank my God for you because of the
grace of God given to you in Christ Jesus, 5 that
you were enriched in him in every way, in all
speech and all knowledge. 6 In this way, the testimony about Christ was confirmed among you,
7 so that you do not lack any spiritual gift as you
eagerly wait for the revelation of our Lord Jesus
Christ. 8 He will also strengthen you to the end, so
that you will be blameless in the day of our Lord
Jesus Christ. 9 God is faithful; you were called by
him into fellowship with his Son, Jesus Christ our
Lord.

Divisions at Corinth

10 Now I urge you, brothers and sisters, in the name
of our Lord Jesus Christ, that all of you agree in
what you say, that there be no divisions among
you, and that you be united with the same understanding and the same conviction. 11 For it has been
reported to me about you, my brothers and sisters,
by members of Chloe's people, that there is rivalry
among you.

1 CORINTHIANS 10:16–17

16 The cup of blessing that we bless, is it not a
sharing in the blood of Christ? The bread that we
break, is it not a sharing in the body of Christ?
17 Because there is one bread, we who are many are
one body, since all of us share the one bread.

1 CORINTHIANS 12:12–20

Unity Yet Diversity in the Body

12 For just as the body is one and has many parts,
and all the parts of that body, though many, are
one body—so also is Christ. 13 For we were all
baptized by one Spirit into one body—whether
Jews or Greeks, whether slaves or free—and we
were all given one Spirit to drink. 14 Indeed, the
body is not one part but many. 15 If the foot should
say, "Because I'm not a hand, I don't belong to the
body," it is not for that reason any less a part of
the body. 16 And if the ear should say, "Because I'm
not an eye, I don't belong to the body," it is not
for that reason any less a part of the body. 17 If the
whole body were an eye, where would the hearing
be? If the whole body were an ear, where would the
sense of smell be? 18 But as it is, God has arranged
each one of the parts in the body just as he wanted.
19 And if they were all the same part, where would
the body be? 20 As it is, there are many parts, but
one body.

1 JOHN 1:1–4

Prologue: Our Declaration

1 What was from the beginning, what we have heard, what we have seen with our eyes, what we have observed and have touched with our hands, concerning the word of life— 2 that life was revealed, and we have seen it and we testify and declare to you the eternal life that was with the Father and was revealed to us— 3 what we have seen and heard we also declare to you, so that you may also have fellowship with us; and indeed our fellowship is with the Father and with his Son, Jesus Christ. 4 We are writing these things so that our joy may be complete.

EPHESIANS 2:14–20

Unity in Christ

14 For he is our peace, who made both groups one and tore down the dividing wall of hostility. In his flesh, 15 he made of no effect the law consisting of commands and expressed in regulations, so that he might create in himself one new man from the two, resulting in peace. 16 He did this so that he might reconcile both to God in one body through the cross by which he put the hostility to death. 17 He came and proclaimed the good news of peace to you who were far away and peace to those who were near. 18 For through him we both have access in one Spirit to the Father. 19 So, then, you are no longer foreigners and strangers, but fellow citizens with the saints, and members of God's household, 20 built on the foundation of the apostles and prophets, with Christ Jesus himself as the cornerstone.

I live with an eleven-year-old chef. When we tell people our son is a chef, their high voice usually kicks in and they respond with something like, "Aww, you're a chef? What do you like to cook?" It doesn't bother me that they do this. He is much smaller than the average kid and also incredibly cute, and I understand the urge to speak to him like he is a tiny pretend chef. But I'm telling you: The kid is an actual chef.

Just this morning, he asked me to sauté some diced onions for him to add to his jalapeno cheddar grits. Later he asked me to add these ingredients to the shopping list: French fried onions, pepper jack cheese, hash browns, and more grits. I'm not sure what he has in mind exactly, but I can guarantee it will be delicious. Having logged hundreds of hours watching cooking shows and another hundred reading menus and cookbooks, he is fluent in the language of food. He has a way of modifying and inventing dishes that don't occur to the rest of us, not to mention the uncanny ability to plate a beautiful meal.

See? Chef.

If we made a menu of the themes in 1 Corinthians, unity would be the main course. The Corinthian church was struggling to stay faithful to the gospel while living as part of the larger non-Christian—even anti-Christian—Corinthian culture. Paul's letter to them gave solutions to specific problems they faced as followers of Jesus, but the underlying answer to every question was the call to live Christ-centered lives in community, no matter the culture or circumstance.

It is easy to imagine why the call to unity was difficult for the Corinthian congregation to hear. They were themselves a mashup of different cultures, with Jews, Gentiles, rich, poor, elites, and commoners all combined into one fledgling Christian community. In addition to these differences, there was also division in how they viewed aspects of the Christian life. "You do not lack any spiritual gift," Paul wrote to them (1 Corinthians 1:7). But rather than using these gifts to work together, they wielded them against one another by ranking some gifts as greater and others as lesser (1 Corinthians 12:21–22).

There will be days when we feel like a group of mismatched ingredients with nothing but our chef in common.

Paul's letter makes it clear that each spiritual gift is useful and needed, just as each member of the body of believers is an important and worthy part of the whole (1 Corinthians 12:19–20). The key to withstanding the external pressures they were facing was to come together, differences and all, to focus first on the cross and resurrection of Jesus.

Unity does not come naturally. There will be days when we feel like a group of mismatched ingredients with nothing but our chef in common. But God, who created us in love and with purpose, brings us together to make something beautiful and culture-changing: the Church. We are "called by him into fellowship with his Son, Jesus Christ our Lord" (1 Corinthians 1:9), and He is faithful.

2 Corinthians

But he said to me, "My grace is sufficient for you, for my power is perfected in weakness." Therefore, I will most gladly boast all the more about my weaknesses, so that Christ's power may reside in me.

2 CORINTHIANS 12:9

2 CORINTHIANS 4:1–10

The Light of the Gospel

1 Therefore, since we have this ministry because we
were shown mercy, we do not give up. 2 Instead,
we have renounced secret and shameful things, not
acting deceitfully or distorting the word of God,
but commending ourselves before God to everyone's conscience by an open display of the truth.
3 But if our gospel is veiled, it is veiled to those
who are perishing. 4 In their case, the god of this
age has blinded the minds of the unbelievers to
keep them from seeing the light of the gospel of
the glory of Christ, who is the image of God. 5 For
we are not proclaiming ourselves but Jesus Christ
as Lord, and ourselves as your servants for Jesus's
sake. 6 For God who said, "Let light shine out of
darkness," has shone in our hearts to give the light
of the knowledge of God's glory in the face of Jesus
Christ.

Treasure in Clay Jars

7 Now we have this treasure in clay jars, so that
this extraordinary power may be from God and
not from us. 8 We are afflicted in every way but not
crushed; we are perplexed but not in despair; 9 we
are persecuted but not abandoned; we are struck
down but not destroyed. 10 We always carry the
death of Jesus in our body, so that the life of Jesus
may also be displayed in our body.

2 CORINTHIANS 12:6–10

Sufficient Grace

6 For if I want to boast, I wouldn't be a fool, because
I would be telling the truth. But I will spare you, so
that no one can credit me with something beyond
what he sees in me or hears from me, 7 especially
because of the extraordinary revelations. Therefore,
so that I would not exalt myself, a thorn in the flesh
was given to me, a messenger of Satan to torment
me so that I would not exalt myself. 8 Concerning
this, I pleaded with the Lord three times that it
would leave me. 9 But he said to me, "My grace
is sufficient for you, for my power is perfected in
weakness."

Therefore, I will most gladly boast all the more
about my weaknesses, so that Christ's power may
reside in me. 10 So I take pleasure in weaknesses,
insults, hardships, persecutions, and in difficulties,
for the sake of Christ. For when I am weak, then
I am strong.

PSALM 27:1–3

My Stronghold

1 The LORD is my light and my salvation—
whom should I fear?
The LORD is the stronghold of my life—
whom should I dread?
2 When evildoers came against me to devour my flesh,
my foes and my enemies stumbled and fell.
3 Though an army deploys against me,
my heart will not be afraid;
though a war breaks out against me,
I will still be confident.

It was just a common cold, then an infection, and then another infection from the antibiotics the doctors had given me to fight the first infection. Then, after being in bed for a week, my lower back started to hurt. To add insult to injury, I cracked one of my molars on a seed in my bread and ended up having to get a root canal. For four weeks it was one thing after another. I don't get sick often, so this debilitating month was like an object lesson in the absolute frailty of my body.

Now, I can manage a simple cold, or even a tweaked back. But when all the world seemed to conspire against me for simply getting out of bed or eating anything harder than yogurt, I began to despair. In that moment, I couldn't remember what it felt like to be well, let alone what it felt like to be cheerful or whole or able to manage anything. I felt like a walking demonstration of weakness.

Have you ever felt like that?

Maybe it's not physical for you; maybe it's emotional. Perhaps it's mental or spiritual—I don't know. But I do know that sometimes God's grace does not feel sufficient for my weakness. Nothing about me, or Him for that matter, seems sufficient in days and weeks and months like these.

Yet in 2 Corinthians 12, Paul listed the weaknesses in which he found contentment: insults, hardships, persecution, and calamities, not to mention the thorn in his flesh God hadn't removed. Paul was not saying these things didn't exist or that they weren't hard. He wasn't putting on a brave face or being courageous in the midst of difficulty. He wasn't even saying it was okay to simply accept the thorn as it was. He begged God to remove it! In the midst of all this very real pain and difficulty, Paul's contentment was not in his ability to weather the storm, bear the hurt, or be brave. His contentment was in the sufficiency of God's grace.

I felt like a walking demonstration of weakness.

When I'm struggling, it's one thing to find contentment in God's sovereign ability to change everything in an instant. It's harder to be content with simply walking through the pain—be it physical, mental, emotional, or spiritual—in the knowledge that He hears me and He is bearing this with me. But in His patience, I am learning that even when He hasn't answered my prayer according to my wishes, His grace is still sufficient.

Have you ever felt like a walking demonstration of weakness? Like me, do you wish God would resolve all your discomfort and save the lesson for another day? As we grow in our faith, let's be women who lean into the Lord in our suffering, who don't waste these opportunities to trust Him and become more like our suffering Savior. Sometimes He doesn't change our circumstances, not even a little. But He does change our hearts, making us more like Him.

Galatians

I do not set aside the grace of God, for if righteousness comes through the law, then Christ died for nothing.

GALATIANS 2:21

GALATIANS 2:20–21

Freedom from the Law

[20] I have been crucified with Christ, and I no longer live, but Christ lives in me. The life I now live in the body, I live by faith in the Son of God, who loved me and gave himself for me. [21] I do not set aside the grace of God, for if righteousness comes through the law, then Christ died for nothing.

GALATIANS 3:24–29

The Purpose of the Law

[24] The law, then, was our guardian until Christ, so that we could be justified by faith. [25] But since that faith has come, we are no longer under a guardian, [26] for through faith you are all sons of God in Christ Jesus.

Sons and Heirs

[27] For those of you who were baptized into Christ have been clothed with Christ. [28] There is no Jew or Greek, slave or free, male and female; since you are all one in Christ Jesus. [29] And if you belong to Christ, then you are Abraham's seed, heirs according to the promise.

GALATIANS 5:13–25

Freedom of the Christian

[13] For you were called to be free, brothers and sisters; only don't use this freedom as an opportunity for the flesh, but serve one another through love. [14] For the whole law is fulfilled in one statement: "Love your neighbor as yourself." [15] But if you bite and devour one another, watch out, or you will be consumed by one another.

The Spirit Versus the Flesh

[16] I say, then, walk by the Spirit and you will certainly not carry out the desire of the flesh. [17] For the flesh desires what is against the Spirit, and the Spirit desires what is against the flesh; these are opposed to each other, so that you don't do what you want. [18] But if you are led by the Spirit, you are not under the law.

[19] Now the works of the flesh are obvious: sexual immorality, moral impurity, promiscuity, [20] idolatry, sorcery, hatreds, strife, jealousy, outbursts of anger, selfish ambitions, dissensions, factions, [21] envy, drunkenness, carousing, and anything similar. I am warning you about these things—as I warned you before—that those who practice such things will not inherit the kingdom of God.

[22] But the fruit of the Spirit is love, joy, peace, patience, kindness, goodness, faithfulness, [23] gentleness, and self-control. The law is not against such things. [24] Now those who belong to Christ Jesus have crucified the flesh with its passions and desires. [25] If we live by the Spirit, let us also keep in step with the Spirit.

2 PETER 1:3–9

Growth in the Faith

3 His divine power has given us everything required for life and godliness through
the knowledge of him who called us by his own glory and goodness. 4 By these
he has given us very great and precious promises, so that through them you may
share in the divine nature, escaping the corruption that is in the world because of
evil desire. 5 For this very reason, make every effort to supplement your faith with
goodness, goodness with knowledge, 6 knowledge with self-control, self-control
with endurance, endurance with godliness, 7 godliness with brotherly affection,
and brotherly affection with love. 8 For if you possess these qualities in increasing
measure, they will keep you from being useless or unfruitful in the knowledge
of our Lord Jesus Christ. 9 The person who lacks these things is blind and shortsighted and has forgotten the cleansing from his past sins.

I grew up on the best street in East Tennessee with neighbors whose families felt like my own. I ate countless sandwiches prepared in the Russells' kitchen, made myself at home in the Burchettes' living room, and ran an imaginary store, office, or school in the Bandys' garage, depending on the day. Technically my family included my brother, our parents, and me, but most days it felt like I had enough siblings for a baseball team, a handful of extra moms and dads, and a rotating assortment of pets.

My only complaint was my age. Most of them were big kids, and I was little. Sure, I could tag along from house to house, have a snack, and hang out in their same general area. They were even nice to me (mostly). But when it came to playing basketball in the driveway, riding bikes down the big hill, or jumping the sled ramps they made any time we got a good snow, I was out. Those were big kid things. And as hard as I tried to act older, there was nothing I could do to change my little kid status.

I wonder if that's what it looks like to God when we try to achieve our own justification—that is, achieve a right and righteous standing with Him. We're like little kids standing on tiptoes, wearing too-big sport coats or dresses that swallow us whole, trying to be our own judge and jury in a court case we can't win. It reminds me of the Corrie ten Boom quote: "When we are powerless to do a thing, it is a great joy that we can come and step inside the ability of Jesus."

This is Paul's message to the churches in Galatia: We cannot justify ourselves before our holy God apart from Christ.

The Galatians knew the gospel; Paul had planted these churches himself. But now there were so-called Christians infiltrating their ranks and insisting that keeping certain Jewish laws were required for salvation. They were redefining the gospel, and Paul was writing to set the record straight. "You foolish Galatians! Who has cast a spell on you?" (Galatians 3:1). I bet you could hear a pin drop in the first-century house church where they first read this letter aloud.

We're like little kids standing on tiptoes, wearing too-big sport coats.

Paul, the former religious zealot himself, declared in no uncertain terms that no amount of religious law-keeping can save a fallen person. Only Jesus can do that. To put anything in place of the saving work of Christ is to "set aside the grace of God, for if righteousness comes through the law, then Christ died for nothing" (Galatians 2:21).

Justification is one of many things we cannot achieve apart from Jesus. Only His sacrifice can move us from death to life. Only His righteousness can reconcile us and make us one. Only His freedom can enable us to truly love. Only His Spirit can keep our hearts in step with His. No status. No achievement. Only Jesus.

What rules are you tempted to add to the gospel for yourself or others? In what ways are you standing on tiptoes trying to look bigger or stronger than you are? Release them to God today. Rediscover the great joy of hiding in Christ alone.

Ephesians

For you are saved by grace through faith, and this is not from yourselves; it is God's gift—not from works, so that no one can boast.

EPHESIANS 2:8–9

EPHESIANS 2:1–22

From Death to Life

1 And you were dead in your trespasses and sins 2 in which you previously walked according to the ways of this world, according to the ruler of the power of the air, the spirit now working in the disobedient. 3 We too all previously lived among them in our fleshly desires, carrying out the inclinations of our flesh and thoughts, and we were by nature children under wrath as the others were also. 4 But God, who is rich in mercy, because of his great love that he had for us, 5 made us alive with Christ even though we were dead in trespasses. You are saved by grace! 6 He also raised us up with him and seated us with him in the heavens in Christ Jesus, 7 so that in the coming ages he might display the immeasurable riches of his grace through his kindness to us in Christ Jesus. 8 For you are saved by grace through faith, and this is not from yourselves; it is God's gift— 9 not from works, so that no one can boast. 10 For we are his workmanship, created in Christ Jesus for good works, which God prepared ahead of time for us to do.

Unity in Christ

11 So, then, remember that at one time you were Gentiles in the flesh—called "the uncircumcised" by those called "the circumcised," which is done in the flesh by human hands. 12 At that time you were without Christ, excluded from the citizenship of Israel, and foreigners to the covenants of promise, without hope and without God in the world. 13 But now in Christ Jesus, you who were far away have been brought near by the blood of Christ. 14 For he is our peace, who made both groups one and tore down the dividing wall of hostility. In his flesh, 15 he made of no effect the law consisting of commands and expressed in regulations, so that he might create in himself one new man from the two, resulting in peace. 16 He did this so that he might reconcile both to God in one body through the cross by which he put the hostility to death. 17 He came and proclaimed the good news of peace to you who were far away and peace to those who were near. 18 For through him we both have access in one Spirit to the Father. 19 So, then, you are no longer foreigners and strangers, but fellow citizens with the saints, and members of God's household, 20 built on the foundation of the apostles and prophets, with Christ Jesus himself as the cornerstone. 21 In him the whole building, being put together, grows into a holy temple in the Lord. 22 In him you are also being built together for God's dwelling in the Spirit.

1 JOHN 5:11–13

The Certainty of God's Testimony

11 And this is the testimony: God has given us eternal life, and this life is in his
Son. 12 The one who has the Son has life. The one who does not have the Son of
God does not have life. 13 I have written these things to you who believe in the
name of the Son of God so that you may know that you have eternal life.

I don't belong here.

I am writing this from the lobby of an exclusive social club in Nashville. I have heard hob-nobby whispers of this place, but I didn't even know where it was and I absolutely doubted I'd ever see the inside of its chic, tinted doors. It is way above my pay grade as well as my coolness grade. But today, I have this loophole. There was an event hosted here this morning that I was invited to, and when it ended and everyone began to shuffle out, I asked at the desk if I could stay and write for a while. When I confessed I wasn't a member, the answer was actually a hard no, but I was invited to sit in the lobby as long as I didn't embarrass myself or them. (That last part isn't 100 percent true, but it feels at least 80 percent true.)

There will be places throughout our lives where we inexplicably feel we don't belong. Maybe it's that you're too old or too young, or maybe it has to do with who you don't know or what you don't have to offer. Whatever the case, *c'est la vie*. (See? I'm speaking French and that's classy. I told you I wouldn't embarrass myself!)

Paul's letter to the Ephesians lays plain the most epic, global example of those who didn't belong, now being treated like VIPs because of the love and blood of Christ. The Gentiles (what we call everybody in the world who wasn't of Jewish descent or a "son of Abraham") were excluded from the citizenship of Israel and "foreigners to the covenants of promise, without hope and without God" (Ephesians 2:12). That was their dark and damning reality. But Christ saw those who were far away and said, *No more.* He had the purpose and power to make both groups one, and that's exactly what He did.

There will be places throughout our lives where we inexplicably feel we don't belong.

Christ came to all of us from all backgrounds, pinkies up and pinkies down, and proclaimed the good news of peace to everyone near and far. "So, then, you are no longer foreigners and strangers, but fellow citizens with the saints, and members of God's household" (Ephesians 2:19). It's incredible to me. Epic doesn't feel like too big a word.

There will be situations and places throughout our lives where we will feel out of place. That's life. We can't belong everywhere on earth because this version of it is not our home. And this afternoon, I may feel like a bit of a fraud in the lobby of an exclusive club, and that's just fine with me. But as a Gentile member of the body of Christ, I don't have a stitch of insecurity or feel as though I don't belong. In fact, Jesus beckons me to come closer. To stay longer. To make my home with Him.

Pinkies down, friend. He came for you and He is your home.

Philippians

For me, to live is Christ
and to die is gain.

PHILIPPIANS 1:21

PHILIPPIANS 1:12–21

Advance of the Gospel

12 Now I want you to know, brothers and sisters, that what has happened to me has actually
advanced the gospel, 13 so that it has become
known throughout the whole imperial guard, and
to everyone else, that my imprisonment is because
I am in Christ. 14 Most of the brothers have gained
confidence in the Lord from my imprisonment
and dare even more to speak the word fearlessly.
15 To be sure, some preach Christ out of envy and
rivalry, but others out of good will. 16 These preach
out of love, knowing that I am appointed for the
defense of the gospel; 17 the others proclaim Christ
out of selfish ambition, not sincerely, thinking
that they will cause me trouble in my imprisonment. 18 What does it matter? Only that in every
way, whether from false motives or true, Christ is
proclaimed, and in this I rejoice. Yes, and I will
continue to rejoice 19 because I know this will lead
to my salvation through your prayers and help
from the Spirit of Jesus Christ. 20 My eager expec-
tation and hope is that I will not be ashamed about
anything, but that now as always, with all courage,
Christ will be highly honored in my body, whether
by life or by death.

Living Is Christ

21 For me, to live is Christ and to die is gain.

PHILIPPIANS 3:7–9

Knowing Christ

7 But everything that was a gain to me, I have considered to be a loss because of Christ. 8 More than
that, I also consider everything to be a loss in view
of the surpassing value of knowing Christ Jesus my
Lord. Because of him I have suffered the loss of all
things and consider them as dung, so that I may
gain Christ 9 and be found in him, not having a
righteousness of my own from the law, but one
that is through faith in Christ—the righteousness
from God based on faith.

PHILIPPIANS 4:4–9

Practical Counsel

4 Rejoice in the Lord always. I will say it again:
Rejoice! 5 Let your graciousness be known to
everyone. The Lord is near. 6 Don't worry about
anything, but in everything, through prayer and
petition with thanksgiving, present your requests
to God. 7 And the peace of God, which surpasses
all understanding, will guard your hearts and
minds in Christ Jesus.

8 Finally brothers and sisters, whatever is true,
whatever is honorable, whatever is just, whatever
is pure, whatever is lovely, whatever is commendable—if there is any moral excellence and if there
is anything praiseworthy—dwell on these things.
9 Do what you have learned and received and
heard from me, and seen in me, and the God of
peace will be with you.

ROMANS 8:35–39

The Believer's Triumph

35 Who can separate us from the love of Christ? Can affliction or distress or persecution or famine or nakedness or danger or sword? 36 As it is written:

> "Because of you
> we are being put to death all day long;
> we are counted as sheep to be slaughtered."

37 No, in all these things we are more than conquerors through him who loved us.
38 For I am persuaded that neither death nor life, nor angels nor rulers, nor things
present nor things to come, nor powers, 39 nor height nor depth, nor any other
created thing will be able to separate us from the love of God that is in Christ
Jesus our Lord.

Years ago, I gave a talk about fear and anxiety. About thirty women settled into a cozy room as I began sharing some of my story.

Looking back on my childhood, I see a little girl who wanted to play it safe, who perpetually problem-solved worst-case scenarios, and who felt shadowed by a vague sense of fear. This stream of anxiety ran steadily throughout my life, but no one would have known. I was the kid who easily made friends, loved school, and didn't cause much trouble. I was the strong, steady one—until I wasn't.

In my late twenties, in the midst of young marriage and new motherhood, the stream of anxiety became a flood. Panic attacks began to torment me. For the first time, my underground anxiety burst out and threatened to take center stage. I felt embarrassed and ashamed. I didn't want to admit my confusing fears, and I certainly didn't want others to see my struggle. After all, I was supposed to be the strong, steady one.

I was the strong, steady one—until I wasn't.

At this point in my talk, I told the women that I had a secret. I began unbuttoning my shirt. Awkward silence filled the room. Underneath my faded, denim top I wore a white T-shirt and cold, bulky metal chains. No one had suspected that I was wearing chains, yet they were there the whole time—pinching, constraining, and weighing me down. We don't always know the chains people are wrapped up in, do we?

The apostle and missionary Paul wore chains too. In his letter to the believers in the city of Philippi, Paul explained that he was "in chains for Christ" as he endured house arrest (Philippians 1:13 NIV). For years he had been misunderstood, criticized, slandered, and beaten, and now he was jailed in Rome.

Some could view Paul as a failure. Some could question his faith or even the power or goodness of God. Yet Paul was convinced that his current suffering was nothing to be ashamed of or to hide. On the contrary, he insisted that his circumstances advanced the gospel message. He told the Philippians, "Because of my chains, most of the brothers and sisters have become confident in the Lord and dare all the more to proclaim the gospel without fear" (Philippians 1:14 NIV). Even in jail, Paul rejoiced that his guards were hearing about Jesus and that other believers were encouraged and empowered.

We may marvel at Paul's perspective, but we can also hold both the redemption of our chains with the pain they cause. In 1 Corinthians 2:3, Paul revealed his own weakness, fear, and trembling. Like Paul, we all chafe and wrestle with painful circumstances, those things we would never choose for ourselves. And like Paul, we can choose to cling to Jesus.

What pinches you, constrains you, or weighs you down? Our anxieties, our fears, and our sufferings are heavy and costly. But we don't have to hide them or be ashamed. Even our struggles can deepen our dependence on Christ and point others to the One who walks us through our darkest valleys and redeems us—chains and all.

Colossians

He is before all things, and by him all things hold together.

COLOSSIANS 1:17

COLOSSIANS 1:9–23

Prayer for Spiritual Growth

9 For this reason also, since the day we heard this,
we haven't stopped praying for you. We are asking
that you may be filled with the knowledge of his
will in all wisdom and spiritual understanding,
10 so that you may walk worthy of the Lord, fully
pleasing to him: bearing fruit in every good work
and growing in the knowledge of God, 11 being
strengthened with all power, according to his
glorious might, so that you may have great endurance and patience, joyfully 12 giving thanks to the
Father, who has enabled you to share in the saints'
inheritance in the light. 13 He has rescued us from
the domain of darkness and transferred us into the
kingdom of the Son he loves. 14 In him we have
redemption, the forgiveness of sins.

The Centrality of Christ

15 He is the image of the invisible God,
the firstborn over all creation.
16 For everything was created by him,
in heaven and on earth,
the visible and the invisible,
whether thrones or dominions
or rulers or authorities—
all things have been created through him
  and for him.
17 He is before all things,
and by him all things hold together.
18 He is also the head of the body, the church;
he is the beginning,
the firstborn from the dead,
so that he might come to have
first place in everything.
19 For God was pleased to have
all his fullness dwell in him,
20 and through him to reconcile
everything to himself,
whether things on earth or things in heaven,
by making peace
through his blood, shed on the cross.

21 Once you were alienated and hostile in
your minds as expressed in your evil actions.
22 But now he has reconciled you by his
physical body through his death, to present
you holy, faultless, and blameless before
him— 23 if indeed you remain grounded
and steadfast in the faith and are not shifted
away from the hope of the gospel that you
heard. This gospel has been proclaimed in
all creation under heaven, and I, Paul, have
become a servant of it.

HEBREWS 1:1–4

The Nature of the Son

1 Long ago God spoke to our ancestors by the prophets at different times and
in different ways. 2 In these last days, he has spoken to us by his Son. God has
appointed him heir of all things and made the universe through him. 3 The Son
is the radiance of God's glory and the exact expression of his nature, sustaining all
things by his powerful word. After making purification for sins, he sat down at the
right hand of the Majesty on high. 4 So he became superior to the angels, just as
the name he inherited is more excellent than theirs.

I guess it was inevitable. All my life, I had 20/20 vision. Distant street signs? No problem. Small print on a menu? I've got this. But then I turned forty. As eyestrain and blurriness became my new normal, I realized how much I had taken the gift of clear vision for granted. Now I have eyeglasses scattered throughout my home and car as I squint to see things up close and far away. Good times.

The problem of aging eyes is one thing, but our spiritual vision is often impaired too. On our own, we strain as we consider who God is and how we can be close to Him. *Can I know God? Does God really love and accept me? Can I trust Him?* The answers to such honest, human questions shape our faith and lives, yet they often seem blurry.

Paul wanted the church in Colossae to see the truth clearly. They had started with gospel clarity, seeing Jesus as the only one able to reconcile sinful people to a holy God, "by making peace through his blood, shed on the cross" (Colossians 1:20). But false teachers were misleading the church. They were instructing the Colossians to rely on their own efforts and enlightenment for right standing with God, instead of relying on the finished work of Jesus's life, death, and resurrection. The issue was a Christ-centered worldview versus their self-centered worldview, which is a futile, tiring way to live. As they sought to find their own wisdom and hold their lives together through their own power, Christ was holding all things together all along.

Truth was being twisted and blurred, so Paul urged the Colossians to look to Christ. Relying on Christ alone was the only way to see and experience God with clarity and certainty. "He is the image of the invisible God, the firstborn over all creation" (Colossians 1:15). Jesus is the very image of God because He *is* God. When we look to Jesus—how He lived, how He loved, how He forgave, how He sacrificed to restore broken, lost people—we see clearly how God relates to us.

Truth was being twisted and blurred, so Paul urged the Colossians to look to Christ.

Looking to Christ is like putting on eyeglasses so we can see God and ourselves more clearly. It means seeing and embracing the truth that He is Creator and King of every single thing—including our salvation, the daily ups and downs of our lives, and the state of the entire world. To be sure, our vision is impaired and life can be a blur: morning-rush meltdowns, job hassles, relationship tensions, deep disappointments, fear of the future. We strain for clarity and control. But let us "not [shift] away from the hope of the gospel" (Colossians 1:23).

Is blurriness about God's love and power becoming your new normal? Are you feeling the strain of relying more and more on yourself to push through each day? Put on your gospel glasses! Look to Christ. He is holding all things together. He is holding you.

1 Thessalonians

Rejoice always, pray constantly, give thanks in everything; for this is God's will for you in Christ Jesus.

1 THESSALONIANS 5:16–18

1 THESSALONIANS 1:2–6

Thanksgiving

2 We always thank God for all of you, making mention of you constantly in our prayers. 3 We recall,
in the presence of our God and Father, your work
produced by faith, your labor motivated by love,
and your endurance inspired by hope in our Lord
Jesus Christ. 4 For we know, brothers and sisters
loved by God, that he has chosen you, 5 because
our gospel did not come to you in word only, but
also in power, in the Holy Spirit, and with full
assurance. You know how we lived among you for
your benefit, 6 and you yourselves became imitators of us and of the Lord when, in spite of severe
persecution, you welcomed the message with joy
from the Holy Spirit.

1 THESSALONIANS 5:1–24

The Day of the Lord

1 About the times and the seasons: Brothers and
sisters, you do not need anything to be written to
you. 2 For you yourselves know very well that the
day of the Lord will come just like a thief in the
night. 3 When they say, "Peace and security," then
sudden destruction will come upon them, like
labor pains on a pregnant woman, and they will
not escape. 4 But you, brothers and sisters, are not
in the dark, for this day to surprise you like a thief.
5 For you are all children of light and children of
the day. We do not belong to the night or the darkness. 6 So then, let us not sleep, like the rest, but let
us stay awake and be self-controlled. 7 For those
who sleep, sleep at night, and those who get drunk,
get drunk at night. 8 But since we belong to the
day, let us be self-controlled and put on the armor
of faith and love, and a helmet of the hope of salvation. 9 For God did not appoint us to wrath, but
to obtain salvation through our Lord Jesus Christ,
10 who died for us, so that whether we are awake or
asleep, we may live together with him. 11 Therefore
encourage one another and build each other up as
you are already doing.

Exhortations and Blessings

12 Now we ask you, brothers and sisters, to give
recognition to those who labor among you and
lead you in the Lord and admonish you, 13 and to
regard them very highly in love because of their
work. Be at peace among yourselves. 14 And we
exhort you, brothers and sisters: warn those who
are idle, comfort the discouraged, help the weak,
be patient with everyone. 15 See to it that no one
repays evil for evil to anyone, but always pursue
what is good for one another and for all. 16 Rejoice
always, 17 pray constantly, 18 give thanks in everything; for this is God's will for you in Christ Jesus.
19 Don't stifle the Spirit. 20 Don't despise prophecies, 21 but test all things. Hold on to what is good.
22 Stay away from every kind of evil.

23 Now may the God of peace himself sanctify you
completely. And may your whole spirit, soul, and
body be kept sound and blameless at the coming
of our Lord Jesus Christ. 24 He who calls you is
faithful; he will do it.

ROMANS 12:1–2

A Living Sacrifice

[1] Therefore, brothers and sisters, in view of the mercies of God, I urge you to present your bodies as a living sacrifice, holy and pleasing to God; this is your true worship. [2] Do not be conformed to this age, but be transformed by the renewing of your mind, so that you may discern what is the good, pleasing, and perfect will of God.

HEBREWS 9:27–28

New Covenant Ministry

[27] And just as it is appointed for people to die once—and after this, judgment— [28] so also Christ, having been offered once to bear the sins of many, will appear a second time, not to bear sin, but to bring salvation to those who are waiting for him.

REVELATION 1:7

"Look, he is coming with the clouds,"
and "every eye will see him,
even those who pierced him.
And all the tribes" of the earth
"will mourn over him."
So it is to be. Amen.

Growing up in a small town in the 80s meant wearing extremely large ruffles on my church socks and taking my turn singing a solo for "special music" a few Sunday evenings each year. Of all the many wonderful and true songs I sang as a child, there were a few that set unrealistic (or perhaps naïve) expectations around what committing to Christ would truly require of me.

I remember belting one tune into the too-heavy microphone that promised a nearly fever-pitch level of happiness, cheer, energy, and relaxation—so much of these things, in fact, that following Jesus would mostly feel like a holiday filled with popcorn and candy and skipping into the sunset.

I'm in my forties now and the ruffles on my socks are now more of a tasteful ripple. And to be completely honest, giving Christ my life these last four decades hasn't been the sugar-covered experience I sang about. Instead, it's been marked by digging deep to forgive not-sorry offenders, waiting on the Lord when the world offered a shortcut, and white-knuckling the hope of the gospel in times of discouragement and grief. Yes, I have also experienced immense joy and peace alongside this pain, but where is the poppy, energetic, ever-fizzy pep in my step I was promised?

If you've been a Christian for any amount of time, then you know that billing this life as all candy and sunshine is false advertising. Sin and sorrow don't disappear when we come to know Jesus, and a world reeling from the effects of the fall is still a very hard place to live. So what do we do when the uncertainties of life collide with our faith? How does our hope in Jesus shape our response in difficult or even painful circumstances?

What do we do when the uncertainties of life collide with our faith?

As new Christians—and some of the first in the world—the first-century church in Thessalonica was facing severe persecution for their beliefs (1 Thessalonians 1:6). Living out their faith wasn't only hard, it was a daily matter of life and death. They needed the steady words of a more experienced brother in Christ to recenter their hope and remind them of the truth they already knew: The Messiah had come, and He was coming back again.

Paul encouraged them not to fret about the timing of Christ's return, but to live fully awake as "children of light and children of the day" (1 Thessalonians 5:5). The promise of Christ's coming was to be fuel for their everyday mission as ambassadors of the gospel, looking to the promised Day of the Lord not with fearful panic but with faithful vigilance and expectant hope.

What does that look like, exactly? Paul had counsel for that as well: "Rejoice always, pray constantly, give thanks in everything; for this is God's will for you in Christ Jesus" (1 Thessalonians 5:16–18).

In the formative years of their faith, amid conflict and persecution, Paul's instructions to his beloved friends may not have been easy, but they were surprisingly simple: Rejoice. Pray. Give thanks.

Are you facing troubles or uncertainties today? Eavesdrop on this letter to the Thessalonians and take the encouragement you need. Your Savior has come, and He is coming again! "Now may the God of peace himself sanctify you completely. And may your whole spirit, soul, and body be kept sound and blameless at the coming of our Lord Jesus Christ. He who calls you is faithful; he will do it" (1 Thessalonians 5:23–24). I'll take that over candy-coated Christianity any day.

2 Thessalonians

May the Lord direct your hearts to God's love and Christ's endurance.

2 THESSALONIANS 3:5

2 THESSALONIANS 2:13–17

Stand Firm

13 But we ought to thank God always for you,
brothers and sisters loved by the Lord, because
from the beginning God has chosen you for
salvation through sanctification by the Spirit and
through belief in the truth. 14 He called you to this
through our gospel, so that you might obtain the
glory of our Lord Jesus Christ. 15 So then, brothers
and sisters, stand firm and hold to the traditions
you were taught, whether by what we said or what
we wrote.

16 May our Lord Jesus Christ himself and God
our Father, who has loved us and given us eternal
encouragement and good hope by grace, 17 encourage your hearts and strengthen you in every good
work and word.

2 THESSALONIANS 3:1–5, 16

Pray for Us

1 In addition, brothers and sisters, pray for us that
the word of the Lord may spread rapidly and be
honored, just as it was with you, 2 and that we
may be delivered from wicked and evil people,
for not all have faith. 3 But the Lord is faithful; he
will strengthen you and guard you from the evil
one. 4 We have confidence in the Lord about you,
that you are doing and will continue to do what
we command. 5 May the Lord direct your hearts to
God's love and Christ's endurance.

. . .

Final Greetings

16 May the Lord of peace himself give you peace
always in every way. The Lord be with all of you.

PSALM 22:27–31

From Suffering to Praise

27 All the ends of the earth will remember
and turn to the LORD.
All the families of the nations
will bow down before you,
28 for kingship belongs to the LORD;
he rules the nations.
29 All who prosper on earth will eat and bow down;
all those who go down to the dust
will kneel before him—
even the one who cannot preserve his life.
30 Their descendants will serve him;
the next generation will be told about the Lord.
31 They will come and declare his righteousness;
to a people yet to be born
they will declare what he has done.

PHILIPPIANS 4:6–7

Practical Counsel

6 Don't worry about anything, but in everything,
through prayer and petition with thanksgiving,
present your requests to God. 7 And the peace of
God, which surpasses all understanding, will guard
your hearts and minds in Christ Jesus.

COLOSSIANS 3:12–17

The Christian Life

12 Therefore, as God's chosen ones, holy and dearly
loved, put on compassion, kindness, humility,
gentleness, and patience, 13 bearing with one
another and forgiving one another if anyone has
a grievance against another. Just as the Lord has
forgiven you, so you are also to forgive. 14 Above
all, put on love, which is the perfect bond of unity.
15 And let the peace of Christ, to which you were
also called in one body, rule your hearts. And be
thankful. 16 Let the word of Christ dwell richly
among you, in all wisdom teaching and admon-
ishing one another through psalms, hymns, and
spiritual songs, singing to God with gratitude in
your hearts. 17 And whatever you do, in word or in
deed, do everything in the name of the Lord Jesus,
giving thanks to God the Father through him.

JAMES 5:7–8

Waiting for the Lord

7 Therefore, brothers and sisters, be patient until
the Lord's coming. See how the farmer waits for
the precious fruit of the earth and is patient with
it until it receives the early and the late rains. 8 You
also must be patient. Strengthen your hearts,
because the Lord's coming is near.

As I write this, it is snowing outside. All my little boys are in snow pants, and I just saw them eating snow off the back bumper of my van—so, I know they are having lovely, strange snow time. My girls are sleeping; the baby is taking her first nap, and the teenager still hasn't woken up yet. We don't often get a blanket of snow in Tennessee, so the sleds tend to appear after a light dusting. I've been known to play English carols and light candles if I even smell snow in the night air.

Snow looks like peace on earth. It hides all the mud and failing boxwood shrubs. It covers downed bicycles and the dog-trot paths in the woods. Snow frosts our little hilltop like a wedding cake, making everything look clean and quiet and peaceful.

Eventually, the snow melts, ducks and dogs track mud, the baby starts to cry, and the responsibilities of life are unveiled once again.

It's sumptuous and delightful to feel peace when the snow falls, and everything looks peaceful. But boy, circumstantial peace sure is hard to come by. Something is always clanging for your attention, while relationships and cars keep showing up broken. Our peace doesn't come from a settled home in the snow or a steady income. (You might have to say that out loud.) Our only true peace comes from Christ. He is the Lord of peace and gives to us generously.

When our heart rates are rapid and our worry increases at all the pressures of the day, God's peace is an answer for us, just as Paul wrote in 2 Thessalonians 3:16: "May the Lord of peace himself give you peace always in every way. The Lord be with all of you." He doesn't mean, "May your breakfasts be uninterrupted by annoying and unanswerable lizard-based questions, and may your evenings be free of emergencies, both toe- and weather-based." The interruptions and emergencies will not stop. Once the babies stop waking you up at night, the pets will do it—and eventually, the bladder will wake us all.

Our peace doesn't come from a settled home or a steady income.

You cannot cultivate true and lasting peace, no matter how hard you try and no matter how many snowstorms you enjoy. Those moments melt away, but for the one whose eyes are fixed on "God's love and Christ's endurance" (2 Thessalonians 3:5), God cultivates peace that only He can bring. Honestly, this kind of peace takes away the pressure! "Don't worry about anything, but in everything, through prayer and petition with thanksgiving, present your requests to God. And the peace of God, which surpasses all understanding, will guard your hearts and minds in Christ Jesus" (Philippians 4:6–7).

Don't worry. Pray. Christ will guard your heart with peace. Snow or hail, filled or hungry, rich or poor—ask God to direct your hearts to Him and the glory of Christ, who endures on your behalf. In Him is true peace.

1 Timothy

This saying is trustworthy and deserving of full acceptance: "Christ Jesus came into the world to save sinners"—and I am the worst of them.

1 TIMOTHY 1:15

1 TIMOTHY 1:1–7, 12–17

Greeting

1 Paul, an apostle of Christ Jesus by the command of God our Savior and of Christ Jesus our hope:

2 To Timothy, my true son in the faith.

Grace, mercy, and peace from God the Father and Christ Jesus our Lord.

False Doctrine and Misuse of the Law

3 As I urged you when I went to Macedonia, remain in Ephesus so that you may instruct certain people not to teach false doctrine 4 or to pay attention to myths and endless genealogies. These promote empty speculations rather than God's plan, which operates by faith. 5 Now the goal of our instruction is love that comes from a pure heart, a good conscience, and a sincere faith. 6 Some have departed from these and turned aside to fruitless discussion. 7 They want to be teachers of the law, although they don't understand what they are saying or what they are insisting on.

. . .

Paul's Testimony

12 I give thanks to Christ Jesus our Lord who has strengthened me, because he considered me faithful, appointing me to the ministry— 13 even though I was formerly a blasphemer, a persecutor, and an arrogant man. But I received mercy because I acted out of ignorance in unbelief, 14 and the grace of our Lord overflowed, along with the faith and love that are in Christ Jesus. 15 This saying is trustworthy and deserving of full acceptance: "Christ Jesus came into the world to save sinners"—and I am the worst of them. 16 But I received mercy for this reason, so that in me, the worst of them, Christ Jesus might demonstrate his extraordinary patience as an example to those who would believe in him for eternal life. 17 Now to the King eternal, immortal, invisible, the only God, be honor and glory forever and ever. Amen.

1 TIMOTHY 4:6–10

A Good Servant of Jesus Christ

6 If you point these things out to the brothers and sisters, you will be a good servant of Christ Jesus, nourished by the words of the faith and the good teaching that you have followed. 7 But have nothing to do with pointless and silly myths. Rather, train yourself in godliness. 8 For the training of the body has limited benefit, but godliness is beneficial in every way, since it holds promise for the present life and also for the life to come. 9 This saying is trustworthy and deserves full acceptance. 10 For this reason we labor and strive, because we have put our hope in the living God, who is the Savior of all people, especially of those who believe.

MATTHEW 7:24–27

The Two Foundations

24 "Therefore, everyone who hears these words of
mine and acts on them will be like a wise man who
built his house on the rock. 25 The rain fell, the
rivers rose, and the winds blew and pounded that
house. Yet it didn't collapse, because its foundation
was on the rock. 26 But everyone who hears these
words of mine and doesn't act on them will be like
a foolish man who built his house on the sand.
27 The rain fell, the rivers rose, the winds blew and
pounded that house, and it collapsed. It collapsed
with a great crash."

ROMANS 1:16–17

The Righteous Will Live by Faith

16 For I am not ashamed of the gospel, because it
is the power of God for salvation to everyone who
believes, first to the Jew, and also to the Greek. 17 For
in it the righteousness of God is revealed from faith
to faith, just as it is written: "The righteous will live
by faith."

2 PETER 1:16–21

The Trustworthy Prophetic Word

16 For we did not follow cleverly contrived myths
when we made known to you the power and
coming of our Lord Jesus Christ; instead, we were
eyewitnesses of his majesty. 17 For he received honor
and glory from God the Father when the voice
came to him from the Majestic Glory, saying "This
is my beloved Son, with whom I am well-pleased!"
18 We ourselves heard this voice when it came from
heaven while we were with him on the holy mountain. 19 We also have the prophetic word strongly
confirmed, and you will do well to pay attention
to it, as to a lamp shining in a dark place, until
the day dawns and the morning star rises in your
hearts. 20 Above all, you know this: No prophecy of
Scripture comes from the prophet's own interpretation, 21 because no prophecy ever came by the will
of man; instead, men spoke from God as they were
carried along by the Holy Spirit.

If you want to test the strength of a marriage, renovate a house with your spouse. Not only will you have to make a million decisions together, small and large, but you'll be forced to define your priorities and perhaps admit to said spouse that a soaking tub is way more important to you than a garage workbench. Hypothetically speaking.

You will also learn far more than you possibly ever cared to learn about home construction. Did you know that the slab of wood known as a "2-by-4" does not actually measure 2 inches by 4 inches? The moniker comes from the general size of the rough wood before it is cut into planks. (How is a novice carpenter supposed to know this, you ask? Great question.) But most importantly, and I cannot stress this enough, there are walls that you cannot remove in a home, no matter how badly you want to enlarge the kitchen or reconfigure the entryway. They're called load-bearing walls, and they do the crucial job of bearing the weight of the house above by transmitting that weight to the foundation below. In other words, knock them down and the whole house eventually comes down with them.

In his first letter to his protegé Timothy, the apostle Paul warns the young pastor of false teachers who are attempting to replace the load-bearing walls of the gospel with flimsy, untrue, and unsound doctrine. They were distracting these new believers from the message of salvation by grace through faith in Jesus Christ by preaching "myths and endless genealogies," even trying to teach them Jewish law but without any true knowledge of it (1 Timothy 1:3–7). Paul, having planted these churches himself and with deep care for their spiritual well-being, was simply not going to stand for it. And he wasn't going to let Timothy stand for it either. "Timothy, guard what has been entrusted to you . . ." (1 Timothy 6:20).

Paul was passionate about the saving grace of Jesus because he had experienced it firsthand. He called himself the worst of sinners (1 Timothy 1:15)—a former blasphemer, persecutor, and all around arrogant guy who nonetheless received mercy and overflowing grace from the Lord (1 Timothy 6:12–15). Paul was saved by nothing less than the radical love and grace of Jesus Christ, and he was not about to let false teachers—even impressive ones—weasel their way into the church and mislead his brothers and sisters in the faith.

There are walls that you cannot remove in a home, no matter how badly you want to enlarge the kitchen or reconfigure the entryway.

Reading Paul's urgent instructions to Timothy, I wonder, *Do I contend this fiercely for the gospel message?* Am I resting my faith on the immovable walls of Jesus's life, death, and resurrection? Or, am I giving "pointless and silly myths" my heart's attention, as if a 2-by-4 can be trusted to hold up the roof over my head?

There will always be false teachers holding out false gospels and false gods. But the true gospel message is clear and unchanging: "Christ Jesus came into the world to save sinners" (1 Timothy 1:15). Just Jesus. He alone is our sure foundation.

2 Timothy

All Scripture is inspired by God and is profitable for teaching, for rebuking, for correcting, for training in righteousness, so that the man of God may be complete, equipped for every good work.

2 TIMOTHY 3:16–17

2 TIMOTHY 1:1–14

Greeting

1 Paul, an apostle of Christ Jesus by God's will, for the sake of the promise of life in Christ Jesus:

2 To Timothy, my dearly loved son.

Grace, mercy, and peace from God the Father and Christ Jesus our Lord.

Thanksgiving

3 I thank God, whom I serve with a clear conscience as my ancestors did, when I constantly remember you in my prayers night and day. 4 Remembering your tears, I long to see you so that I may be filled with joy. 5 I recall your sincere faith that first lived in your grandmother Lois and in your mother Eunice and now, I am convinced, is in you also.

6 Therefore, I remind you to rekindle the gift of God that is in you through the laying on of my hands. 7 For God has not given us a spirit of fear, but one of power, love, and sound judgment.

Not Ashamed of the Gospel

8 So don't be ashamed of the testimony about our Lord, or of me his prisoner. Instead, share in suffering for the gospel, relying on the power of God. 9 He has saved us and called us with a holy calling, not according to our works, but according to his own purpose and grace, which was given to us in Christ Jesus before time began. 10 This has now been made evident through the appearing of our Savior Christ Jesus, who has abolished death and has brought life and immortality to light through the gospel. 11 For this gospel I was appointed a herald, apostle, and teacher, 12 and that is why I suffer these things. But I am not ashamed, because I know whom I have believed and am persuaded that he is able to guard what has been entrusted to me until that day.

Be Loyal to the Faith

13 Hold on to the pattern of sound teaching that you have heard from me, in the faith and love that are in Christ Jesus. 14 Guard the good deposit through the Holy Spirit who lives in us.

2 TIMOTHY 3:12–17

Struggles in the Christian Life

12 In fact, all who want to live a godly life in Christ Jesus will be persecuted. 13 Evil people and impostors will become worse, deceiving and being deceived. 14 But as for you, continue in what you have learned and firmly believed. You know those who taught you, 15 and you know that from infancy you have known the sacred Scriptures, which are able to give you wisdom for salvation through faith in Christ Jesus. 16 All Scripture is inspired by God and is profitable for teaching, for rebuking, for correcting, for training in righteousness, 17 so that the man of God may be complete, equipped for every good work.

2 TIMOTHY 4:1–8

Fulfill Your Ministry

1 I solemnly charge you before God and Christ Jesus, who is going to judge the living and the dead, and because of his appearing and his kingdom: 2 Preach the word; be ready in season and out of season; correct, rebuke, and encourage with great patience and teaching. 3 For the time will come when people will not tolerate sound doctrine, but according to their own desires, will multiply teachers for themselves because they have an itch to hear what they want to hear. 4 They will turn away from hearing the truth and will turn aside to myths. 5 But as for you, exercise self-control in everything, endure hardship, do the work of an evangelist, fulfill your ministry.

6 For I am already being poured out as a drink offering, and the time for my departure is close. 7 I have fought the good fight, I have finished the race, I have kept the faith. 8 There is reserved for me the crown of righteousness, which the Lord, the righteous Judge, will give me on that day, and not only to me, but to all those who have loved his appearing.

JOSHUA 1:7–9

Encouragement of Joshua

7 "Above all, be strong and very courageous to
observe carefully the whole instruction my servant
Moses commanded you. Do not turn from it to
the right or the left, so that you will have success
wherever you go. 8 This book of instruction must
not depart from your mouth; you are to meditate
on it day and night so that you may carefully
observe everything written in it. For then you will
prosper and succeed in whatever you do. 9 Haven't
I commanded you: be strong and courageous? Do
not be afraid or discouraged, for the LORD your
God is with you wherever you go."

ROMANS 15:4–6

4 For whatever was written in the past was written for our instruction, so that we may have hope
through endurance and through the encouragement from the Scriptures. 5 Now may the God
who gives endurance and encouragement grant
you to live in harmony with one another, according to Christ Jesus, 6 so that you may glorify the
God and Father of our Lord Jesus Christ with one
mind and one voice.

My son was just born.

Technically, he was born eighteen years ago. But to me, I don't know—it just all happened so fast. In my mind, I still need my husband to pick up diapers on his way home from work because I have to keep an eye on the kids in the pool and cut their sandwiches into dinosaur shapes.

The apostle Paul didn't have children, but he was a significant father in the faith to many, especially Timothy. I don't know if you're allowed to play favorites with your spiritual children, but I get the sense that Paul's love for Timothy and concern for his spiritual growth rivaled that of the most dedicated parent. Maybe this is why I have always connected so deeply with the book of 2 Timothy.

Paul wrote, I would guess, dozens of letters. Thirteen of them are included in the New Testament. The book of 2 Timothy, as far as we know, is Paul's last letter before he was martyred in Rome, and Paul knew it would likely be his last letter to Timothy (2 Timothy 4:6).

Imagine knowing you are near the end of your race on earth, and you can write one final letter to your child. At this particular stage of motherhood, it's not so difficult to envision. We're on the 12-month countdown to dropping off our boy at college. His high school is already asking us for things like "first day of kindergarten" pictures, senior yearbook ads, and, yes, letters to be given to him upon graduation. What on earth do you write in a final letter to your son before he no longer sleeps upstairs?

As for Paul, he says what matters, and he doesn't waste time.

> *". . . rekindle the gift of God that is in you . . ." (1:6).*
>
> *". . . God has not given us a spirit of fear, but one of power, love, and sound judgment" (1:7).*
>
> *". . . don't be ashamed of the testimony about our Lord . . ." (1:8).*
>
> *". . . rely on the power of God" (1:8).*
>
> *"Hold on to the pattern of sound teaching that you have heard from me . . ." (1:13).*
>
> *"Evil people and imposters will become worse . . . but as for you, continue in what you have learned and firmly believed" (3:13–14).*
>
> And my favorite: *"Proclaim the message; persist in it whether convenient or not . . . endure hardship, do the work of an evangelist, fulfill your ministry" (4:2, 5 HCSB).*

He reiterates the gospel (2 Timothy 1:10), holds the Scriptures high (2 Timothy 3:15), and warns his spiritual son of what will come (2 Timothy 4:3–4). I think Paul just wrote my senior letter for me!

But before I pass this letter to my own son, I want to stop and receive it for myself. I want to read Paul's words, inspired by the Holy Spirit, as a challenge and encouragement to me, a daughter of God and co-heir with Christ.

Persist whether it's convenient or not.

Rekindle the gift of God that is in you, Raechel. Rely on His power. Proclaim the message, Raechel. Persist whether it's convenient or not.

What about you? When you read Paul's letter for yourself, what challenges you? What changes you? What do you want to pass on to the people you love? What matters? Friend, don't waste time.

Titus

He saved us—not by
works of righteousness
that we had done, but
according to his mercy—
through the washing of
regeneration and renewal
by the Holy Spirit.

TITUS 3:5

TITUS 2:11–15

Sound Teaching and Christian Living

11 For the grace of God has appeared, bringing
salvation for all people, 12 instructing us to deny
godlessness and worldly lusts and to live in a
sensible, righteous, and godly way in the present
age, 13 while we wait for the blessed hope, the
appearing of the glory of our great God and Savior,
Jesus Christ. 14 He gave himself for us to redeem
us from all lawlessness and to cleanse for himself
a people for his own possession, eager to do good
works.

15 Proclaim these things; encourage and rebuke
with all authority. Let no one disregard you.

TITUS 3:1–7

Christian Living Among Outsiders

1 Remind them to submit to rulers and authorities, to obey, to be ready for every good work,
2 to slander no one, to avoid fighting, and to be
kind, always showing gentleness to all people. 3 For
we too were once foolish, disobedient, deceived,
enslaved by various passions and pleasures, living
in malice and envy, hateful, detesting one another.

4 But when the kindness of God our Savior and
his love for mankind appeared, 5 he saved us—not
by works of righteousness that we had done, but
according to his mercy—through the washing of
regeneration and renewal by the Holy Spirit. 6 He
poured out his Spirit on us abundantly through
Jesus Christ our Savior 7 so that, having been justified by his grace, we may become heirs with the
hope of eternal life.

MICAH 7:18–19

Micah's Prayer Answered

18 Who is a God like you,
forgiving iniquity and passing over rebellion
for the remnant of his inheritance?
He does not hold on to his anger forever
because he delights in faithful love.
19 He will again have compassion on us;
he will vanquish our iniquities.
You will cast all our sins
into the depths of the sea.

MATTHEW 5:13–16

Believers Are Salt and Light

13 "You are the salt of the earth. But if the salt should lose its taste, how can it be made salty? It's no longer good for anything but to be thrown out and trampled under people's feet.

14 "You are the light of the world. A city situated on
a hill cannot be hidden. 15 No one lights a lamp and
puts it under a basket, but rather on a lampstand,
and it gives light for all who are in the house. 16 In
the same way, let your light shine before others, so that they may see your good works and give glory to your Father in heaven."

EPHESIANS 2:8–10

From Death to Life

8 For you are saved by grace through faith, and
this is not from yourselves; it is God's gift— 9 not
from works, so that no one can boast. 10 For we
are his workmanship, created in Christ Jesus for good works, which God prepared ahead of time for us to do.

I've received a lot of advice in my life, some of it helpful. Things like:

> *Lay the baby on her front. (Read: late 80s.)*
>
> *Lay the baby on her back. (Read: early 90s.)*
>
> *Don't sit on cold concrete. (Why?)*
>
> *Clean the baseboards every week. (Please don't make me.)*
>
> *If you don't have anything nice to say, don't say anything at all. (This is actually pretty good advice.)*
>
> *Never miss an opportunity to go to the lavatory. (It's just true.)*

Of course, receiving good advice and following it are two very different things. (I definitely don't keep my baseboards properly cleaned.) We are often tempted to think that simply knowing the right thing should be enough, a kind of salvation-by-information or salvation-by-education. But, as Paul points out, we don't need another good bit of advice. We aren't following the good advice we've already heard.

We don't need another good bit of advice.

In fact, Paul's letter to Titus is something much different from an advice column. He is talking about a transformation of life. We, left to ourselves "were once foolish, disobedient, deceived, enslaved by various passions and pleasures" (Titus 3:3). And it wasn't merely a bit of good advice that saved us. It was not someone offering an odious, "Here's what you oughta do . . ." No, it was grace. God poured out His Spirit on us through Jesus Christ. We were justified—not by following a nifty list of suggestions, not by our works in any way, but purely by grace.

This salvation by grace, through Christ, by the work of His Spirit, is what we are to insist on. And this is not truth we are simply to know, but truth that transforms us by knowing Him. Yes, there are things we ought to do and ought not to do, but grace alone is sufficient to transform us from fools who refuse sound wisdom, to sons and daughters who walk in the righteousness of Christ. "Insist on these things," Paul says, "so that those who have believed God might be careful to devote themselves to good works" (Titus 3:8). Devotion to good works is the fruit of God's gracious work of transformation.

Don't worry about advice. It's tempting to read Paul's words as a list of how we are falling short and how we need to change our behavior so we fit in as God's kind of people. We are already God's people. "While we were still sinners, Christ died for us" (Romans 5:8). And because of His sacrifice and His grace, He is changing us from the inside out.

The work is done by Him. Step into the waters of regeneration (Titus 3:5), and walk out a new creation.

Philemon

For this reason, although I
have great boldness in Christ to
command you to do what
is right, I appeal to you,
instead, on the basis of love.

PHILEMON 8–9a

PHILEMON 4–22

Philemon's Love and Faith

[4] I always thank my God when I mention you in my prayers, [5] because I hear of
your love for all the saints and the faith that you have in the Lord Jesus. [6] I pray that
your participation in the faith may become effective through knowing every good
thing that is in us for the glory of Christ. [7] For I have great joy and encouragement
from your love, because the hearts of the saints have been refreshed through you,
brother.

An Appeal for Onesimus

[8] For this reason, although I have great boldness in Christ to command you to
do what is right, [9] I appeal to you, instead, on the basis of love. I, Paul, as an
elderly man and now also as a prisoner of Christ Jesus, [10] appeal to you for my
son, Onesimus. I became his father while I was in chains. [11] Once he was useless
to you, but now he is useful both to you and to me. [12] I am sending him back to
you—I am sending my very own heart. [13] I wanted to keep him with me, so that
in my imprisonment for the gospel he might serve me in your place. [14] But I didn't
want to do anything without your consent, so that your good deed might not
be out of obligation, but of your own free will. [15] For perhaps this is why he was
separated from you for a brief time, so that you might get him back permanently,
[16] no longer as a slave, but more than a slave—as a dearly loved brother. He is
especially so to me, but how much more to you, both in the flesh and in the Lord.

[17] So if you consider me a partner, welcome him as you would me. [18] And if he
has wronged you in any way, or owes you anything, charge that to my account.
[19] I, Paul, write this with my own hand: I will repay it—not to mention to you
that you owe me even your very self. [20] Yes, brother, may I benefit from you in
the Lord; refresh my heart in Christ. [21] Since I am confident of your obedience, I
am writing to you, knowing that you will do even more than I say. [22] Meanwhile,
also prepare a guest room for me, since I hope that through your prayers I will be
restored to you.

MATTHEW 18:21–35

The Parable of the Unforgiving Servant

21 Then Peter approached him and asked, "Lord,
how many times must I forgive my brother or sister who sins against me? As many as seven times?"

22 "I tell you, not as many as seven," Jesus replied,
"but seventy times seven.

23 "For this reason, the kingdom of heaven can be
compared to a king who wanted to settle accounts
with his servants. 24 When he began to settle
accounts, one who owed ten thousand talents was
brought before him. 25 Since he did not have the
money to pay it back, his master commanded that
he, his wife, his children, and everything he had be
sold to pay the debt.

26 "At this, the servant fell facedown before him
and said, 'Be patient with me, and I will pay you
everything.' 27 Then the master of that servant had
compassion, released him, and forgave him the
loan.

28 "That servant went out and found one of his
fellow servants who owed him a hundred denarii.
He grabbed him, started choking him, and said,
'Pay what you owe!'

29 "At this, his fellow servant fell down and began
begging him, 'Be patient with me, and I will pay
you back.' 30 But he wasn't willing. Instead, he went
and threw him into prison until he could pay what
was owed. 31 When the other servants saw what
had taken place, they were deeply distressed and
went and reported to their master everything that
had happened. 32 Then, after he had summoned
him, his master said to him, 'You wicked servant!
I forgave you all that debt because you begged me.
33 Shouldn't you also have had mercy on your fellow
servant, as I had mercy on you?' 34 And because he
was angry, his master handed him over to the jailers
to be tortured until he could pay everything that
was owed. 35 So also my heavenly Father will do to
you unless every one of you forgives his brother or
sister from your heart."

GALATIANS 6:1–2

Carry One Another's Burden

1 Brothers and sisters, if someone is overtaken in
any wrongdoing, you who are spiritual, restore
such a person with a gentle spirit, watching out
for yourselves so that you also won't be tempted.
2 Carry one another's burdens; in this way you will
fulfill the law of Christ.

COLOSSIANS 3:12–14

The Christian Life

12 Therefore, as God's chosen ones, holy and dearly
loved, put on compassion, kindness, humility,
gentleness, and patience, 13 bearing with one
another and forgiving one another if anyone has
a grievance against another. Just as the Lord has
forgiven you, so you are also to forgive. 14 Above
all, put on love, which is the perfect bond of unity.

The book of Philemon has something you don't often find in Scripture: some comedy.

Here's the backstory. Philemon was a wealthy Christian in the city of Colossae, and Onesimus was his bondservant. One day, Onesimus fled to Rome. Some say it was because he stole property or money from Philemon. Others think the two men had a dispute and Onesimus sought out Paul to be their mediator. But one thing is certain: While in Rome, Onesimus encountered the gospel and became a Christian.

As helpful as Onesimus was to Paul's ministry, he was also still a slave with a broken relationship with his master. Whatever wrongdoing happened between him and Philemon, they needed reconciliation, specifically as brothers in Christ. So, Paul wrote to Philemon and offered to pay whatever debt Onesimus might owe him.

This is where the comedy comes in. Paul leaves it for Philemon to call in that debt with a question I'd paraphrase like this: "Onesimus's debt is now mine, Philemon. I'll repay it. But don't forget, I gave you the gospel, so you owe me your life. In light of the fact that I've taken his debt and you owe me your life, tell me, how much do I owe you?" (Philemon 17–20).

That right there is funny. But it's also rightly serious. Paul wants Philemon to do for Onesimus what Jesus did for Philemon: Set him free.

For love's sake, Onesimus and Paul agreed that it was time to reconcile, and Onesimus prepared to return to Philemon and make things right. It was time for distance to give way to forgiveness and reunification as brothers in Christ, on both sides.

Forgiveness is a work of liberation, and it will be necessary at some point between people who spend any length of time together. Spouses, friends, church members—we will hurt each other, intentionally or unintentionally. Paul's letter to Philemon reminds us that forgiveness is an exercise of love. We have all borne the pain of someone else's anger, bitterness, or disappointment, just as we have taken others captive by our own. To forgive is not merely to dismiss an offense. It is to release someone, so that we might both live in freedom.

Forgiveness is a work of liberation.

As sinners saved by grace, we never go first with forgiveness—we can only ever pay it forward. Without exception we are people who have been forgiven a greater debt than we can ever repay. Who are we to withhold forgiveness for smaller debts to others?

How is the Holy Spirit nudging you as you read Philemon today? Have you hurt someone and need to seek their forgiveness? Or, do you have the opportunity to release someone from the burden of your bitterness? Do what Jesus has done for you: Set them free. This is what it means to live like someone who has been forgiven.

Hebrews

Let us run with endurance the race that lies before us, keeping our eyes on Jesus, the pioneer and perfecter of our faith. For the joy that lay before him, he endured the cross, despising the shame, and sat down at the right hand of the throne of God.

HEBREWS 12:1b–2

HEBREWS 1:1–3

The Nature of the Son

1 Long ago God spoke to our ancestors by the prophets at different times and in different ways. 2 In these last days, he has spoken to us by his Son. God has appointed him heir of all things and made the universe through him. 3 The Son is the radiance of God's glory and the exact expression of his nature, sustaining all things by his powerful word. After making purification for sins, he sat down at the right hand of the Majesty on high.

HEBREWS 5:1–10

Christ, a High Priest

1 For every high priest taken from among men is appointed in matters pertaining to God for the people, to offer both gifts and sacrifices for sins. 2 He is able to deal gently with those who are ignorant and are going astray, since he is also clothed with weakness. 3 Because of this, he must make an offering for his own sins as well as for the people. 4 No one takes this honor on himself; instead, a person is called by God, just as Aaron was. 5 In the same way, Christ did not exalt himself to become a high priest, but God who said to him,

> "You are my Son;
> today I have become your Father,"

6 also says in another place,

> "You are a priest forever
> according to the order of Melchizedek."

7 During his earthly life, he offered prayers and appeals with loud cries and tears to the one who was able to save him from death, and he was heard because of his reverence. 8 Although he was the Son, he learned obedience from what he suffered. 9 After he was perfected, he became the source of eternal salvation for all who obey him, 10 and he was declared by God a high priest according to the order of Melchizedek.

HEBREWS 10:19–25

Exhortations to Godliness

19 Therefore, brothers and sisters, since we have boldness to enter the sanctuary through the blood of Jesus— 20 he has inaugurated for us a new and living way through the curtain (that is, through his flesh)— 21 and since we have a great high priest over the house of God, 22 let us draw near with a true heart in full assurance of faith, with our hearts sprinkled clean from an evil conscience and our bodies washed in pure water. 23 Let us hold on to the confession of our hope without wavering, since he who promised is faithful. 24 And let us consider one another in order to provoke love and good works, 25 not neglecting to gather together, as some are in the habit of doing, but encouraging each other, and all the more as you see the day approaching.

HEBREWS 12:1–2

The Call to Endurance

1 Therefore, since we also have such a large cloud of witnesses surrounding us, let us lay aside every hindrance and the sin that so easily ensnares us. Let us run with endurance the race that lies before us, 2 keeping our eyes on Jesus, the pioneer and perfecter of our faith. For the joy that lay before him, he endured the cross, despising the shame, and sat down at the right hand of the throne of God.

ROMANS 8:31–34

The Believer's Triumph

31 What, then, are we to say about these things?
If God is for us, who is against us? 32 He did not
even spare his own Son but gave him up for us all.
How will he not also with him grant us everything?
33 Who can bring an accusation against God's
elect? God is the one who justifies. 34 Who is the
one who condemns? Christ Jesus is the one who
died, but even more, has been raised; he also is at
the right hand of God and intercedes for us.

1 CORINTHIANS 9:24–27

24 Don't you know that the runners in a stadium
all race, but only one receives the prize? Run in
such a way to win the prize. 25 Now everyone
who competes exercises self-control in everything.
They do it to receive a perishable crown, but we
an imperishable crown. 26 So I do not run like one
who runs aimlessly or box like one beating the air.
27 Instead, I discipline my body and bring it under
strict control, so that after preaching to others, I
myself will not be disqualified.

PHILIPPIANS 3:10–14

Knowing Christ

10 My goal is to know him and the power of his
resurrection and the fellowship of his sufferings,
being conformed to his death, 11 assuming that I
will somehow reach the resurrection from among
the dead.

Reaching Forward to God's Goal

12 Not that I have already reached the goal or am
already perfect, but I make every effort to take
hold of it because I also have been taken hold of
by Christ Jesus. 13 Brothers and sisters, I do not
consider myself to have taken hold of it. But one
thing I do: Forgetting what is behind and reaching
forward to what is ahead, 14 I pursue as my goal
the prize promised by God's heavenly call in Christ
Jesus.

Have you ever watched someone's dream come true in real time?

One summer night Raechel and I had the joy of watching the Olympic swimming trials together from the eighth row of the arena. Heat after heat, swimmers took their places on the starting blocks for a chance to earn a spot on Team USA. With a printed program in one hand and the other waving wildly in the air, we cheered and jumped and screamed and yes, even cried a little, as athletes who had devoted their whole lives to a sport competed for one of its highest achievements. In his post-race interview, one young man still in shock from his win said to the poolside reporter, "Now I don't have to pretend or dream about being an Olympian. I *am* an Olympian."[8] Cue more tears.

I've thought of that night many times since, and I can still feel the wonder of watching those athletes give their all for the revered title of Olympian. I can hear the distinctly unified sound of the crowd, cheering not against one another but for one another. And I can almost feel the goosebumps again from seeing that first-time Olympian receive his qualifying medal from none other than twenty-three-time Olympic gold medalist, Michael Phelps. Talk about a dream come true.

Scripture speaks of the Christian life as a race—only, our eyes and hopes are not set on a world record or Olympic medal. Our eyes are fixed on Jesus. Hebrews calls Him "the pioneer and perfecter of our faith" (Hebrews 12:2), meaning He has not onlyΔ run the race before us, but He is the one who enables us to run it too.

But what does it mean to "win" the Christian life? Does it mean to have an unbroken streak of quiet times, always rising with the sun to read our Bibles? Does it mean to volunteer a certain number of hours at our local church, or put a specific amount of money in the offering plate each week? Does it mean to be lauded for our faithfulness or admired for our goodness? Does it mean being known as a "gold medal" Christian?

I can hear the distinctly unified sound of the crowd, cheering not against one another but for one another.

As hard as it can be to accept, our victory as followers of Jesus does not come by our own dedication, status, or sacrifice. Our victory comes by relying fully and completely on the achievements of another. For the joy set before Him, Jesus ran the race on our behalf. He endured the temptation, trials, and sorrow of this human life, all without sin. He endured death—even death on a cross (Philippians 2:8)—to atone for our sin and secure for us eternal life and peace with God.

Surrounded by those who have gone before us and those who run beside us we race together toward the prize already won by Jesus. He alone is both our sacrifice and our Great High Priest, our joy and our crown. The greatest of all time invites you up onto the podium with Him today to receive an eternal award you could never earn. How will you respond?

James

Consider it a great joy, my brothers and sisters, whenever you experience various trials, because you know that the testing of your faith produces endurance. And let endurance have its full effect, so that you may be mature and complete, lacking nothing.

JAMES 1:2–4

JAMES 1:1–18

Greeting

1 James, a servant of God and of the Lord Jesus Christ:

To the twelve tribes dispersed abroad.

Greetings.

Trials and Maturity

2 Consider it a great joy, my brothers and sisters, whenever you experience various trials, 3 because you know that the testing of your faith produces endurance. 4 And let endurance have its full effect, so that you may be mature and complete, lacking nothing.

5 Now if any of you lacks wisdom, he should ask God—who gives to all generously and ungrudgingly—and it will be given to him. 6 But let him ask in faith without doubting. For the doubter is like the surging sea, driven and tossed by the wind. 7 That person should not expect to receive anything from the Lord, 8 being double-minded and unstable in all his ways.

9 Let the brother of humble circumstances boast in his exaltation, 10 but let the rich boast in his humiliation because he will pass away like a flower of the field. 11 For the sun rises and, together with the scorching wind, dries up the grass; its flower falls off, and its beautiful appearance perishes. In the same way, the rich person will wither away while pursuing his activities.

12 Blessed is the one who endures trials, because when he has stood the test he will receive the crown of life that God has promised to those who love him.

13 No one undergoing a trial should say, "I am being tempted by God," since God is not tempted by evil, and he himself doesn't tempt anyone. 14 But each person is tempted when he is drawn away and enticed by his own evil desire. 15 Then after desire has conceived, it gives birth to sin, and when sin is fully grown, it gives birth to death.

16 Don't be deceived, my dear brothers and sisters. 17 Every good and perfect gift is from above, coming down from the Father of lights, who does not change like shifting shadows. 18 By his own choice, he gave us birth by the word of truth so that we would be a kind of firstfruits of his creatures.

JOHN 16:33

"I have told you these things so that in me you may have peace. You will have suffering in this world. Be courageous! I have conquered the world."

ROMANS 8:18–23

From Groans to Glory

18 For I consider that the sufferings of this present
time are not worth comparing with the glory that
is going to be revealed to us. 19 For the creation
eagerly waits with anticipation for God's sons to
be revealed. 20 For the creation was subjected to
futility—not willingly, but because of him who
subjected it—in the hope 21 that the creation itself
will also be set free from the bondage to decay into
the glorious freedom of God's children. 22 For we
know that the whole creation has been groaning
together with labor pains until now. 23 Not only
that, but we ourselves who have the Spirit as the
firstfruits—we also groan within ourselves, eagerly
waiting for adoption, the redemption of our
bodies.

1 PETER 4:12–19

Christian Suffering

12 Dear friends, don't be surprised when the fiery
ordeal comes among you to test you, as if something unusual were happening to you. 13 Instead,
rejoice as you share in the sufferings of Christ,
so that you may also rejoice with great joy when
his glory is revealed. 14 If you are ridiculed for the
name of Christ, you are blessed, because the Spirit
of glory and of God rests on you. 15 Let none of
you suffer as a murderer, a thief, an evildoer, or
a meddler. 16 But if anyone suffers as a Christian,
let him not be ashamed but let him glorify God
in having that name. 17 For the time has come for
judgment to begin with God's household, and if it
begins with us, what will the outcome be for those
who disobey the gospel of God?

> 18 And "if a righteous person is saved
> with difficulty,
> what will become of the ungodly and the
> sinner?"

19 So then, let those who suffer according to God's
will entrust themselves to a faithful Creator while
doing what is good.

Twenty-two and newly married, I placed my bag of lemons on the grocery belt along with the rest of my groceries. If being a homemaker was an Olympic sport, I was determined to medal in it. So when the cashier asked as she weighed my lemons, "I don't get it. What on earth do people do with a dozen lemons?" I responded with incredulity, "You make lemonade!"

I laughed to myself on the way home. *Obviously, there is only one right way to make lemonade in the summertime.* Now, two decades and countless reality checks later, I've learned that a home is not made with fresh-squeezed lemonade, and it's possible that cashier was also laughing to herself about me.

The book of James offers a host of brass-tacks directions for the Christian life—including directions on suffering. Reading James's words on this subject has always reminded me of that interaction at the grocery store. When he tells us to "Consider it a great joy . . . whenever you experience various trials" (James 1:2), he most certainly isn't telling us to make lemonade out of lemons. No, as is always true of the world's promises versus the Word's, God's promises are even better.

James didn't say, "Consider it a personal challenge, brothers and sisters, to make sense of the suffering you experience, because that's what will make the pain go away." Deep down, we all know better. Hard things are real, and they won't be made untrue until Jesus makes all things new (Revelation 21:5). But in the meantime, James testifies that "the testing of your faith produces endurance. And let endurance have its full effect, so that you may be mature and complete, lacking nothing" (James 1:3–4). When we have truly learned how to endure—how to let the hope of Jesus be our only comfort—then we will have everything we need. Now that's a promise.

It's not up to you to squeeze lemonade out of the lemons in your life as if you need to figure out how to turn fiery trials and heartache into something sweet. If it was my job to turn tripping on the sidewalk of life into a fancy dance, I'm afraid you'd find me face down in the mud. But the good news is this: We serve a God who is in the business of redemption. It is His specialty.

We serve a God who is in the business of redemption. It is His specialty.

As believers, we have a calling to look trials in the face, then face our Father and say a joyful "thank you." And yet, my inclination is to stand up and run around, trying to make sense of things myself. Perhaps it's yours too. But it isn't our job to make things make sense. He's already on it! And His purposes are His to know. God is producing fruit in ways we may not understand until we see Him face-to-face.

Do you feel the relief as James removes the juicer from your hands? Where is the Lord producing endurance in your life—maturing you and completing you? Count it as joy.

1 Peter

Blessed be the God and Father of our Lord Jesus Christ. Because of his great mercy he has given us new birth into a living hope through the resurrection of Jesus Christ from the dead and into an inheritance that is imperishable, undefiled, and unfading, kept in heaven for you.

1 PETER 1:3–4

1 PETER 1:3–25

A Living Hope

3 Blessed be the God and Father of our Lord Jesus Christ. Because of his great mercy he has given us new birth into a living hope through the resurrection of Jesus Christ from the dead 4 and into an inheritance that is imperishable, undefiled, and unfading, kept in heaven for you. 5 You are being guarded by God's power through faith for a salvation that is ready to be revealed in the last time. 6 You rejoice in this, even though now for a short time, if necessary, you suffer grief in various trials 7 so that the proven character of your faith—more valuable than gold which, though perishable, is refined by fire—may result in praise, glory, and honor at the revelation of Jesus Christ. 8 Though you have not seen him, you love him; though not seeing him now, you believe in him, and you rejoice with inexpressible and glorious joy, 9 because you are receiving the goal of your faith, the salvation of your souls.

10 Concerning this salvation, the prophets, who prophesied about the grace that would come to you, searched and carefully investigated. 11 They inquired into what time or what circumstances the Spirit of Christ within them was indicating when he testified in advance to the sufferings of Christ and the glories that would follow. 12 It was revealed to them that they were not serving themselves but you. These things have now been announced to you through those who preached the gospel to you by the Holy Spirit sent from heaven—angels long to catch a glimpse of these things.

A Call to Holy Living

13 Therefore, with your minds ready for action, be sober-minded and set your hope completely on the grace to be brought to you at the revelation of Jesus Christ. 14 As obedient children, do not be conformed to the desires of your former ignorance. 15 But as the one who called you is holy, you also are to be holy in all your conduct; 16 for it is written, "Be holy, because I am holy." 17 If you appeal to the Father who judges impartially according to each one's work, you are to conduct yourselves in reverence during your time living as strangers. 18 For you know that you were redeemed from your empty way of life inherited from your ancestors, not with perishable things like silver or gold, 19 but with the precious blood of Christ, like that of an unblemished and spotless lamb. 20 He was foreknown before the foundation of the world but was revealed in these last times for you. 21 Through him you believe in God, who raised him from the dead and gave him glory, so that your faith and hope are in God.

22 Since you have purified yourselves by your obedience to the truth, so that you show sincere brotherly love for each other, from a pure heart love one another constantly, 23 because you have been born again—not of perishable seed but of imperishable—through the living and enduring word of God. 24 For

> "All flesh is like grass,
> and all its glory like a flower of the grass.
> The grass withers, and the flower falls,
> 25 but the word of the Lord endures forever."

And this word is the gospel that was proclaimed to you.

LEVITICUS 20:7–8

7 "Consecrate yourselves and be holy, for I am the LORD your God. 8 Keep my statutes and do them; I am the LORD who sets you apart."

ROMANS 5:1–11

Faith Triumphs

1 Therefore, since we have been justified by faith,
we have peace with God through our Lord Jesus
Christ. 2 We have also obtained access through
him by faith into this grace in which we stand, and
we boast in the hope of the glory of God. 3 And
not only that, but we also boast in our afflictions,
because we know that affliction produces endurance, 4 endurance produces proven character, and
proven character produces hope. 5 This hope will
not disappoint us, because God's love has been
poured out in our hearts through the Holy Spirit
who was given to us.

The Justified Are Reconciled

6 For while we were still helpless, at the right
time, Christ died for the ungodly. 7 For rarely will
someone die for a just person—though for a good
person perhaps someone might even dare to die.
8 But God proves his own love for us in that while
we were still sinners, Christ died for us. 9 How
much more then, since we have now been justified
by his blood, will we be saved through him from
wrath. 10 For if, while we were enemies, we were
reconciled to God through the death of his Son,
then how much more, having been reconciled,
will we be saved by his life. 11 And not only that,
but we also boast in God through our Lord Jesus
Christ, through whom we have now received this
reconciliation.

My mother-in-law is the proudest mother and grandmother on earth. We love that about her. Her sons? The best and brightest, capable of no wrong. Her grandchildren? The finest athletes, students, and artists to grace the great states of South Carolina and Tennessee. And her daughters-in-law? Unparalleled in kindness and charm.

It feels good to be loved and prized so fiercely, but we on the receiving end of such admiration know ourselves too well to believe all the hype.

I wonder how Peter felt when Jesus gave him his new name. "You are Peter, and on this rock I will build my church, and the gates of hell shall not prevail against it" (Matthew 16:18). *Say what now?*

I imagine Peter was a good man. Hard working and honest, a good friend and, yes, maybe even a son his mama could brag to her friends about. But *the* rock on which Jesus would build *the* Church? It seems a little extreme, especially for a regular ole fisherman who will one day deny even knowing Jesus.

This is why I have fallen head over heels for these letters from Peter the apostle. Not only do they deliver essential encouragement and admonition to the Church, they are gospel reminders spoken by a product of the gospel himself. Peter is sold out for spreading the message of Jesus Christ because he has lived it. He walked alongside the Savior; followed Him throughout His ministry; and saw His miracles and His death, resurrection, and ascension as they happened. Peter knows the story of the Church because it is his personal story.

When he says, *Your inheritance in Christ will never fade,* he is saying it to himself, too. When he says, *Don't listen to the liars; they want to destroy you but Jesus gives you life,* he remembers how those same voices tried to woo him, too (1 Peter 1:4; 4:4–6, my paraphrase).

When Peter tells us that we, the Church, can rejoice in our suffering, he says it as one who watched the Son of Man suffer in real-time on the cross, bearing the sins of you and me. He also says it as one who would face imprisonment and ultimately death for his faith in Christ. Despite his sometimes-fickle faith, the gospel was the anchor that never gave way, the solid ground in a world of sinking sand.

Despite Peter's sometimes-fickle faith, the gospel was the anchor that never gave way.

Peter was a man made new by Jesus, a man looking forward to "an inheritance that is imperishable, undefiled, and unfading" (1 Peter 1:4), secured in heaven by his Savior and friend. He is the same man who, despite rocky circumstances, became the strong rock Jesus declared him to be, strengthening the Church through his letters in their most difficult times.

Today, no matter what you face, you have a living hope that will not disappoint, an inheritance that no trial can tarnish. And when you wonder if you'll ever become the faith-filled disciple you want to be, remember Peter. God grew a denying disciple into a sage shepherd, and He will finish the good work He's started in you.

2 Peter

His divine power has given us
everything required for life and
godliness through the knowledge
of him who called us by his
own glory and goodness.

2 PETER 1:3

2 PETER 1:3–15

Growth in the Faith

3 His divine power has given us everything
required for life and godliness through the knowledge of him who called us by his own glory and
goodness. 4 By these he has given us very great and
precious promises, so that through them you may
share in the divine nature, escaping the corruption
that is in the world because of evil desire. 5 For this
very reason, make every effort to supplement your
faith with goodness, goodness with knowledge,
6 knowledge with self-control, self-control with
endurance, endurance with godliness, 7 godliness
with brotherly affection, and brotherly affection
with love. 8 For if you possess these qualities in
increasing measure, they will keep you from being
useless or unfruitful in the knowledge of our Lord
Jesus Christ. 9 The person who lacks these things
is blind and shortsighted and has forgotten the
cleansing from his past sins. 10 Therefore, brothers
and sisters, make every effort to confirm your calling and election, because if you do these things you
will never stumble. 11 For in this way, entry into
the eternal kingdom of our Lord and Savior Jesus
Christ will be richly provided for you.

12 Therefore I will always remind you about these
things, even though you know them and are established in the truth you now have. 13 I think it is
right, as long as I am in this bodily tent, to wake
you up with a reminder, 14 since I know that I will
soon lay aside my tent, as our Lord Jesus Christ has
indeed made clear to me. 15 And I will also make
every effort so that you are able to recall these
things at any time after my departure.

2 PETER 3:1–18

The Day of the Lord

1 Dear friends, this is now the second letter I have
written to you; in both letters, I want to stir up
your sincere understanding by way of reminder,
2 so that you recall the words previously spoken by
the holy prophets and the command of our Lord
and Savior given through your apostles. 3 Above
all, be aware of this: Scoffers will come in the last
days scoffing and following their own evil desires,
4 saying, "Where is his 'coming' that he promised?
Ever since our ancestors fell asleep, all things
continue as they have been since the beginning of
creation." 5 They deliberately overlook this: By the
word of God the heavens came into being long ago
and the earth was brought about from water and
through water. 6 Through these the world of that
time perished when it was flooded. 7 By the same
word, the present heavens and earth are stored up
for fire, being kept for the day of judgment and
destruction of the ungodly.

8 Dear friends, don't overlook this one fact: With
the Lord one day is like a thousand years, and a
thousand years like one day. 9 The Lord does not
delay his promise, as some understand delay, but is
patient with you, not wanting any to perish but all
to come to repentance.

10 But the day of the Lord will come like a thief;
on that day the heavens will pass away with a loud
noise, the elements will burn and be dissolved, and
the earth and the works on it will be disclosed.
11 Since all these things are to be dissolved in this
way, it is clear what sort of people you should be in
holy conduct and godliness 12 as you wait for the
day of God and hasten its coming. Because of that
day, the heavens will be dissolved with fire and the
elements will melt with heat. 13 But based on his
promise, we wait for new heavens and a new earth,
where righteousness dwells.

Conclusion

14 Therefore, dear friends, while you wait for these
things, make every effort to be found without spot
or blemish in his sight, at peace. 15 Also, regard the
patience of our Lord as salvation, just as our dear
brother Paul has written to you according to the
wisdom given to him. 16 He speaks about these
things in all his letters. There are some things hard
to understand in them. The untaught and unstable
will twist them to their own destruction, as they
also do with the rest of the Scriptures.

17 Therefore, dear friends, since you know this in
advance, be on your guard, so that you are not
led away by the error of lawless people and fall
from your own stable position. 18 But grow in the
grace and knowledge of our Lord and Savior Jesus
Christ. To him be the glory both now and to the
day of eternity.

PSALM 77:11–12

Confidence in a Time of Crisis

[11] I will remember the LORD's works;
yes, I will remember your ancient wonders.
[12] I will reflect on all you have done
and meditate on your actions.

1 CORINTHIANS 15:58

Victorious Resurrection

Therefore, my dear brothers and sisters, be steadfast, immovable, always excelling in the Lord's work, because you know that your labor in the Lord is not in vain.

GALATIANS 5:1

Freedom of the Christian

For freedom, Christ set us free. Stand firm, then, and don't submit again to a yoke of slavery.

PHILIPPIANS 1:27–28

Living Is Christ

[27] Just one thing: As citizens of heaven, live your life worthy of the gospel of Christ. Then, whether I come and see you or am absent, I will hear about you that you are standing firm in one spirit, in one accord, contending together for the faith of the
gospel, [28] not being frightened in any way by your opponents. This is a sign of destruction for them, but of your salvation—and this is from God.

Little known fact: I was a percussionist in the school band from ages eleven to eighteen. And before you think percussion is just drums, you should know that I also played a mediocre xylophone, jangled the jingle bells every year at Christmastime, and (though I never quite got the hang of tuning them) I absolutely loved rolling in and out of a mighty crescendo on the tympani.

But what I really loved was the bass drum. There was something about that low, underlying rhythm. I was setting the pace, critical yet almost undetected, eyes locked on the conductor, keeping the entire band playing in unity.

I was setting the pace, critical yet almost undetected, eyes locked on the conductor.

When we read about Peter's life in the Gospels, it's like we're watching a faint yet steady gospel drumbeat begin to pound in Peter's soul. And as I read the book of 2 Peter, a letter written in the apostle's own voice, the beat grows from faint to forefront. *Remember. Remember. Remember.* Eyes locked on the Conductor, keeping the band in unity.

And as he pounds the drum it sounds like this: The gospel is sure. Stand firm. The gospel is sure. Stand firm.

"Therefore I will always remind you about these things, even though you know them and are established in the truth you now have" (1:12).

The gospel is sure. Stand firm.

"I think it right as long as I am in this body, to stir you up by way of reminder, since I know the putting off of my body will be soon" (1:13 ESV).

The gospel is sure. Stand firm.

"And I will also make every effort so that you are able to recall these things at any time after my departure." (1:15).

The gospel is sure. Stand firm.

Dear friends, this is now the second letter I have written to you; in both letters, I want to stir up your sincere understanding by way of reminder . . ." (3:1).

Remember. Don't forget. This is what unites us. This is what the Conductor is doing.

Better than any simple yet earnest high school percussionist with a piece of relatively straightforward sheet music, Peter knows things are going to get complicated. He expects other drummers to show up with drums and beats of their own. They won't regard the Conductor. They will be "untaught and unstable" and will twist the music not only "to their own destruction" but also to the destruction of others (2 Peter 3:16).

But Peter's warning comes with a charge to "be on your guard, so that you are not led away by the error of lawless people and fall from your own stable position" (2 Peter 3:17), and that charge is for you and me today. Keep your ear tuned to the drum beat of the gospel, eyes locked on the Conductor.

The gospel is sure. Stand firm.

1 John

If we confess our sins, he is faithful and righteous to forgive us our sins and to cleanse us from all unrighteousness.

1 JOHN 1:9

1 JOHN 1:5–10

Fellowship with God

5 This is the message we have heard from him and declare to you: God is light, and there is absolutely no darkness in him. 6 If we say, "We have fellowship with him," and yet we walk in darkness, we are lying and are not practicing the truth. 7 If we walk in the light as he himself is in the light, we have fellowship with one another, and the blood of Jesus his Son cleanses us from all sin. 8 If we say, "We have no sin," we are deceiving ourselves, and the truth is not in us. 9 If we confess our sins, he is faithful and righteous to forgive us our sins and to cleanse us from all unrighteousness. 10 If we say, "We have not sinned," we make him a liar, and his word is not in us.

1 JOHN 3:1a

God's Children

See what great love the Father has given us that we should be called God's children—and we are!

1 JOHN 4:7–11, 16b–21

Knowing God Through Love

7 Dear friends, let us love one another, because love is from God, and everyone who loves has been born of God and knows God. 8 The one who does not love does not know God, because God is love. 9 God's love was revealed among us in this way: God sent his one and only Son into the world so that we might live through him. 10 Love consists in this: not that we loved God, but that he loved us and sent his Son to be the atoning sacrifice for our sins. 11 Dear friends, if God loved us in this way, we also must love one another.

. . .

16 God is love, and the one who remains in love remains in God, and God remains in him. 17 In this, love is made complete with us so that we may have confidence in the day of judgment, because as he is, so also are we in this world. 18 There is no fear in love; instead, perfect love drives out fear, because fear involves punishment. So the one who fears is not complete in love. 19 We love because he first loved us. 20 If anyone says, "I love God," and yet hates his brother or sister, he is a liar. For the person who does not love his brother or sister whom he has seen cannot love God whom he has not seen. 21 And we have this command from him: The one who loves God must also love his brother and sister.

LEVITICUS 19:18

Laws of Holiness

"Do not take revenge or bear a grudge against members of your community, but love your neighbor as yourself; I am the LORD."

MATTHEW 22:34–40

The Primary Commands

34 When the Pharisees heard that he had silenced
the Sadducees, they came together. 35 And one of
them, an expert in the law, asked a question to test
him: 36 "Teacher, which command in the law is the
greatest?"

37 He said to him, "'Love the Lord your God
with all your heart, with all your soul, and with
all your mind.' 38 This is the greatest and most
important command. 39 The second is like it: 'Love
your neighbor as yourself.' 40 All the Law and the
Prophets depend on these two commands."

ROMANS 12:10

Christian Ethics

Love one another deeply as brothers and sisters. Take the lead in honoring one another.

EPHESIANS 5:1–2

Living the New Life

1 Therefore, be imitators of God, as dearly loved
children, 2 and walk in love, as Christ also loved us
and gave himself for us, a sacrificial and fragrant
offering to God.

1 PETER 4:8

End-Time Ethics

Above all, maintain constant love for one another, since "love covers a multitude of sins."

One of my favorite stories from the early Church fathers is about the teaching ministry of the apostle John, who penned three letters (1, 2, and 3 John), plus the Gospel of John and the book of Revelation.

The story holds that John lived in Ephesus until he was very, very old. Despite his advanced age, he still made it a priority to teach the brothers and sisters in Ephesus at church gatherings, even if it meant his disciples had to carry him there and back. And of course they did, because imagine all the things John could share. After all, John was the guy Jesus called to leave his fishing nets and follow Him (Matthew 4:21–22). John was the guy who walked with Jesus during His earthly ministry, listening to His teaching every day and witnessing His miracles. John was one of only three disciples to see Jesus in His transfigured glory and the only one of the Twelve who stayed near Jesus at the cross (Mark 9:2–10; John 19:25–27). John was the disciple who outran Peter in his eagerness to see the empty tomb, and ate fish on the beach with the risen Christ (John 20:1–9; 21:1–14).

But, according to tradition, John did not teach on these things. Instead, he would say the same thing at every gathering, every single time: "Little children, love one another." Finally, those in attendance asked him why he didn't vary in his message. John replied, "Because it is the Lord's commandment to us, and if it alone is kept, it is sufficient."[9]

Now, this story is more legend than proven history. But across John's three letters, you'll notice that he returns to the importance of love repeatedly—over fifty times in 133 verses! John's Gospel records Jesus giving His disciples this command: "Love one another. Just as I have loved you, you are also to love one another. By this everyone will know that you are my disciples" (John 13:34–36). Here, and in 1 John 4:10, we find the "why" of this command. It is not simply so Christians are seen as kind or long-suffering with those who are hard to love. The reason behind our love is the overwhelming love we've received from God, even before we loved Him.

He would say the same thing at every gathering, every single time.

This overwhelming love is seen in the overwhelming suffering of Christ on the cross as He atoned for our sins with His blood and experienced God's wrath on our behalf—all so we might have life with Him forever. Yes, love one another, but love because you have been so loved that it has changed you. Love because you know your sin does not deserve this type of love, and yet Jesus gave it anyway. Love because His affection for you is so strong you cannot help but be a picture of that love to others.

What if we repeated John's message to ourselves every day? "Little children, love one another." It is the Lord's commandment to us, and it is sufficient.

2 John

This is love: that we walk
according to his commands.
This is the command as you have
heard it from the beginning:
that you walk in love.

2 JOHN 6

2 JOHN

Greeting

1 The elder:

To the elect lady and her children, whom I love in the truth—and not only I, but
also all who know the truth— 2 because of the truth that remains in us and will
be with us forever.

3 Grace, mercy, and peace will be with us from God the Father and from Jesus
Christ, the Son of the Father, in truth and love.

Truth and Deception

4 I was very glad to find some of your children walking in truth, in keeping with a
command we have received from the Father. 5 So now I ask you, dear lady—not as
if I were writing you a new command, but one we have had from the beginning—
that we love one another. 6 This is love: that we walk according to his commands.
This is the command as you have heard it from the beginning: that you walk in
love.

7 Many deceivers have gone out into the world; they do not confess the coming of
Jesus Christ in the flesh. This is the deceiver and the antichrist. 8 Watch yourselves
so that you don't lose what we have worked for, but that you may receive a full
reward. 9 Anyone who does not remain in Christ's teaching but goes beyond it
does not have God. The one who remains in that teaching, this one has both the
Father and the Son. 10 If anyone comes to you and does not bring this teaching, do
not receive him into your home, and do not greet him; 11 for the one who greets
him shares in his evil works.

Farewell

12 Though I have many things to write to you, I don't want to use paper and
ink. Instead, I hope to come to you and talk face to face so that our joy may be
complete.

13 The children of your elect sister send you greetings.

JOHN 13:34–35

The New Command

34 "I give you a new command: Love one another.
Just as I have loved you, you are also to love one
another. 35 By this everyone will know that you are
my disciples, if you love one another."

GALATIANS 5:16–26

The Spirit Versus the Flesh

16 I say, then, walk by the Spirit and you will certainly not carry out the desire of the flesh. 17 For
the flesh desires what is against the Spirit, and the
Spirit desires what is against the flesh; these are
opposed to each other, so that you don't do what
you want. 18 But if you are led by the Spirit, you are
not under the law.

19 Now the works of the flesh are obvious: sexual
immorality, moral impurity, promiscuity, 20 idolatry, sorcery, hatreds, strife, jealousy, outbursts
of anger, selfish ambitions, dissensions, factions,
21 envy, drunkenness, carousing, and anything
similar. I am warning you about these things—as I
warned you before—that those who practice such
things will not inherit the kingdom of God.

22 But the fruit of the Spirit is love, joy, peace,
patience, kindness, goodness, faithfulness, 23 gentleness, and self-control. The law is not against
such things. 24 Now those who belong to Christ
Jesus have crucified the flesh with its passions
and desires. 25 If we live by the Spirit, let us also
keep in step with the Spirit. 26 Let us not become
conceited, provoking one another, envying one
another.

There is a foot of height between us, but I have learned to keep up, quicken my step, and match my stride to my husband's. He ran Division 1 Track and Field for his university, and, to this day, he can run a mile while I'm still changing into my sneakers.

But when we walk, we walk at a matched pace: He's a little slower than normal and I'm a little faster. When he asks me to go for a walk, he does it because he loves me and he loves spending time with me. Walking at different paces—though more comfortable for each of us—would not be the loving thing to do.

The book of 2 John speaks of walking in love, matching the stride of Christ in the way we live. "This is love: that we walk according to his commands," John writes. "This is the command as you have heard it from the beginning: that you walk in love" (2 John 6). As followers of Jesus, we don't walk ahead or lag behind or make our own path, but we look more and more like the love of Jesus with every step. Yet, John is not only concerned with our everyday steps, but also our everyday abiding in the truth of Christ, never wandering from His good path because our eyes are fixed on Him.

For me, it's easy to grow distracted by what's around me or impatient for what's ahead of me. But John says, *Beloved, walk. Match your pace to the One who loved you first. Walk, one step in front of another, faithful in practice—not for a particular result, but simply to walk with your Father and enjoy His presence* (my paraphrase).

Beloved, walk. Match your pace to the One who loved you first.

The Bible offers examples of those who have done this extremely well—and those who have had to correct their step. Enoch's life, for example, was summed up in Genesis with this line: "Enoch walked faithfully with God" (Genesis 5:24 NIV). Peter, on the other hand, might be a little more relatable. While he certainly had seasons of walking in step with Christ, he also had moments when his walk with God was clearly "not in step with the truth of the gospel" (Galatians 2:14 ESV).

The demands and pressures of life can cause us to forget what's real, true, and eternal, and we sometimes fail to match our stride to the love of God. He slowed His pace to meet ours, to teach us how to walk, and even run the race set before us (Hebrews 12:1–2). By His grace, may we live as those who walk faithfully with God. In the end, may our own lives echo these words:

I have fought the good fight,
I have finished the race,
I have kept the faith (2 Timothy 4:7).

Are your steps matched with those of Jesus? What can you do today to walk with your Father and enjoy His presence?

3 John

I have no greater joy than
this: to hear that my children
are walking in truth.

3 JOHN 4

3 JOHN

Greeting

[1] The elder:

To my dear friend Gaius, whom I love in the truth.

[2] Dear friend, I pray that you are prospering in every way and are in good health,
just as your whole life is going well. [3] For I was very glad when fellow believers
came and testified to your fidelity to the truth—how you are walking in truth.
[4] I have no greater joy than this: to hear that my children are walking in truth.

Gaius Commended

[5] Dear friend, you are acting faithfully in whatever you do for the brothers and
sisters, especially when they are strangers. [6] They have testified to your love before
the church. You will do well to send them on their journey in a manner worthy
of God, [7] since they set out for the sake of the Name, accepting nothing from
pagans. [8] Therefore, we ought to support such people so that we can be coworkers
with the truth.

Diotrephes and Demetrius

[9] I wrote something to the church, but Diotrephes, who loves to have first place
among them, does not receive our authority. [10] This is why, if I come, I will remind
him of the works he is doing, slandering us with malicious words. And he is not
satisfied with that! He not only refuses to welcome fellow believers, but he even
stops those who want to do so and expels them from the church.

[11] Dear friend, do not imitate what is evil, but what is good. The one who does
good is of God; the one who does evil has not seen God. [12] Everyone speaks well
of Demetrius—even the truth itself. And we also speak well of him, and you know
that our testimony is true.

Farewell

[13] I have many things to write you, but I don't want to write to you with pen and
ink. [14] I hope to see you soon, and we will talk face to face.

[15] Peace to you. The friends send you greetings. Greet the friends by name

DEUTERONOMY 15:10–11

Lending to the Poor

10 "Give to him, and don't have a stingy heart when you give, and because of this the LORD your God will bless you in all your work and in everything you do. 11 For there will never cease to be poor people in the land; that is why I am commanding you, 'Open your hand willingly to your poor and needy brother in your land.'"

PSALM 15:1–5

A Description of the Godly

1 LORD, who can dwell in your tent?
Who can live on your holy mountain?

2 The one who lives blamelessly, practices righteousness,
and acknowledges the truth in his heart—
3 who does not slander with his tongue,
who does not harm his friend
or discredit his neighbor,
4 who despises the one rejected by the LORD
but honors those who fear the LORD,
who keeps his word whatever the cost,
5 who does not lend his silver at interest
or take a bribe against the innocent—
the one who does these things will never be shaken.

EPHESIANS 2:11–20

Unity in Christ

11 So, then, remember that at one time you were Gentiles in the flesh—called "the uncircumcised" by those called "the circumcised," which is done in the flesh by human hands. 12 At that time you were without Christ, excluded from the citizenship of Israel, and foreigners to the covenants of promise, without hope and without God in the world. 13 But now in Christ Jesus, you who were far away have been brought near by the blood of Christ. 14 For he is our peace, who made both groups one and tore down the dividing wall of hostility. In his flesh, 15 he made of no effect the law consisting of commands and expressed in regulations, so that he might create in himself one new man from the two, resulting in peace. 16 He did this so that he might reconcile both to God in one body through the cross by which he put the hostility to death. 17 He came and proclaimed the good news of peace to you who were far away and peace to those who were near. 18 For through him we both have access in one Spirit to the Father. 19 So, then, you are no longer foreigners and strangers, but fellow citizens with the saints, and members of God's household, 20 built on the foundation of the apostles and prophets, with Christ Jesus himself as the cornerstone.

I remember the day when my daughter, only eight years old at the time, came home from school to tell me she'd been bullied by a classmate.

I was skeptical at first. *Who could ever be mean to my favorite girl?* Many follow-up questions and a few confirming reports later, I'd gone from mildly concerned mom to full-on mama bear. Someone was shoving my kid around, and I was not okay with it.

Of course, this wouldn't be the last time I felt the visceral urge to shield my child from hurt. Grade school gave way to middle school, with its lunchtime cliques and pressure to fit in. Then came the push and pull of the teenage years, when harsh words fly indiscriminately through the air like a host of arrows and some of the worst word-wounds are self-inflicted. The truth is, every season of growth involves struggle, and parenting our children through adversity is hard at every age. (Parents of adult kids, does it get any easier? Never mind—don't answer that.)

In his last letter to the church, addressed to his friend and fellow-believer Gaius, the apostle John takes the tone of a loving and protective father as he urges the church to "not imitate what is evil, but what is good" (3 John 11). John punctuates his point by contrasting Gaius's faithfulness to the gospel with the way a fellow congregant, a man named Diotrephes, weaponizes it.

The gospel is not a power play—the biggest and baddest have no advantage in the kingdom of God.

Diotrephes fancied himself to be quite a powerful figure in the church, so powerful that he took it upon himself to decide who was in and who was out. While Gaius welcomed strangers and co-workers in the faith, Diotrephes considered himself the gatekeeper of the gospel: He welcomed only those he wanted to welcome, and he pushed out those who opposed him (3 John 10). Diotrephes failed to understand that the gospel is not a power play—the biggest and baddest have no advantage in the kingdom of God. The life Jesus calls us to is one of love, service, and peace. He invites us to live in unity with one another, not pushing and shoving, but walking in truth as we follow Him together (3 John 4).

I've never kicked anyone out of church, but I have played the part of Diotrephes in my own ways. I've tried to twist the gospel into something it isn't, tried shaping truth to fit my preferences or prioritize my comfort. I have misrepresented Christ by looking at others and even myself with eyes that are not truthful or loving. But praise God, I cannot rewrite the gospel! It does not shift with my insecurities or shrink according to my understanding. No, it is always and forever "the power of God for salvation to everyone who believes" (Romans 1:16).

There is no self-appointed gatekeeper who can keep you from the love of God in Christ Jesus. There is no lie so loud that it can diminish the truth of the gospel. How does John's heartfelt message challenge and encourage you today?

Jude

Now to him who is able to protect you from stumbling and to make you stand in the presence of his glory, without blemish and with great joy, to the only God our Savior, through Jesus Christ our Lord, be glory, majesty, power, and authority before all time, now and forever. Amen.

JUDE 24–25

JUDE

Greeting

1 Jude, a servant of Jesus Christ and a brother of James:

To those who are the called, loved by God the Father and kept for Jesus Christ.

2 May mercy, peace, and love be multiplied to you.

Jude's Purpose in Writing

3 Dear friends, although I was eager to write you about the salvation we share, I found it necessary to write, appealing to you to contend for the faith that was delivered to the saints once for all. 4 For some people, who were designated for this judgment long ago, have come in by stealth; they are ungodly, turning the grace of our God into sensuality and denying Jesus Christ, our only Master and Lord.

Apostates: Past and Present

5 Now I want to remind you, although you came to know all these things once and for all, that Jesus saved a people out of Egypt and later destroyed those who did not believe; 6 and the angels who did not keep their own position but abandoned their proper dwelling, he has kept in eternal chains in deep darkness for the judgment on the great day. 7 Likewise, Sodom and Gomorrah and the surrounding towns committed sexual immorality and perversions, and serve as an example by undergoing the punishment of eternal fire.

8 In the same way these people—relying on their dreams—defile their flesh, reject authority, and slander glorious ones. 9 Yet when Michael the archangel was disputing with the devil in an argument about Moses's body, he did not dare utter a slanderous condemnation against him but said, "The Lord rebuke you!" 10 But these people blaspheme anything they do not understand. And what they do understand by instinct—like irrational animals—by these things they are destroyed. 11 Woe to them! For they have gone the way of Cain, have plunged into Balaam's error for profit, and have perished in Korah's rebellion.

The Apostates' Doom

12 These people are dangerous reefs at your love feasts as they eat with you without reverence. They are shepherds who only look after themselves. They are waterless clouds carried along by winds; trees in late autumn—fruitless, twice dead and uprooted. 13 They are wild waves of the sea, foaming up their shameful deeds; wandering stars for whom the blackness of darkness is reserved forever.

14 It was about these that Enoch, in the seventh generation from Adam, prophesied: "Look! The Lord comes with tens of thousands of his holy ones 15 to execute judgment on all and to convict all the ungodly concerning all the ungodly acts that they have done in an ungodly way, and concerning all the harsh things ungodly sinners have said against him." 16 These people are discontented grumblers, living according to their desires; their mouths utter arrogant words, flattering people for their own advantage.

17 But you, dear friends, remember what was predicted by the apostles of our Lord Jesus Christ. 18 They told you, "In the end time there will be scoffers living according to their own ungodly desires." 19 These people create divisions and are worldly, not having the Spirit.

Exhortation and Benediction

20 But you, dear friends, as you build yourselves up in your most holy faith, praying in the Holy Spirit, 21 keep yourselves in the love of God, waiting expectantly for the mercy of our Lord Jesus Christ for eternal life. 22 Have mercy on those who waver; 23 save others by snatching them from the fire; have mercy on others but with fear, hating even the garment defiled by the flesh.

24 Now to him who is able to protect you from stumbling and to make you stand in the presence of his glory, without blemish and with great joy, 25 to the only God our Savior, through Jesus Christ our Lord, be glory, majesty, power, and authority before all time, now and forever. Amen.

ISAIAH 5:20

Judah's Sin Denounced

"Woe to those who call evil good
and good evil,
who substitute darkness for light
and light for darkness,
who substitute bitter for sweet
and sweet for bitter."

MARK 9:42

Warnings from Jesus

"But whoever causes one of these little ones who believe in me to fall away—it would be better for him if a heavy millstone were hung around his neck and he were thrown into the sea."

EPHESIANS 2:1–5

From Death to Life

1 And you were dead in your trespasses and sins
2 in which you previously walked according to
the ways of this world, according to the ruler of
he power of the air, the spirit now working in the
disobedient. 3 We too all previously lived among
them in our fleshly desires, carrying out the inclinations of our flesh and thoughts, and we were by
nature children under wrath as the others were
also. 4 But God, who is rich in mercy, because of
his great love that he had for us, 5 made us alive
with Christ even though we were dead in trespasses. You are saved by grace!

2 TIMOTHY 1:13–14

Be Loyal to the Faith

13 Hold on to the pattern of sound teaching that
you have heard from me, in the faith and love
that are in Christ Jesus. 14 Guard the good deposit
through the Holy Spirit who lives in us.

JAMES 5:19–20

Effective Prayer

19 My brothers and sisters, if any among you strays
from the truth, and someone turns him back, 20 let
that person know that whoever turns a sinner from
the error of his way will save his soul from death
and cover a multitude of sins.

We all need at least one friend who will give it to us straight—someone to tell us to put down the scissors when we want to cut our own bangs, to speak up when they don't have a good feeling about the guy we think we like, and to check in on our prayer life when we feel like we're floundering. They don't sugar coat things, and they don't often hold back. And we're so glad we have them.

In the New Testament, that straight-shooting friend is Jude. His message may be short, but it's one of the most pull-no-punches letters in the Bible (and in the company of Paul, that's saying something!).

Jude writes to warn believers of *apostates*, or people who are intentionally leading believers away from the truth of the gospel. He describes these people as those who are "relying on their dreams," those who "defile their flesh, reject authority, and . . . slander glorious ones," only looking out for themselves instead of shepherding others with care (Jude 8). They may think they're living in the light, but in reality, they're "turning the grace of God into sensuality" as "scoffers living according to their own ungodly desires" (Jude 4, 18). Jude calls these people "waterless clouds . . . trees in late autumn . . . twice dead," and "wandering stars for whom the blackness of darkness is reserved forever" (Jude 12–13). He takes this threat to the Christian faith seriously, and he's hoping his readers do, too.

So what do we do with Jude's warning? How do we recognize false teachers when we see them? A wolf in sheep's clothing often looks like a sheep, after all. And how do we take care not to become an apostate ourselves?

First, we remind ourselves of the truth of the gospel, and that begins by remembering that every believer was once a scoffer (Ephesians 2:3). We were the "wild waves of the seas, foaming up [our] shameful deeds" (Jude 13). We were self-deceived and pretending. You, me, and everybody else. *But God.* Being rich in mercy, because of His great love for us, Christ died for the ungodly (Ephesians 2:4; Romans 5:6). We were all in darkness. We were all dead. And by His mysterious mercy, God made us His. He takes the waterless cloud and transforms it to bring rain. He takes twice dead trees and causes them to live again.

He takes the waterless cloud and transforms it to bring rain.

Second, we remain in Him. You know that moment in the shower when you simply stand still under the falling water, letting it wash over you? Jude says to "keep yourselves in the love of God, waiting expectantly for the mercy of our Lord Jesus Christ for eternal life" (Jude 20). Remain in His love as though you're standing under a waterfall, letting it soak you to the bone. Only then can you be a minister of Christ's mercy, snatching those who waver from the fire (Jude 22).

Jude's warning is strong, but his trust in God's ability to "protect you from stumbling" is stronger (Jude 24). This is how we heed his urgent warning and this is how we, the scoffers made saints, embody the gospel message.

How are you keeping yourself in the love of God today?

Revelation

Then he said to me, "It is done! I am the Alpha and the Omega, the beginning and the end. I will freely give to the thirsty from the spring of the water of life."

REVELATION 21:6

REVELATION 21:1–11, 22–27

The New Creation

1 Then I saw a new heaven and a new earth; for the
first heaven and the first earth had passed away,
and the sea was no more. 2 I also saw the holy city,
the new Jerusalem, coming down out of heaven
from God, prepared like a bride adorned for her
husband.

3 Then I heard a loud voice from the throne: Look,
God's dwelling is with humanity, and he will live
with them. They will be his peoples, and God himself will be with them and will be their God. 4 He
will wipe away every tear from their eyes. Death
will be no more; grief, crying, and pain will be
no more, because the previous things have passed
away.

5 Then the one seated on the throne said, "Look,
I am making everything new." He also said, "Write,
because these words are faithful and true." 6 Then
he said to me, "It is done! I am the Alpha and the
Omega, the beginning and the end. I will freely
give to the thirsty from the spring of the water
of life. 7 The one who conquers will inherit these
things, and I will be his God, and he will be my
son. 8 But the cowards, faithless, detestable, mur-
derers, sexually immoral, sorcerers, idolaters, and
all liars—their share will be in the lake that burns
with fire and sulfur, which is the second death."

The New Jerusalem

9 Then one of the seven angels, who had held the
seven bowls filled with the seven last plagues, came
and spoke with me: "Come, I will show you the
bride, the wife of the Lamb." 10 He then carried me
away in the Spirit to a great, high mountain and
showed me the holy city, Jerusalem, coming down
out of heaven from God, 11 arrayed with God's
glory. Her radiance was like a precious jewel, like a
jasper stone, clear as crystal.

. . .

22 I did not see a temple in it, because the Lord
God the Almighty and the Lamb are its temple.
23 The city does not need the sun or the moon to
shine on it, because the glory of God illuminates
it, and its lamp is the Lamb. 24 The nations will
walk by its light, and the kings of the earth will
bring their glory into it. 25 Its gates will never close
by day because it will never be night there. 26 They
will bring the glory and honor of the nations into
it. 27 Nothing unclean will ever enter it, nor anyone who does what is detestable or false, but only
those written in the Lamb's book of life.

REVELATION 22:1–5, 16–21

The Source of Life

1 Then he showed me the river of the water of life,
clear as crystal, flowing from the throne of God
and of the Lamb 2 down the middle of the city's
main street. The tree of life was on each side of
the river, bearing twelve kinds of fruit, producing
its fruit every month. The leaves of the tree are for
healing the nations, 3 and there will no longer be
any curse. The throne of God and of the Lamb will
be in the city, and his servants will worship him.
4 They will see his face, and his name will be on
their foreheads. 5 Night will be no more; people
will not need the light of a lamp or the light of the
sun, because the Lord God will give them light,
and they will reign forever and ever.

. . .

16 "I, Jesus, have sent my angel to attest these
things to you for the churches. I am the Root and
descendant of David, the bright morning star."

17 Both the Spirit and the bride say, "Come!" Let
anyone who hears, say, "Come!" Let the one who
is thirsty come. Let the one who desires take the
water of life freely.

18 I testify to everyone who hears the words of the
prophecy of this book: If anyone adds to them,
God will add to him the plagues that are written
in this book. 19 And if anyone takes away from the
words of the book of this prophecy, God will take
away his share of the tree of life and the holy city,
which are written about in this book.

20 He who testifies about these things says, "Yes,
I am coming soon."

Amen! Come, Lord Jesus!

21 The grace of the Lord Jesus be with everyone.
Amen.

ISAIAH 2:2–4

The City of Peace

[2] In the last days
the mountain of the LORD's house will be
established
at the top of the mountains
and will be raised above the hills.
All nations will stream to it,

[3] and many peoples will come and say,
"Come, let's go up to the mountain of the LORD,
to the house of the God of Jacob.
He will teach us about his ways
so that we may walk in his paths."
For instruction will go out of Zion
and the word of the LORD from Jerusalem.

[4] He will settle disputes among the nations
and provide arbitration for many peoples.
They will beat their swords into plows
and their spears into pruning knives.
Nation will not take up the sword against nation,
and they will never again train for war.

ISAIAH 65:17–19, 24–25

A New Creation

[17] "For I will create new heavens and a new earth;
the past events will not be remembered or
come to mind.
[18] Then be glad and rejoice forever
in what I am creating;
for I will create Jerusalem to be a joy
and its people to be a delight.
[19] I will rejoice in Jerusalem
and be glad in my people.
The sound of weeping and crying
will no longer be heard in her."

. . .

[24] "Even before they call, I will answer;
while they are still speaking, I will hear.
[25] The wolf and the lamb will feed together,
and the lion will eat straw like cattle,
but the serpent's food will be dust!
They will not do what is evil or destroy
on my entire holy mountain,"
says the LORD.

EZEKIEL 37:26–27

The Reunification of Israel

[26] "I will make a covenant of peace with them; it
will be a permanent covenant with them. I will
establish and multiply them and will set my sanctuary among them forever. [27] My dwelling place
will be with them; I will be their God, and they
will be my people."

We wash dishes by hand at our house. We are a big family, so it's a bit of work, but after years of loading and unloading dishwashers only to find dirty dishes inside, it's worth it for us.

I have three sink basins; in the first I rinse, the second is filled with hot soapy water for washing, and the third is for rinsing again. Above the sink, mounted to the wall, are four big drying racks. Everything smells like lemon and optimism. Once my dishes are shiny and dripping on the metal racks, a child usually brings in one last bowl and spoon. After that, someone finds a stray coffee cup, and before my dishes have dried, the first sink is full again with ladles, milk glasses, and unnecessary straws.

Our work is never done on this side of heaven. Life is better when I don't expect a full stop from things that do not stop. The dishes will never be done. The garden does not stay weeded. The beds need to be made every morning. Even King Solomon with his limitless wealth, massive power, and access to every imaginable pleasure came to the conclusion that it's all vanity. "All things are wearisome, more than anyone can say" (Ecclesiastes 1:8). And if that guy, with all his resources, realized that our hope is not found under the sun, do we think that we're going to discover something different?

Now, don't misunderstand me. The fresh glory of a sunrise over mountains and the squishy skin of a new baby and the arms of my husband all hold a true and inexpressible joy for me. But none of it will satisfy my deepest longings. None of it will make me complete. There will always be dishes to wash and our favorite ones will continue to break, and our dogs will die, and our houses will deteriorate, and we will bury everyone we love until they bury us.

Life is better when I don't expect a full stop from things that do not stop.

But there is a land where there is no death, no sickness, no depravity, and no shame. And, boy, I hope we will see our pets, because there's a good girl I sure wish I could see again. We will lay down our tools and run home, into the arms of our Father. He has promised us this: "Look, God's dwelling is with humanity, and he will live with them. They will be his peoples, and God himself will be with them and will be their God" (Revelation 21:3).

One day, in the new heaven and new earth, God will dwell with His people as He did in the beginning. We were created for life in our holy God's presence. Our sin keeps us from coming close to Him, but He comes to us and brings us home. There we find our settled rest, not like guests or strangers, but like a child who is truly home.

How are you longing for this true home today?

NOTES

1. J. R. R. Tolkien, *The Hobbit* (Houghton Mifflin, 2012), 3.
2. J. M. Barrie, *Peter Pan: The Original 1911 Classic* (Reader's Library Classics, 2022), 1.
3. Charles Dickens, *A Tale of Two Cities* (Penguin, 1970), 35.
4. *The Confessions of St. Augustine: Modern English Version* (Baker, 2005), 15–16.
5. C. S. Lewis, *The Weight of Glory and Other Addresses* (Macmillian, 1949), 5.
6. J. R. R. Tolkien, *Tree and Leaf* (Houghton Mifflin, 1965), 68.
7. Eric Walter White, *Stravinsky: The Composer and His Works* (University of California Press: 1984), 105.
8. Isa Almeida, "Shaine Casas, Carson Foster Earn Spot in U.S. Swimming Olympic Team," June 22, 2024, texaslonghorns.com.
9. St. Jerome, *Commentary on Galatians*, trans. Andrew Cain (Catholic University of American Press, 2010), 260.

ABOUT THE AUTHORS

Raechel Myers is always on the lookout for beauty, goodness, and truth in everyday life. Founder of She Reads Truth, Raechel can often be found cooking up a project in her kitchen, puzzling at her dining room table, or tending the flowers and vegetables in her garden and making gospel connections with the soil. Raechel has always enjoyed travel and the art of hospitality. She and her husband Ryan make their home south of Nashville, Tennessee, where their right-now highest calling is preparing their two teenage kids to launch well into their next chapters of life.

Amanda Bible Williams is co-founder of She Reads Truth. When she isn't writing, editing, or podcasting, Amanda enjoys working crosswords, laughing at sitcoms with her family, and catching up on her reading for seminary, where she is pursuing her lifelong dream of being a professional student. Amanda and her husband David live in Franklin, Tennessee, with their four kids—three teenagers and a medically fragile yet dauntlessly joyful eleven-year-old who they are pretty sure is from Neverland. And yes, her maiden name really is Bible.

Raechel and Amanda are both general editors of the *She Reads Truth Bible* and *He Reads Truth Bible*, co-authors of the book *She Reads Truth: Holding Tight to Permanent in a World That's Passing Away*, and co-hosts of the *She Reads Truth Podcast*.

About the Contributors

The devotionals in this book are a collected effort. While most were written by Raechel or Amanda, some have been adapted or edited from existing pieces written by members of the She Reads Truth devotional writing team. We are grateful for these added perspectives and life experiences that serve to make this journey through the Bible even richer and more well-rounded than it could have been without them. These contributors are noted and celebrated on the following page.

CONTRIBUTORS

OLD TESTAMENT

Genesis	Jessica Lamb
Exodus	Raechel Myers
Leviticus	Tameshia Williams
Numbers	Amanda Bible Williams
Deuteronomy	Jessica Lamb
Joshua	Amanda Bible Williams
Judges	Raechel Myers & Amanda Bible Williams
Ruth	Raechel Myers & Amanda Bible Williams
1 Samuel	Raechel Myers
2 Samuel	Russ Ramsey
1 Kings	Raechel Myers, adapted from Russ Ramsey
2 Kings	Amanda Bible Williams
1 Chronicles	Amanda Bible Williams, adapted from Jessica Lamb
2 Chronicles	Seana Scott
Ezra	Raechel Myers
Nehemiah	Amanda Bible Williams
Esther	Amanda Bible Williams, adapted from Rebecca Faires
Job	Erin Davis
Psalms	Amanda Bible Williams
Proverbs	Amanda Bible Williams
Ecclesiastes	Amanda Bible Williams
Song of Songs	Amanda Bible Williams
Isaiah	Amanda Bible Williams
Jeremiah	Erin Davis
Lamentations	Patti Sauls
Ezekiel	Bailey Gillespie Throssel
Daniel	Amanda Bible Williams
Hosea	Amanda Bible Williams
Joel	Rebecca Faires
Amos	Tameshia Williams
Obadiah	Amanda Bible Williams
Jonah	Erin Davis
Micah	Raechel Myers
Nahum	Jessica Lamb
Habakkuk	Lore Ferguson Wilbert
Zephaniah	Raechel Myers
Haggai	Erin Davis
Zechariah	Raechel Myers & Amanda Bible Williams
Malachi	Ashley Gorman & Raechel Myers

NEW TESTAMENT

Matthew	Rebecca Faires
Mark	Amanda Bible Williams
Luke	Raechel Myers
John	Raechel Myers
Acts	Amanda Bible Williams
Romans	Raechel Myers
1 Corinthians	Amanda Bible Williams
2 Corinthians	Lore Ferguson Wilbert
Galatians	Amanda Bible Williams
Ephesians	Raechel Myers
Philippians	Patti Sauls
Colossians	Patti Sauls
1 Thessalonians	Amanda Bible Williams & Raechel Myers
2 Thessalonians	Rebecca Faires
1 Timothy	Amanda Bible Williams
2 Timothy	Raechel Myers
Titus	Rebecca Faires
Philemon	Russ Ramsey
Hebrews	Amanda Bible Williams
James	Raechel Myers
1 Peter	Amanda Bible Williams
2 Peter	Raechel Myers
1 John	Jessica Lamb
2 John	Lore Ferguson Wilbert
3 John	Amanda Bible Williams
Jude	Raechel Myers
Revelation	Rebecca Faires

SHE READS TRUTH

JOIN THE COMMUNITY

The worldwide She Reads Truth community is reading Scripture together TODAY. Join the synchronized daily reading by downloading the She Reads Truth app or visiting SheReadsTruth.com. Or, visit ShopSheReadsTruth.com to find hundreds of Daily Reading Guides that cover whole books of the Bible explore important topics of the Christian faith, and celebrate seasons of the Church calendar.

The Bible isn't just a book. It is living and active, given to us by God so that we can know Him. You are meant to read it. And you can start today.

DOWNLOAD
the She Reads Truth app

VISIT
shereadstruth.com

SHOP
shopshereadstruth.com

CONTACT
hello@shereadstruth.com

CONNECT
@shereadstruth

LISTEN
to the She Reads Truth Podcast